1. Raises good questions, Answers are theological!
2. Down on "scientific" historians of religions.
3. Wants to see African religion as worshipping
the Supreme God. Polytheism its corruption.

AFRICAN TRADITIONAL RELIGION

E. BOLAJI IDOWU

AFRICAN TRADITIONAL RELIGION

A Definition

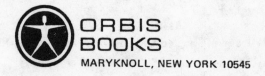

ORBIS BOOKS

MARYKNOLL, NEW YORK 10545

Nupe -- African people -- Religion

Second Printing, Orbis Books, 1975

© SCM Press Ltd 1973
ISBN 0-88344-005-9
Library of Congress Catalog Card Number 72-96951
Manufactured in the United States of America

For My Beloved Wife

YEWANDE

Contents

Preface

Do not be misled by the title of this book. Its purpose is emphasized by the sub-title. It is a book which results from years of experience in the study of African traditional religion – experience gathered through research, teaching, seminars, and discussions, at home and abroad.

It is a book which has come forth when the time has 'fully come'. There are several factors which call for it. First, for several reasons, attention is being focussed on Africa and a special interest has been aroused in what is generally described in the academic world as African Studies. Even though in most places this discipline is still to be defined clearly, it already has a place in the curriculum of many universities in Europe and America. And the indigenous religion of Africa is being mentioned as an element in the studies. It has, therefore, become quite clear to those of us who are experienced in the field of African traditional religion that, in the circumstances, the right technical tools are needed for dealing with the religion by way of research, teaching, and learning with understanding.

Over the years, it has been noticed that the first difficulty with which the world outside Africa has to grapple is what to make of the indigenous religion. That world still has to be convinced that there is an indigenous religion of Africa and that, by right, it deserves the name of religion. Those who are organizing societies and congresses or conferences with particular reference to the history, or even the phenomenology, of religion have always regarded African traditional religion as of little account, except where they choose to deal with it as an illustration of what is 'primitive'. A recent congress on the history of religion was a good example: in a conference which lasted several days, the religion was just squeezed in and perfunctorily touched upon among other matters.

Thus, the world outside Africa still has to wake up to the fact that African traditional religion is *the* religion which resulted from the sustaining faith held by the forbears of the present Africans, which is being practised today by the majority of Africans in various forms and various shades and intensities, nakedly in most cases; but also, in some cases, under the veneers supplied by Westernism and Arabism; it is also a religion which is receiving a new vitality in certain areas in consequence of nationalism plus inspiration by other religions.

Secondly, the important question of what *is* the indigenous religion of Africa has become an urgent one. The question expands itself to include 'what is the nature of religion?' and 'of what elements is it made up?' Experience has revealed that this is an area in which there has been much perplexity and confusion, which have resulted in the coinage of wrong descriptive nomenclatures for the religion.

Thirdly, the eyes of African peoples, especially African scholars, are being opened to the fact that they have a certain God-given heritage which has its own intrinsic values with which is bound the destiny of their racial soul. These values they are seeking to recover or refurbish. This is the meaning of the philosophies of identity known as '*négritude*', 'African personality', etc., with their counterparts in Black Power, Black Religion, etc.

Besides, African scholars are beginning to engage themselves in serious researches into the indigenous beliefs of their peoples; African traditional religion is now a recognized course in African universities, training colleges, and seminaries. Recently, it has been listed among the courses to be taught in the upper classes of secondary schools and examined for the General Certificate of Education.

An urgent need has arisen, therefore, for a guide book, if the task of research is to be carried out thoroughly and teaching done effectively.

Fourthly, African traditional religion is religion indeed; therefore, it is necessary for both teachers and students to see it where it really belongs. Thus, it has been necessary to begin this book with a general introduction to religion – a beaten and perhaps well-trodden track to several scholars; but a necessary path to be trodden for many. It is a vital exercise for those who still need to be convinced of the claim of African traditional religion. There is also a need for beginners who have not been brought up in the basic disciplines of the study of religion to be informed of certain basic terminologies and positions.

Fifthly, the day of theology in the perspective of Africa is dawning. There are African scholars and men of faith who are finding the prefabricated theology imported into Africa inadequate for her spiritual and academic needs. These are now strong advocates and promoters of the theology which bears the stamp of original thinking and meditation of Africans. And the only way by which this worthy end can be attained is for African theologians to apprehend African spiritual values with the African mind while, at the same time, they possess the requisite knowledge of the fundamental facts of the faith which they are seeking to express and disseminate in indigenous idiom.

This book is thus definitive and interpretative. In that consists its basic aim. It is also methodological, inasmuch as it points out a way by which the religion should be studied from the inside and in true perspective. Therefore, as it shows the difficulties and pitfalls, so also does it define the religion positively, saying what it is not and what it is, and revealing its anatomical components.

I am very grateful to the Secretariat staff of the Department of Religious Studies, who have given generously and freely of their time and energy to help in the production of the book; Mr I. K. Dawodu, who organized its typing from the draft stages to its completion; Mr S. A. Olatunji for his part in preparing the drafts; and Mr Leonard Obeifoh for producing so perfectly the entire final typescript.

My deep gratitude is also due to the following: Professor E. A. Ayandele of the Department of History and Dr Ayọ Banjọ of the Department of English for reading the draft typescript and making valuable and useful suggestions with regard to matter and style; the Revs. J. O. Kayọde and S. A. Adewale, postgraduate students in the Department of Religious Studies, and Miss Faramọbi Ọlalẹmi, a student in the same Department, for checking the typescripts carefully and thoroughly; the Rev. S. A. Adewale for undertaking the onerous task of preparing the index; and, finally the Managing Director and Editor of SCM Press, the Rev. John Bowden, and his staff for their understanding sympathy and the production of the book.

It is my hope that all who use the book will fill the framework which it supplies with the flesh of illustrative and descriptive facts from their own native localities, or defined area of study, anywhere on the continent.

University of Ibadan   E. Bolaji Idowu

I

The Study of Religion

Religion is very much and always with us. It is with us at every moment of life – in our innermost beings and with regard to the great or minor events of life; it is discussed daily in the newspapers, through the radio and television, and in our conversations. It is with all of us inevitably, whatever may be our individual, avowed attitudes to it.

That is why everybody is interested in 'religion', be he a believer to whom his faith is a matter of ultimate concern, or a person who thinks that he does not believe and cannot believe in the divine rulership of the universe.

Religion, *qua* religion, needs no apologetics to establish the fact of its existence and that it has been a concomitant of almost every sphere of human activity from time immemorial. That it has always been a sphere of human activity is not debatable, even though there are those who argue whether it is a *proper* sphere of human activity or not. In fact, A. C. Bouquet would go so far as to say :

Religion cannot wisely or safely be ignored or neglected as it is by so many frivolous persons today. Even a defective or obsolete scheme of religion will serve the individual better than none at all. This is why so many old-fashioned persons possess, in spite of their defective views on some topics. a wholeness and completeness of character which is absent from the young ultra-moderns.[1]

While Bouquet might probably wish to modify his statement about 'a defective or obsolete scheme of religion' if he were writing now, there is no doubt about the validity of the essential point of his statement. Religion has always served a purpose – a purpose which belongs to the very fabric of life itself – and this is a fact of history as of experience.

Sir Arthur Keith, as chairman when Julian Huxley was delivering the Conway Memorial Lecture in October 1930, found it necessary to say at the end of his introductory speech:

> His lecture is so packed with ideas and his reasoning so close that there is a point which may escape your immediate notice. It is a point which makes a special appeal to me, and which I dare hope will gain your acceptance. He holds that we who wish to make reason the guide of life can no longer afford to be mere breakers of images; if our way of thinking is to make progress in the world we must set up as well as cast down. Our lecturer, you will find, realizes to the full that we have no more right to deprive men and women of their religion than of their favourite drinks unless we can provide reasonable and acceptable substitutes.

Earlier in the introduction, Sir Arthur had said that Julian Huxley considered this matter of casting down orthodox religion in order to set up a substitute religion to be of such urgency and importance that he had had to turn himself to a freelance scientist, who only retained a foothold in his laboratory.[2] The comparison of religion to 'favourite drinks' is immaterial for the moment; what is of significance is that there is recognition of the fact that there is bound to be an aching void in life if people are deprived of their religion and are not provided with 'reasonable and acceptable substitutes'. A. C. Bouquet puts it more truly and forcefully when he says that 'any one who is inside a working scheme of religion is well aware that to deprive him of that scheme is to a large extent, so to speak, to disembowel his life'.[3]

A definition of religion by H. G. Wells proves further the universal recognition of the fact that religion is inescapable and that man tries to escape it at his own peril.

> Nearly all of us want something to hold us together, something to dominate this swarming confusion and save us from the black misery of wounded and exploded pride, of thwarted desire, of futile conclusions ... We want more oneness, some steadying thing that will afford an escape from fluctuations ... It seems to me that this desire to get the complex of life simplified is essentially what has been called the religious motive, and the manner in which a man achieves that simplification, if he does achieve it, and imposes an order upon his life, is his religion.[4]

Religion is an inescapable involvement of every member of the human race. We are all of us religious in the sense that we believe in the sacred and are committed to one 'faith' or another; in the sense of those who seek and try to establish a 'reasonable and acceptable substitute' religion; or in the sense of those who think that they are only interested in 'religion' without being involved in religion, except in so far as they seek to fill up life's aching void with spiritualism, astrology, magic, or some other forms of occultism. Several idols have come into being as a result of man's effort to try to escape the inescapable. 'Try as it may, iconoclasm has often succeeded, by some miscarriage of purpose, only in clearing the house for new, perhaps more subtle or more absurd, images.'[5] 'Humanism', 'efficiency', 'the organization of the collective man', 'the cult of the state' and 'the cult of personality' (which two are mutually involved but, curiously, are never, or very rarely, called by their proper designations), are current examples.

The answer to the question why religion is so inevitable as a sphere of human life and activity is deep down in the nature of every person: there is an inherent urge in man which makes religion a matter of ultimate concern. It makes also for the common 'interest' in religion – whether the interest is in embracing it or in fighting a defensive battle against it.

The fact must be faced, however, that there have been in 'religion' certain things against which the best instincts in man rebel, especially as man learns to bring his emotions under control and apply his critical judgment even to the experiences of life. This indicates that we must be sure of what is in our minds when we think or speak of religion. It would seem that in every case of man's revolt against 'religion', the revolt is invariably not against religion *qua* religion, but against a scheme of religion or a religious institution which is a prostitution of essential religion, or something in religion that contradicts its basic spiritual and moral claims. Priestcraft with all its insult and disgusting sins against humanity, abuse of the authority recognized by people because it is religious, 'holy' cruelty, stealing, immorality, and other ghastly forms of inhumanity perpetrated in the name of Deity – these have been a constant embarrassment to religion and have raised questions as to its worthwhileness. How can history forget the Crusades, the *Jihads*, the Inquisition, those burnings and mutilations and devastations?

Communist Russia is believed to be an example of a nation which has officially revolted successfully against religion and repudiated it completely. I believe that it is, in fact, written in the Communist constitution of Russia that every initiated, practising Communist *must* be an atheist. In Russia one is confronted externally almost everywhere with the evidence of national substitutes for the 'traditional' or orthodox rituals and the cult-objects of religion. Nevertheless, it is possible to discern through the history of the revolutionary movement, and even through certain evidence in the current situation, that the complex situation in Russia with reference to religion has been oversimplified. The original revolt was not against religion *qua* religion (although it may be doubted whether the authors of the revolution ever rationalized it in this way), but against 'religion' which had departed grossly from the fulfilment of the ennobling, uplifting, peace-giving task that should be the role of religion: it was against a 'religion' which had become an instrument of enslavement and oppression – a religion which was indeed a diabolic 'opium'. Unfortunately religion *qua* religion and religion as practised are most difficult, if not impossible, to separate from each other. This is why those who find religion a traitor to itself often adopt either the radical method of 'throwing out the baby with the bath-water' or else find for themselves wittingly or unwittingly what amounts to a substitute religion. It is for this reason that 'the Dialectical Process' could be interpreted at the same time as a repudiation of religion and as a ' "radical displacement", the discontinuous substitution of one religion for another'.[6]

The universal 'interest' in religion has to a great extent damaged the understanding of what it really is and means. Religion in practice and the word 'religion' are so much with us that it is taken for granted that we all know what it is and what it is all about. The danger of this universal 'interest' may be seen from three different directions.

First, appearance is easily taken for reality. This happens only too often. What, for example, do we mean when we say that a person is 'very religious'? There may be very little in the statement, even though it immediately raises an expectation of virtue. What is probably meant is that the person professes a certain 'faith' and observes certain rituals; he may nevertheless be a rogue or a veritable blackguard. This is what Jesus warns against when he says, 'Not everyone who says to me, "Lord, Lord", shall enter the kingdom of heaven, but he who does the will of my Father who is in heaven ...'[7] There could be a distinction between having a religion and living a life the motive force of which is a dynamic faith. 'The former state is unfortunately commoner than the latter, and we may compare the relationship of the two to that prevailing between the rich parvenu who collects beautiful things without understanding them, and the individual who, however poor, has been trained to love and perceive the significance of beauty.'[8]

From the point of view of scholarship in the study of religion, this is a very serious point. W. Cantwell Smith expresses clearly the issue at stake when he says that certain

... objective study of religion leaves out the very part of religion that counts; it analyses the externals but misses the core of the matter, studying the only aspect of religious history that is available for study – namely, the mundane manifestation – but neglecting, or not understanding, or anyway unable to deal effectively with, the only part that <u>essentially signifies</u>. The student must be warned lest, from a study of symbols, he come, perhaps with painstaking brilliance, to <u>conclusions that are true but</u>, so far as concerns the references of those symbols, <u>irrelevant</u>; or if he confuses the symbols with what is symbolized, then to conclusions that are absurd.

Such scholars might uncharitably be compared to flies crawling on the outside of the goldfish bowl, making accurate and complete observations on the fish inside, measuring their scales meticulously, and indeed contributing much to the knowledge of the subject, but never asking themselves, and never finding out, <u>how it feels to be a goldfish.</u>[9]

<u>Secondly, religion and culture are often confused.</u> This often leads to faulty conclusions. To Dr Samuel Johnson, 'There are two objects of curiosity, the Christian world and the Mohammedan world – all the rest may be considered as barbarous.'[10] It is true that any religion and culture are involved in each other and that it is <u>often difficult to draw a precise line of demarcation between the two,</u> if that is ever possible, especially in places where people still consider life as one indivisible whole and have not reached the stage of artificially dividing reality into the sacred and the secular. <u>A fair attempt at differentiation may be that while culture covers the whole of a people's scheme of life, religion gives direction and complexion to the scheme.</u> It is doubtful if one should accept wholesale W. Cantwell Smith's statement that, in the Western world, religion and culture are different in origin.[11] It would seem that what happened in the Western world, as it is now happening in Asia and Africa, was that one early religion, more or less aboriginal, formed the cohesive factor of, and gave the foundation complexion to, culture, while another culture was, or other cultures were, superimposed on this. In this way the fabric of life became a thing made up of strands of various hues and stresses each of which has gone inextricably into the warp and weft of the complex whole.

As we shall see later, several errors of identity with reference to religion in Africa are results of this confusion between religion and culture. 'Heathenism' or 'paganism',[2] which we shall consider later on, is an apt illustration.

Thirdly, there is the ever-menacing habit of biassed comparison, witting or unwitting, of other people's religions with one's own. When a scholar falls into this habit, his research has become vitiated from the start; for anything which is not in conformity with his own tradition is rejected by him either as meaningless or substandard. The usual tendency is to regard whatever is undeniably of real value in those religions as something borrowed from another culture and to dismiss what does not conform to the investigator's own pattern as barbarous. And the matter can degenerate to such an absurd level as in the case of the German professor of anatomy who illustrated good and bad formations of the human anatomy respectively with the picture of a Hollywood film star and that of an ugly, fat woman which, according to him, was from the interior of Africa!

Another important consideration in the study of religion is to select the right person and the proper tool to prosecute and execute the task. This is delicate ground which must be trodden with caution. At the same time we must face the fact that not every person who is 'interested' in religion is equipped for a scholarly study of religion, and not just any available tool will do for the task.

There are two complementary categories of writers who have always been a menace to the study of religion: the traveller who takes back, among other things, reports on the religions of the foreign countries of his travels, and the stay-at-home investigator who waits eagerly at the other end for the supply of information of which the traveller is always full to overflowing. The traveller, ever true to type, tells his *tales* from strange lands with characteristic exaggerations or distortions, simply because his interest is little more than that of a collector of curios to boost his own ego as traveller and for the entertainment of the stay-at-homes; he is more often than not very ill-equipped for the study of religion. And how frequently have travellers' tales found their way *as facts* into writings which claim to be scholarly works! Visitors from the Western world have come briefly to this or that locality in Africa, or have been jet-propelled through the continent, only immediately afterwards to constitute themselves competent authorities on the way and wisdom of the whole of Africa, confidently giving lectures and writing books and dishing out information.

For example, in 1963, when I was at Mindolo, Northern Rhodesia (now Zambia), as a leading theologian in connection with a seminar on 'Christian Home and Family Life', I was visited one morning by two Americans. They had been told in the course of their research travel in Africa that I was there and had come to consult me about the state of the church in Nigeria. After the formal preliminaries had been quickly disposed of, they announced to me cheerfully that they were not going to take much of my time because they were pressed for time! And then, with note-book opened and pen poised, one of them fired an order at me: 'Now tell us five things that are most important about the church in Nigeria.' I am sure that my readers would appreciate my predicament. I had to make an effort to show a reasonable amount of courtesy as I told them as gently as I could that their quest was not a matter that could be dealt with in five minutes. However, as they insisted on hearing something from me and I found it difficult to send them away rudely, I had to tell them *something*. What they have made of that all-too-brief investigation, I am still wondering. But this is something that often happens, with near-tragic results in print.

The stay-at-home investigator deals solely in material supplied by the traveller or any literature that he can find on the subject of his investigation. Since he has never been out in the 'strange land' himself, he has little means of checking the accuracy or otherwise of the material he is using. Of his tribe it has been aptly observed:

There is a type of thinking which remains safely at home, merely receiving reports, maps, and photographs of what is beyond the garden wall, and speculates often with great cleverness, on the basis of such dispatches received. Thinking and living are thus divorced, or rather, thinking is made into an instrument of escape from involvement with life. Why dive into the sea, if you can talk about it so well and think about it so clearly? But in such circumstances the object of thought becomes no more than an imaginary toy.[13]

Evans-Pritchard is more to the point:

It is a remarkable fact that none of the anthropologists whose theories about primitive religion have been most influential had ever been near a primitive people. It is as though a chemist had never thought it necessary to enter a laboratory. They had consequently to rely for their information on what European explorers, missionaries, administrators, and traders told them. Now, I want to make it clear that this evidence is highly suspect ... much of it was false and almost all unreliable and, by modern standards of professional research, casual, superficial, out of perspective, out of context; and to some extent this was true even of the earlier professional anthropologists.[14]

He goes further to rebuke the deliberate denigration which characterized these earlier statements: the 'ill-formed misconceptions, or, in other words, so much rubbish' all of which 'fitted in very well with colonialist and other interests', some of this 'discredit must go to the ... ethnologists who wanted an excuse for slavery, and some also to those who desired to find a missing link between men and monkeys.'[15]

The menace of this unwitting collaboration between the traveller and the stay-at-home investigator is in the oracular way in which their joint effort produces pronouncements which are unfortunately swallowed bodily by a gullible public. And once such pronouncements are made and accepted, it becomes next to impossible to correct the mischief.

I once visited the Faculty of African Studies headed by an *eminent* professor in a university situated in a European capital. During my discussion with the staff, I asked whether any of them had ever done any field-work in Africa and whether, currently, the faculty had any field-workers in Africa. The answer was that no member of the staff had ever done any field-work in Africa and that the faculty had never had, and did not have, any field-workers in Africa. All their information they collected from books on Africa, a few of which, or extracts from a few of which, had been translated into their own language!

Then there are the serious scholars, several of them specialists in their chosen fields, who inevitably encounter religion in their researches. To this category belong the genuine anthropologist or sociologist whose work is the study of man or society. The debt which scholarship owes to anthropology and sociology, including ethnology, is incalculable. Their scholars and investigators have today penetrated almost every area of the world, remote or near, easy or difficult of access. As a result of their researches, copious amounts of information have been compiled and made available on areas which used to be considered by the Western world as 'dark' and which were imagined to be entirely without any cultures.

Investigators in this category study religion only by the way. It is not their main occupation. They are interested in it only as an element within the spheres of human activity, whether man be taken as an individual or his kind considered as forming the entity known as society. Because of this, neither their qualifications nor their tools are adequate to deal with the essential element of religion. That is why W. Cantwell Smith observes:

> The psychologist or sociologist has probed the externals or the aberrations of faith; but has missed the heart of the matter that has kept the externals living, or the norms from which the abnormal, perhaps all too readily, deviates.[16]

This may cover their circumstances better:

> Social scientists have discerned that in order to understand man, his religion should be taken into account. Inevitably, however, they have had to study religion as one element in the masses of material which they have to collect, sort out, and collate, in order to reach their conclusions. One cannot blame them, therefore, if they find themselves unable to accord it (religion) the cultural place which is its due. At least, they have the virtue of recognizing that one cannot ignore religion if one is to understand man at all.[17]

But here we should allow the anthropologist to speak for himself:

> He is not concerned, *qua* anthropologist, with the truth or falsity of religious thought. As I understand the matter, there is no possibility of his *knowing* whether the spiritual beings of primitive religions or of any others have any existence or not, and since that is the case he cannot take the question into consideration. The beliefs are for him sociological facts, not theological facts, and his sole concern is with their relation to each other and to other social facts ... It was precisely because so many anthropological writers did take up a theological position, albeit a negative and implicit one, that they felt that an explanation of primitive religious phenomena in causal terms was required, going, it seems to me, beyond the legitimate bounds of the subject.[18]

Thus we can see that the shortcomings resulting from the approach of this category of scholars to the study of religion arise from the fact that they do not give enough heed to the wisdom in the saying that 'a genius becomes ordinary when he steps from his proper frame...'

Those who adopt the humanistic approach to the study of religion should be considered as a class, although they are to be found within almost every school of thought. Julian Huxley represents their position well when he says that '... our chief concern is with the humanistic approach to religion – the consideration of religion as a function of the human organism, a natural product of human nature ...'[19] This approach is not entirely without merit as religion has 'ever approximated to being of positive value in proportion as it has succeeded in making man at home in the universe'.[20] Its main problem, however, is that what began as an over-emphasis of the manward end of religion became crystallized into a complete elimination of every other factor in religion, particularly the factor that counts most. The school appears to have accepted the fact of religion in human affairs simply because that fact is so stubborn that it cannot be blinked, ignored, or denied. And true to the tradition of the rationalist school, it has found a compensation in accounting for the undeniable existence of religion with reference solely to man and his mundane preoccupations.

We now come to the theologian who by his designation, properly defined, should be well equipped to enter into the field of the study of religion and be sensitive enough to discern that which is the metaphysic of religion, that which makes religion *religion*, and the individual and social response or reaction which is, paradoxically, the factor in consequence of which one religion is different from another.

Unfortunately, by and large, the theologian of today is a very handicapped person. To begin with, he still lives with the age-old, erroneous notion that only one religion, namely Christianity, has theology; which makes nonsense of the linguistic and connotational significance of the word. Recently, the question of the degree of Doctor of Divinity as one of the higher degrees to be awarded in one of the universities of Africa arose, and the demurrer was raised that the DD has 'always' been awarded in connection with Christian theology; that therefore it might compromise a department whose avowed position was that of religious studies as a comprehensive discipline. The corollary to this is obvious: a doctorate of divinity is incompatible with Islamic Studies, and very much less so with a thing like African traditional religion!

Worse still, the theologian of today considers himself modern if he adopts the laboratory methods in the sense of researching and teaching without being personally and emotionally involved. Thus, he is becoming more and more theoretical and abstract to the detriment of the truth which he is expected to be seeking and imparting. It is this sad situation that gives point to Julian Huxley's remark about 'many divines who have ... diluted the idea of God with philosophical milk-and-water' and probably contributes to his idea of God who 'is tending to fade away, like the Cheshire cat in *Alice*, until only a faint cosmic smile remains ...'[21] When in the study of religion the very heart of religion is disregarded, where is the hope of a profitable study?

On the other hand a serious theologian is constantly beset by the temptation to over-emphasize the divine factor in religion to the detriment of the fact of man as the one who holds faith and apart from whom religion has no meaning. This means that a theologian who yields to this temptation is maintaining a half-truth opposite to that held by the humanist or the rationalist.

We can conclude this section by pointing out that the three great handicaps to the study of religion are ignorance, prejudice, and the 'scientific method' narrowly defined. Of these it is only on the scientific method that it is necessary to say a few more words.

A further quotation from Sir Arthur Keith will be illuminating here.

For the better understanding of man's nature both [Julian Huxley and his grandfather] applied the same methods – the methods of the biological laboratory. Manifestations of the religious spirit were for them biological phenomena, and had to be studied by appropriate methods.[22]

In reply to this we may quote A. C. Bouquet:

It may be questioned whether a world-view expressing itself in an habitual attitude can be deduced from scientific enquiry as commonly conceived; for science is not concerned with values but with phenomena irrespective of quality. Its processes are those of classification and analysis, or of construction as a result of the latter. Thus it analyses the working of the body-machine, with results which are of interest for the chemist and the engineer. But the bodies of the sane man, the criminal, the lunatic, the genius and the prophet, are all equally matter for scientific analysis, and scientific research does not pronounce any qualitative judgment upon their respective brains. It merely says that they differ, and indicates the nature of the difference ... A world-view on a *purely* scientific basis would seem to be impossible, unless by science we mean more than physical science, and make it embrace an impartial observation of human *thought*, with deductions therefrom.[23]

More precisely, Bouquet says with this limitation in mind, 'No doubt the study has its dangers. It may sink to the level of collecting dead insects or pressed flowers, which in the process lose all their colour and reality.'[24] As we have observed elsewhere,

The 'scientific method' has certainly been a blessing to scholarship in that

it has served the salutary purpose of minimizing the amount of emotion
which usually gets mixed up with what should be an objective study; it
has led to more careful verification of data, and created also an urge towards
accuracy in the documentation of observed or verified facts. We must realize,
however, that as in all human things, the 'scientific method' has its limitations; otherwise we shall be according it undue significance and making of
it an infallible tool of divination. There are certain things which this method,
strictly defined, cannot probe. And there are things which are to be reached
and known only through the appropriate apparatus of the human faculties.[25]

Russell Brain sums up the argument by saying,

> The scientific answer is relevant so far as concerns the sense-impressions
> interlocked with the stirring of the spirit, which indeed form an important
> part of the mental content. For the rest the human spirit must turn to the
> unseen world to which it itself belongs.[26]

It is of the utmost importance for the scholar to realize that
religion is living and organic. Dead or extinct religion is dead and
extinct; and the dead should be left to bury their dead. The religion
that is worth studying is religion as practised by living men. Sir
Arthur Keith makes a point when he says, 'Human nature is a vast
complex – not easily analysed. If we are to understand religion, we
must first know human nature.'[27] Whether or not he would accept
the tremendous import that we see in his words is another question.
Huston Smith concludes the opening chapter of his book, *The
Religions of Man* with the significant paragraph:

> A great anatomist used to close his first lecture to beginning medical
> students with some words whose tenor applies equally well to our own
> undertaking. 'In this course,' he would say, 'we shall be dealing with flesh
> and bones and cells and sinews, and there are going to be times when it's
> all going to seem terribly cold blooded. But never forget – it's alive!'[28]

There can be nothing like religion in the abstract or religion
considered apart from persons who worship and practise the tenets
of their faith. Without the mind and consciousness of man and the
consequent ability to apprehend the world of nature and link this
with Something through which that world takes on a meaning and
a significance which cannot be accounted for in mundane terms,
there can be no religion to speak of.

But in considering religion in connection only with worshipping
and practising persons, we must inevitably reckon with the disturbing and at the same time fascinating phenomena of change. The
universe in which man lives expands and contracts almost simul-

taneously, and his world-views are affected accordingly. The change and his world-views may take the form of enlightenment which gives him a better understanding and confirmation of his faith; or it may disturb him so much that its result is a perversion or loss of faith. It is certain that a people whose culture has come into contact with another culture from outside can never *really* be the same again. The culture is either enriched in accordance with its power to withstand the assault of other cultures while assimilating something of their best qualities, or impoverished because of its weakness in consequence of which it succumbs to them by losing its own genius. The power of adaptation in the light of current circumstances is probably a power inherent in every culture; and so, by and large, cultural contact is a matter at the same time of addition and subtraction. When we take into account with the factor of culture-contacts the fact of scientific enlightenment and the technological achievements in which every corner of the world shares in greater or lesser degree, we see how it is impossible for modern man everywhere any longer to be purely conservative with regard to his religious tradition.

It is the duty of the scholar to take account of this factor of change and give it due regard in his study. To study the actual situation of religion is essential to his task. That is why W. Cantwell Smith says:

> I would advise any Western scholar who sets out to study modern religious processes in the Islamic world, not to imagine that he either knows or can find out what Islam formally or essentially is before he starts, so that his task is to survey the current scene and simply to report on what is happening to *that* Islam in the tumult of today's whirlwind ... The Islam that is significant today lies, as it has always lain, in the heart of Muslims; and not necessarily in the inherited forms.[29]

At the same time (and we cannot stress this too often or too much), whatever changes may overtake religion, there is that which is constant and unchanging about every living religion: that which connects the present with the past and reaches out to eternity. Without this, religion ceases to be what it claims to be. 'Every religion maintains that it is not only a state of mind in those who practise it, but an apprehension of the Truth which is independent of their minds altogether; and its whole significance for them resides in this.'[30] The sacred, the holy, this is the factor which is not only the cause but also that which gives religion its ethos, its meaning, its cohesion; it is this which unceasingly grips and transmutes life for man, which remains constantly the heart of religion, whatever changes may take place in its external form.

Thus, in every religion, there are always the elements of change-lessness and change. Religion in what may be known of its pristine state and religion as practised today form one tapestry showing how a person's religion gives meaning and purpose to his world at every moment of time and how the changes in his world affect his theo-logical formulation without necessarily changing the essence of religion for him. There is the constant, creative effort of man's spirit to maintain communion with the Ever-abiding whose mani-festations as seen through the world and through the accommodating mind of man are ever-changing – '... because of the comprehensive nature of religious response, ... a person's faith is the meaning that life has for him, in the light of his tradition'.[31] In this consists the temporality and timelessness of faith.

> For any man whose faith is vivid, even whose faith is at all alive, there are two qualities of that faith ... that stand out, so far as questions of temporality are concerned: first, that it is timeless, second, that it is present. If religion is anything at all, it is something that links the present moment to eternity. Not to understand this is to have no feel for religion at all.[32]

This immediately raises the question of the relation between faith – living faith – and inherited forms and dogma. The general pattern is that dogma tends to remain permanent and unchanging, the custodians of the tradition in each religion being loath to see it disturbed or changed in any way. This has often resulted in dogma becoming a bondage and has led to grave disasters in human history. Consequently, there have been those extremists who would see all dogma scrapped and all adherents of religion left to think 'freely' about their faith. But free-thinking never remains free-thinking for very long: in its turn it crystallizes into set patterns and develops into formulations; and man is back where he was – with new dogma in place of the old.

The history of dogma shows that it comes as a matter of course in every religion. It is laid upon every religion sooner or later to formulate its articles of faith in order to teach and maintain its tenets. Before systematic theology became an academic profession with a tendency to abstraction, the prophets, the seers, the apostles and the disciples were the agents to whom it was given to make statements about the basic tenets of religions and to guide believers about the articles of faith. Thus, the formulations of religious doctrines began with prophecy (forth-telling with reference to orthodoxy) and preaching (proclamation of the truth of religion), which were for the purpose of conversion, of preventing, or calling people from, apostasy and of providing doctrinal material for teaching and the correction or checking of 'heresy'. What began in this way developed and took concrete, permanent shapes, and gathered accretions especially with the marriage of religion and politics and with the development of competitive, proselytizing interests.

Thus the original intention of dogma was that of checking, correcting, and sustaining faith. In a way, the 'theologian' brings or restores order into the chaos which is always a threat to beliefs and practices. Further, dogma and faith are at bottom inextricably related, in that dogma emerged out of the basic experiences of religion. It is certain that, at the beginning, man worshipped he [?] *certain?* knew not what. A person of special perceptive ability had an experience which gripped him and changed the course of life for him, and he could not help making this known; in consequence a generality of his people followed his spiritual and moral leadership. But it would [?] not be enough for him to say, 'Oh, I have had an experience, come and share it with me!' He had to try and put his experience into words. Here, reflection came in, and theological formulations resulted. Moses can only be fully understood when he is seen as Moses of Egypt, of the land of the Midianites, of the place of the burning bush, and all the way through the stages of his theological development until it came to flowering at Mount Sinai; Muhammad who received the revelations which resulted in the Qur'an and the ḥadīth can be fully understood only in the light of Muhammad of the retirement and the solitude of Mount Ḥira. Even as one probes the oral literatures of the traditional religion in Africa, one sees this same process of revelation, reflection, and theological formulation.

Thus, dogma is basically a systematic statement about the beliefs of a particular religion, emphasizing its genius and its tenets. But fundamentally, the man of faith does not set out to obey a law but to practise the law as divine command. His obedience and allegiance are to the Transcendent, to God.[33] Where a religion becomes cramped within the framework of dogma and thus a law to be obeyed, and *true religion's* not a life to be lived, such religion has become an aberration; it *"not in cramping* ceases, in fact, to be religion and has become a mere system, 'a yoke *framework* upon the neck ... which neither our fathers nor we have been able *of dogma"* to bear'.[34] It is necessary to bear all this in mind in order to avoid the distraction too often created by the fact of faith *vis-à-vis* inherited formulation.

Let us conclude this chapter with the following highway code.

In the study of religion, the first rule in the scholar's highway code should be *caution*. The evidence so far is not very encouraging. Scholars in the field of the study of religion appear to know *too much* before they even begin; there is too much show of knowledge and cocksureness about other people's beliefs. I have often watched and listened with feelings wavering between amusement, irritation, or annoyance when foreigners discuss *their own beliefs* about the concept of God and the tenets of religion in my country. The more they can make a debating point of the discussion, the happier they appear to be: after all, an abstraction lends itself easily to a debate! It is a wise warning that:

> Particularly in a study of a major civilization other than one's own, and most of all, of the religions of that civilization, one must learn not to set out seeking answers to questions that one has formulated previously. One must learn rather – slowly, perceptively, painfully, creatively – to ask new questions; to discern new categories; to sense new visions ... One of the most important requirements of our study is a recognition that we do not quite know what it is that we are observing – so that our first struggle is to find out.[35]

It will thus be a restraining influence to know that no scholar who is worth the name should create the impression that his own is the last word on the subject of religious studies. The limit of research is not yet reached and may never be reached by finite man. We live in a universe where reality is constantly revealing itself, where new facets of it are being discovered from time to time. The days of absolute certainty in regard to the universe and human things are gone, and this is in consequence of the disillusionments which have made foolish the wisdom of the 'oracles' of the past, even during their own life time. As fresh visions are vouchsafed to man, new material is added to existing knowledge to modify, enrich, or correct our views with regard to past acquisitions and intellectual positions. Especially is it necessary to be cautious with regard to statements which have to do with Deity in relation to man. To those who conceive Deity as *personal*, it should be easy from their experiences of persons on the mundane level – friends, husbands, or wives – to see that knowledge of a person is never complete. There is a Yoruba saying to the effect that you only know a person by the side of him which he turns to you. Even those who have been married for years continue from time to time to surprise each other by some unexpected revelation of human nature. St Paul's words, 'For now we see in a mirror dimly', should be heeded by everyone who is dealing with the very delicate matter which concerns life in time and in eternity.

The second rule in the highway code for the scholar should be openness and sympathy. Religion cannot be properly studied unless it is studied from the inside; and only those who are prepared to allow truth to reveal itself to them, and those who are prepared to enter into the feelings of worshippers, as much as possible 'sit where they sit', can make any profitable study of religion. It is only in this way that the scholar can appreciate the genius of religion as known to the worshipper. Thus, each religion must be seen 'in terms of its own perspective', otherwise what is studied cannot be the real thing. *

Openness and sympathy presuppose a mind which exposes itself to reality, whatever place reality may happen to have chosen as one of its earthly habitations; a mind which accepts without inhibitions the revelation *in the actual situation*. A committee of the World Council of Churches on the study of Evangelism once adopted the slogan, 'The world provides the agenda'. This is a wise approach in that, if properly followed, it ensures that one does not enter the field with any preconceived notions. The study of religion should follow this approach and let the actual situation 'provide the agenda', that is, let the religion reveal itself. It is not what we think about a religion or what people say about it that is of moment. In fact there is a good deal of what has been called 'extravagant nonsense' in our conceited imaginings about other people's beliefs. What is of moment is what a religion says about itself: and it is upon this that an estimate of it should be based.

At this point the question is rightly asked, 'How does one know what religion is saying about itself amidst its bewildering variety, not only with reference to religions in its various forms, each with its own particular genius which marks it out from other religions, but also with regard to the variety and "deviations" within each religion?' This phenomenon of variety can become so complex and so baffling that one can easily adopt one of three points of view. First, one might be tempted to take appearance for reality: we have already commented on this. Secondly, one might fix upon one particular form of a religion and conclude that this represents the whole of that religion. For example, Methodism or the Eastern Orthodox Church might be seen as holding itself up as representing the whole world of Christianity. Thirdly, one might give up altogether the attempt to understand religion, because here is seen something so confusing and therefore so impossible of disentanglement that it is a waste of valuable time to make the attempt: and from this it is only a step to repudiating religion altogether.

The scholar who seeks to pursue the study of religion is thus beset with a great difficulty from the start in consequence of the ever-growing predicaments inherent in religious situations.

The rich panorama of man's religious life over the centuries presents the observer with a bewildering variety of phenomena, and the studies of those phenomena present him with a cacophony of interpretation. Those who would understand, and those who would intelligently participate, are confronted with a task of no mean proportions.[36]

The scholar will survive the ordeal, however, if he does not confuse himself further by putting self-made obstacles in his own way.

There are those, of course, for whom this openness and sympathy are for ever impossible: they enter the field of study with a spirit of cultural pride and disdain, or as curio collectors. What the curio seeker picks up depends upon why he wants a curio – is it to amuse himself and his friends? Is it to be used as a foil to show off the superiority of his own culture when he is back at home? Is it merely to be able to prove that he has indeed visited a foreign country? Or is it to prove his appreciation of the value in the culture of that foreign country, different from his own as it may be? Yes, the curio seeker may be permitted his possible choices according to his motive; but a true scholar in the study of religion is not permitted to be such a freelance. He is committed to the truth of *the actual situation*, which he should seek until he finds it. But he cannot take this truth by storm. This is where he is kept waiting, and must wait, if he is in earnest, asking until he is given, patiently seeking until he finds, and knocking until the door is open to him. Thus, a necessary passport into that sacred country is imaginative sympathy and constant readiness to learn; that is, the scholar must try and enter into the feelings of the people and see with their eyes in order to grasp and possess the knowledge of what they actually know and believe about the supersensible world.

If religion is essentially of the inner life, it follows that it can be truly grasped only from within. But beyond a doubt, this can be better done by one in whose inward consciousness an experience of religion plays a part. There is but too much danger that the other [the non-believer] will talk of religion as a blind man might of colours, or one totally devoid of ear, of a beautiful musical composition.[37]

It is to be lamented that too often, certain scholars' formulations of other people's faiths are no more than prescriptions of what such scholars in their own wisdom would commend as faith-formulae for those people, without regard to their historical and cultural situation! What is really demanded of the scholar is not this oracular attitude of this-cannot-be-so, this-is-how-it-should-be, but what has been summed up in the words 'imaginative sympathy, appreciative understanding, and (where possible) experiential participation'.

The third rule is *reverence.* 'It has been said that one must tread softly here. For one is treading on men's dreams.'[38] Dreams here must, of course, mean the things of supreme concern to men, the things that they hold dear, which in fact mean life, or which give meaning to life for them both on earth and for eternity. This is the point at which it is difficult for people of certain dispositions – and their name is legion – to understand what religion, especially other people's faith, is all about. They are just not conditioned to enter reverently into other people's homes and observe every sacred rule of hospitality, especially where they have convinced themselves that such people are racially, culturally, or religiously of inferior status to themselves. Whereas the most indifferent of such investigators probably have in their own homes or private lives certain corners where they put off their shoes from their feet, for the place on which they are standing is holy ground, they hold it inconceivable that such holy ground could exist elsewhere for others or within the premises of another faith. They are just spiritually and emotionally unqualified to enter the field of the study of religion, for they cannot help treading blindly and making a mess of things.

Once, a Christian minister accompanied me into one of the principal temple-seminaries at Badagry. From the moment that we entered the place, the minister openly showed his disdain and contempt for the custodian of the cult and everything in the temple. This became increasingly and embarrassingly manifest as the conversation between the custodian and me progressed. The minister kept muttering loudly, 'Oh, ignorance!' 'What darkness!' 'What a pity !', etc. Needless to say, a person of that minister's calibre can learn little about other people's faiths.

The aim of the seeker should be to reach the thing which is of enduring value in religion. It is true that there is no religion whose full story could be all rosy or all insight and inspiration : the catalogue of perversions or vices which each religion has harboured at one time or another during the course of its history will probably be endless; it certainly will not make edifying reading. But there is no point in focussing on the strange, the bizarre and the fantastic, 'lifting it out of context and waving it before the public drool', thus committing 'straight sacrilege, the crudest kind of vulgarization'.[39] Many researchers in the field of religion do not have even the doubtful wisdom of Lady Britomart : 'Will nothing make you behave yourself, Charles? Remember that this is a sacred place, though the misguided worshippers are heathen idolators.'[40]

We can summarize all that we have said about this highway code with the words of Steven Runciman :

Of all the roads that a historian may tread none passes through more difficult country than that of religious history. To a believer religious truths are eternal. The doctrine that he preaches and accepts gives expression to their everlasting validity. To him the historian who seeks to discover and explain why the doctrine should have appeared at a particular moment of time seems guilty of unwarranted determinism ... The historian himself is mortal, restricted by the limitations of temporality; and he must have the modesty to know his limitations. His business is to tell the story and to make it, as best he can, intelligible to humanity.

Nevertheless, if the story is to be intelligible, more is needed than a presentation of mundane facts. Many great and wise men have told us that history is a science and no more. It is true that in the collection of historical evidence accuracy and objectivity are required, especially when the subject concerns religion, a sphere in which judgement is too often influenced by personal conviction and prejudice. But the historian's methods cannot be entirely empirical. Human behaviour defies scientific laws; human nature has not yet been tidily analysed; human beliefs disregard logic and reason. The historian must attempt to add to his objective study the qualities of intuitive sympathy and imaginative perception without which he cannot hope to comprehend the fears and aspirations and convictions that have moved past generations. These qualities are, may be, gifts of the spirit, gifts which can be experienced and felt but not explained in human terms.[41]

R. S. Rattray is a good teacher in this matter, in that he translated our code into practice in his approach to the study of the religion of the Akan :

I approached these old people and this difficult subject [their religious beliefs] in the spirit of one who came to them as a seeker after truths, the key to which I told them they alone possessed, which not all the learning nor all the books of the white man could ever give to me.

I made it clear to them [the Ashanti] that I asked access to their religious rites ... for this reason I attended their ceremonies with all the reverence and respect I could well accord to something which I felt to have been already very old, before the religion of my country had yet been born as a new thought, yet not so entirely new, but that even its roots stretched back and were fed from the same stream which still flows in Ashanti today.[42]

II

Religion

1. The etymological connotation

H. Fielding Hall observes:

> When you find confusion of argument in a book, want of clearness of expression, when you see men arguing and misunderstanding each other, there is nearly always one reason. Either they are using words in different senses or they have no clear idea themselves of what they mean by their words. Ask ten men what they mean when they say art, beauty, civilization, right, wrong, or any other abstract term, and see if one can give a satisfactory explanation.
>
> This is an error I am trying to avoid.[1]

In writing this chapter, we are availing ourselves of Hall's warning; but we do not necessarily accept his implied pessimism with reference to other persons; and we must also bear in mind the saying that 'Philosophy gives little help when it speaks with uncertan voice'.[2]

'Religion' is a difficult topic to handle, whether we are considering its root-meaning, its connotation, its origin, or its definition. Our treatment of the topic of the study of religion in the previous chapter has indicated this much. In this chapter, we must go warily; but nevertheless we must try to elucidate the subject.

In his *Comparative Religion*,[3] A. C. Bouquet examines the etymological meaning of the word 'religion'. 'Religion' he says, 'is a European word, and it is a European convention which has led to its employment as a general term to embrace certain human interests all the world over.' He observes that ancient scholars were divided with regard to its basic meaning:

Of Roman writers Cicero held that it came from a root 'leg–' – meaning 'to take up, gather, count, or observe', i.e. 'to observe the signs of Divine communication'. Servius, on the other hand, held that it came from another root, 'lig–', 'to bind', so that 'religio' meant 'a relationship', i.e. 'a communion between the human and Super-Human'.

The word 'religion' came to embrace both meanings either interchangeably or in combination.

While Bouquet thinks that the root 'leg–' might be the original one of the two, on the ground of comparison with the Greek word *paratērēsis* – 'the scrupulous observation of omens and the performance of ritual', he is nevertheless inclined to derive from the word 'religio' the meaning of 'a fixed relationship between the human self and some non-human entity, the Sacred, the Supernatural, the Self-Existent, the Absolute, or simply "God".'

J. Estlin Carpenter records:

A new use of it [religio] passes into Roman literature in the writings of Cicero. The feeling of awe still lies in the background, but the word takes on a reference to the acts which it prompts, and thus comes to denote the whole group of rites performed in the honour of the divine being. These make up a particular cult or worship, ordained and sanctioned by authority or tradition. 'Religion' thus comes to mean a body of religious duties, the entire series of sacred acts in which the primitive act is expressed.[4]

Recently, W. Cantwell Smith has re-examined the word 'religio' and its use 'in a great variety of senses':

Cicero ... has Balbus the Stoic propound a derivation of the adjective from *relegere*, with the implication that a 'religious' person is one who is careful in his worship and is, as it were, the opposite of a 'neglectful' one. The Christian writer Lactantius ... rejects this on the grounds that piety turns not on the subjective question of how men worship, but rather on the objective one of whom; that there are real obligations to be fulfilled, and this is the root of the matter. He accordingly derives it from *religare* 'to bind'.[5]

Cantwell Smith observes that a great deal of all study of religion since these writers, including the most modern, could be arranged in effect on one side or the other of this dichotomy. Further:

On the etymological question earlier pronouncements were made with no basis for any learned decision: the ideas put forward by any writer reflect his own position on the significance of religion in human life, rather than any philological wisdom about its name. These writers' expositions are valuable to the modern student as indicating authoritatively, and often quite forcefully, what *religio* (more recently, 'religion') meant to them.[6]

He then proceeds to express what amounts to agreement with Bouquet that 'the two roots ["leg-" and "lig-"] may have coalesced in the Latin *religio*'.

Nevertheless, Cantwell Smith rejects the word 'religion'. In a well worded, powerfully argued, fully documented thesis,[7] he seeks to persuade us to drop the word. I do not know how many of his readers would be in the same position as I; that is, left in the end with great admiration for the writer of a truly scholarly work, but still baffled and with little conviction as to the worthwhileness of dropping 'religion', at least for the time being, on the terms of his suggested substitute. It seems that with his substitute we shall be left more confused and far more intellectually frustrated than we are now with 'religion'. The following points raised by his thesis may be considered.

First, it is astonishing that he wishes to drop 'religion' and retain its direct, immediate adjective, 'religious'. It might have been thought logical that if piety, as he suggests,[8] might form a reasonable substitute for 'religion', then 'pious', a direct and immediate adjective of 'piety', should function adequately where he wishes so earnestly to retain 'religious'. Just as 'living religiously is an attribute of persons'[9] (his main argument for retaining 'religious') so also, as far as our knowledge of living creatures go, 'being pious' is attributable only to persons. Just as 'pious' may refer to an active participation in what he describes as 'transcendence', or (loosely) to a passive or negative attitude, so also may 'religious'.

Secondly, 'An historical "cumulative tradition", and the personal faith of men and women', abbreviated to 'tradition and faith',[10] which is his suggested substitute for 'religion', is cumbersome. But, more seriously, what does 'cumulative tradition' mean? Does it refer to the 'history' of a people all down the ages, culture in general and in all its dimensions as it dates back to remembered beginnings, or to the many elements of oral and written traditions which, in spite of any form of sophistication, continue to be the sustaining factor in the culture of each people? 'Cumulative tradition', when it stands out of a context where it is strictly defined to carry a particular meaning for the moment, could have various meanings and connotations. Moreover, even where it refers specifically to a people's belief, in what way could it leave out those concomitant practices, or that accumulation of them which is the usual ground of the quarrel with 'religion'? If 'tradition' is not being given a completely new meaning, then it must be admitted that what is handed down from generation to generation as 'religion' is not only 'the faith once for all delivered' or the dynamic faith which operates in and actuates men and women, but also faith as it expresses itself in interpretation, response, and ceremonial practices.

Thirdly, he proposes 'the personal faith of men and women' as a buttress for 'cumulative tradition'. 'Faith' as a title or concept is attractive as emphasizing that what signifies is that which men and women hold dear, a thing of the inner being, dynamic, actuating, and motivating to the whole of life for them:

> Our Friend, our Brother, and our Lord,
> What may Thy service be?
> Nor name, nor form, nor ritual word,
> But simply following Thee.[11]

That is all very well! But with each religious situation, we happen to be faced not only with God who reveals himself (and not religion), but also with a concrete, visible, tangible, phenomenological and existential fact. 'Faith' means, no doubt, personal trust in the living, transcendental Being; committal in self-surrender to the divine will, with the result that life is divinely controlled and guided. It is precisely here, however, that we run into difficulty. This difficulty concerns the age-long puzzle with regard to form and content or content and form – a puzzle which is not merely for idle speculation or intellectual gymnastics; a puzzle which is an urgent question posed by the actual state of things with regard to man as a being living in a created (or physical) order, who knows, nevertheless, that there is something which to him is more than matter: something outside himself which evokes not a mere response but an active or acted response. Thus, 'faith', both as 'once for all delivered', and as lived out practically by men and women in the course of the spiritual and intellectual pilgrimage of the race, has always sought to express itself in acts of devotion and service. It should not take much research to see how several 'faiths', in trying to express themselves, have had to make use of elements identical with, or similar to, those of older 'faiths'. For example, take the 'movement' inaugurated by Gautama Buddha. The great reformer taught to his followers what had been revealed to him, with the specific aim of a radical departure from the surrounding religious practices and the formation of what might be in fact described as 'religionless' faith. But we know how even before his death, his own practices had come to be regarded as normative and thus taken as a foundation for a ritual structure; from this it was only a step to acquiring from other ways of worship elements which were considered appropriate. Thus, a 'faith' which set out to deliver men and women from the abuses of religion by repudiating 'religion', and by setting up a 'system' of faith in moral practice and spiritual (or mental) discipline *only*, soon found that in order to fulfil certain emotional needs in incurably worshipping man, it must adopt certain forms of ritual as a vehicle of devotional expression.

A not unfair assessment will see in the structure of Christian cultus something of the paraphernalia of the ancient Roman *Pontifex Maximus*, of the ancient cult of the Mother Goddess, and of the oriental mysteries of Mithra. The Christian Church began with no intention of involving its original *koinonia* in any aspects of the cultus of its surrounding religions. But the originator of Christianity had already showed by practice that he was not averse to joining in the worship of the temple or of the synagogue, provided the place was and remained 'a house of prayer' and was not turned to 'a den of robbers'. The early church adopted the rite of baptism which had taken various forms from the *taurobolium* of Mithraism to immersion by John the Baptist in the river Jordan; so also has the sacrament of the holy communion its ancient predecessors. Thus, the church soon found itself caught in the web of the ancient practices with which it was surrounded at its birth, with the result that a 'movement' not originally intended to be priestly in the traditional sense came to acquire priesthood; it began to speak of sacrifice, and even brought itself under the suspicion of seeking salvation by magic.

Still to substantiate our point, we shall quote Bernard Shaw:

Anyone who has been in a mosque can testify that though there is nominally no priest there, the Imams who lead the prayers and conduct the ceremonies fill, in the imagination of the worshippers of Allah, the place of the clergy and priests in the Christian churches, and that a Moorish Marabout has all the powers and all the sanctity of a medieval Christian bishop. True, there are no graven images or likeness of anything that is in heaven above or in the earth beneath or in the water under the earth; but the elaborate decoration, the symbols and texts, the majestic architecture that is made homelike for Allah by the carpeted floor, are capable of influencing the mind of the spectators quite as powerfully as the imagery in Christian Cathedrals.

The mass of mankind must have something to worship that the senses can comprehend.[12]

It would, in fact, be interesting to see what shape the currently advertised 'religionless Christianity' takes, if it ever catches on, in a few years from now !

The cogent fact here is that no one has ever seen or touched 'faith'. Faith only becomes known as it realizes or actualizes itself in expressions. And expressions of faith by persons must reduce themselves into forms which can be described in categories. One category may be changed for another, depending on a current outlook or a state of development; but categories we must employ. This is becoming more so in our form-filling, labelling, pigeon-holing computerizing world !

[margin note: Faith, not a thing to be touched]

When faith expresses itself, the expression manifests itself either spontaneously or by acquiring ever-recurring ritual patterns and practices which are common phenomena throughout the world. The cultural achievement of the human race has a way of repeating or diffusing itself in every place 'where two or three are gathered together ...'. Such are human things; no one lives to himself, no one dies to himself. The words of Eugene Carson Blake are apposite here :

Of course it is true that the organization of religion is not the same thing as faith itself or worship. Of course it is true that the depths of Christian experience are plumbed and the heights of Christian experience are attained, not by majority votes or by church executives in official edicts, but by individual 'God-intoxicated' men and women. But some would have us believe that it would be better if there were no Church organizations at all; that to organize religion destroys it; that though God is great and Christ is good, the Christian Church, like all organized religion, is evil. It is in direct opposition to this too-prevalent mood ... that I speak ... suggesting that without organization Christianity would be as formless and futile as a body without its bones, as man without his spine and its attached and necessary appendages ...[13]

As we have observed earlier in this book, the fact of the phenomena of change must be kept before us all the time in our study or discussion of this subject. But inexorable as the factor of change is, it has never been able to prevail against the persistent, stubborn tendency towards uniformity, for better or for worse, which distinguishes religious expressions of faith from every other phenomenon of human activity. As with an organism, anything that has life – a person, the corporate personality known as society or nation – so it is with faith-in-self-expression. There is a sense in which 'I die every day' is true of each such organism. We speak of a changed man : the man of yesterday, is biologically, the same and yet not the same today; nevertheless, this does not excuse us from calling him a man. Trace the history of a nation, its circumstances and vicissitudes – in a sense it continues to be the same 'through all the changing scenes of life', even though there is a sense in which it will never be the same again. For example, Africa today is undergoing a phenomenal change, not only in parts but as a whole; as an organism it maintains its Africanness, and as a living, dynamic organism it is undergoing, and will continue to undergo, inevitable changes. This all goes to show that one cannot plead the changes which are taking place in religious situations as a reason, or one of the reasons, warranting the dropping of the word 'religion'.

One of the major factors with regard to attitudes to 'religion' is that each category of persons which is concerned about it finds it difficult to be wholly classless. Somehow, each category finds itself, maybe not without struggle, an adherent of this or that school of thought. This may be inevitable; it is possible also that the scholars' own thinking and conclusions have only accidentally coincided with the tenets of one or another of such schools. But it is a point to be watched.

'Religion' has, consequently, been attacked or criticized by at least four categories of thinkers – the atheist or the secularist, those who are reacting against religion in consequence of priestcraft and the abuses and evils promoted or perpetuated in connection with religion, the exclusivist, and currently, the posthumous school in honour of Bonhoeffer.

It is not uncommon to hear the categorical statement that there are no genuine atheists. The question is, however, 'How do we know that?' For this is a statement as difficult to prove as it is difficult to disprove the claim of those who say that they believe in God. It would seem that there have always been the few – call them abnormal or aberrations, if you must judge ! – who can laugh at the very idea of God or gods, be they intellectuals or in the category of 'the village atheists'. It is certainly not impossible that there are those who on moral or intellectual grounds find that they cannot believe in God; or those who, for some inexplicable reason, are just incapable of believing. This does not mean that God is not real or that such disbelief could affect his nature or deity. It does mean, however, that for such atheists God has no demonstrable existence and that they find no occasion or reason to bring him into the practical business of life or to expect anything from him. To them the material world – the visible, tangible world – holds all reality and they do not look elsewhere for it, whether such reality has to do with life in general or with themselves in their existential situations. This class of people has always been represented in the race and its views have been expressed in varying terms. 'The absurd man' created by Albert Camus will be a fair representative of the class: 'the absurd man' lives outside God and therefore 'prefers his courage and his reasoning. The first teaches him to live *without appeal* and get along with what he has; the second informs him of his limits ...' In preference to God he chooses an absorbing passion ... as man he is his own end ... Whatever comes to him or upon him he accepts as fate without grumbling, for a fate is not a punishment ... To him 'nothing is vanity except the hope of another life', for 'what comes after death is futile'; ... Therefore, between history and the eternal he chooses history because he likes certainties ... his mind is made up that he will live out his adventure within the span of his life time ... 'The wise man ... lives on what he has without speculating on what he has not.' He has no concern with ideas or with the eternal. The truths that come within his scope can be touched with the hand – he cannot separate from them ... It is 'royal power' to 'know how to live in harmony with a universe without future and without weakness', to 'think clearly and cease to hope.' Thus 'the absurd man' refuses to take a leap, 'rushing into the divine or the eternal', or to afford himself of any screens which may hide the true facts of life from him.[14]

To those who are represented in 'the absurd man', religion, especially where it has to do with Deity, could have no existential or pragmatic meaning; no useful, desirable purpose. At best, it could only be regarded as an unnecessary human device for the purpose of beguiling a toilsome life or preserving chaos-prone society from the constant threats of disruption. They therefore make religion, with all that it implies both for this life and for the hereafter, a target for severe attack, either because this class of persons has no patience with such a universal epidemic of folly, or in self-defence because it shows them up as odd.

The Roman Lucretius will find a place in between the secularist-atheist and those who abhor 'religion' because of priestcraft and the abuses and evils connected with it. It would seem that his main quarrel was with the kind of religion which makes savage gods its objects of devotion and the perpetration of atrocities and oppression its 'reasonable service':

Human life lay visibly before men's eyes foully crushed to earth under the weight of Religion, who showed her head from the quarters of heaven with hideous aspect lowering upon men ... O hapless race of men! when they attributed such deeds to the gods and added cruel anger thereto! What groanings did they then beget for themselves, what wounds for us, what tears for our children! No act of piety is it to be often seen with veiled head turning towards a stone, to haunt every altar, to lie prostrate on the ground with hands outspread before the shrines of gods, to sprinkle the altars with much blood of beasts and link vow to vow – no! rather to be able to look on all things with a mind at peace.[15]

Anyone who is acquainted with the chequered history of religion with the 'sanctified' monstrosities – murder, cheating, lying, theft, and devastations – which have been committed in the name of Deity will at least sympathize with the critics who are represented in Lucretius.

The exclusivist has always found his refuge in particularity. Properly defined, particularity is a safeguard to the integrity of the faith. It can, nevertheless, become, and has more often than not become, a cloak for odium and rancour with regard to other people's beliefs. The exclusivist sees his own faith as *the* faith, the one and only way to salvation with reference both to life here on earth and life in the hereafter.

Karl Barth, as an outstanding exclusivist of this age, based his whole thesis against 'religion' on the fact that it is a thing which ranges itself alongside falsehood, illusion, and unbelief against Christianity or, to be precise, revelation in Christ which is the *only* means of salvation, on the other side:

There is only one revelation ... Apart from and without Jesus Christ, we can say nothing at all about God and man and their relationship one with another ... From the standpoint of revelation religion is clearly seen to be a human attempt to anticipate what God in His revelation wills to do and does do. It is the attempted replacement of the divine work by a human manufacture ... religion is unbelief ... It is a feeble but defiant, and arrogant but hopeless, attempt to create ... the knowledge of the truth, the knowledge of God ...

Jesus Christ, as He attested to us in Holy Scripture, is the one Word of

God, whom we have to hear and whom we have to trust and obey in life
and in death.

We condemn the false doctrine that the Church can and must recognize
as God's revelation other events and powers, forms and truths, apart from
and alongside this one Word of God.[16]

Orthodox Islam, from the point of view of the exclusivist, makes
the same claim that there can be no other religion but Islam, that
this was *the* religion delivered once for all to Abraham and entrusted
to Muhammad as the *final* revelation.

The rejection of 'religion' by the exclusivist is based upon the
principle that to recognize any other religion or faith is to renounce
the exclusive claim of his own faith. Thus, he cannot accept that
his own faith should be enclosed in the same terminological brackets
as other faiths without at the same time repudiating his exclusivist
claims. Moreover, with the faiths which make such exclusivist claims
there is always the urge to seek to purify their own faith-in-practice
of what they consider to be needless accretions, and this has led
frequently to schisms and rancour among adherents of the same
faith. This brings us to the fourth category.

The martyrdom of Dietrich Bonhoeffer in a German concentration
camp has made a deserved Christian and theological hero of him
and drawn attention to the collection of his writings from prison. His
Letters and Papers from Prison[17] have become especially the quarry
from which elements of what is regarded as his 'new' theology are
being dug out. Of all that the collection of writings contains, the
most attractive for universal consideration seem to be those dis-
connected pieces or sections dealing with his 'suggestions' for 'religionless Christianity'. One wonders, however, if everyone who in-
vokes him on this subject really interprets him correctly, or considers
the background to the sporadic statements which appear to imply a
radical change from his earlier theological position. Be that as it may,
one interpretation of 'religionless Christianity' as read into Bonhoeffer amounts to a discounting of the God who has been hitherto
known to men and women of faith, and to taking sides almost with
'the absurd man' of Albert Camus, with the difference that it would
seem that God still exists in a deistic sense: God is, but this very
God has brought about an order of things in such a way that man has
come of age and can now do without him.

God would have us know that we must live as men who manage our
lives without him ... The world that has come of age is more godless, and

perhaps it is for that very reason nearer to God, than the world before its coming of age.[18]

This is not the place to discuss Bonhoeffer in detail. Our purpose here is to recognize the category of people who cluster round him more or less closely, understanding or *mis*understanding him, but all somehow forming this particular machinery of assault on 'religion'.

It would seem that Cantwell Smith derives from this school his inspiration for saying:

> I am bold enough to speculate whether this term (religion) will not in fact have disappeared from serious writing and careful speech within twenty-five years. Such disappearance could mean for the devout a truer faith in God and a truer love of their neighbour; and for scholars, a clearer understanding of the religious phenomena that they are studying.[19]

He should, however, have added a third category who might 'benefit' from such a disappearance, even triumphantly, and that would be the secularist-atheist. For we must not evade the fact that the real assault on religion is the world of self-sufficient technology: that is, in the interim period before technology has been given full recognition as deity. When the Son of Man comes, will he find faith on earth?'[20] There will always be some kind of 'faith', of course, human nature being what it is, even if it be a 'faith' which has changed 'our Lord' to 'our Ford', altered AD to AF, and makes 'Oh, Ford' serve instead of 'Oh, Lord!'.[21]

We thus conclude this discussion.

'Religion', from the Latin *religio* is a European word. It has come to embrace a reference to the transcendental Reality of faith, the inner reality of faith, as well as the rituals and ceremonies which, basically, are means of communion and communication with Deity. Thus, it carries the unmistakable reference to faith and 'the way of worship' which may aptly be described as 'divine service'.[22]

The term religion as implying 'a great objective something' is phenomenological: it is a working handle for taking hold of a universal phenomenon which, however variegated may be its forms, presents a more or less uniformly recognizable structure and identity of elements. 'Religion' as a concept is based upon an observed, observable fact of a particular sphere of human activity. This is a fact which must not be ignored in our consideration of this delicate subject.

The tendency of the human spirit is to revert to type: 'the faiths' which came into being within a strong cultus area would not have found it difficult to make use of elements from their surrounding cultus in order to express themselves; those which at first resolved that they would have no cultus at all soon found themselves being driven to catch up with their world counterparts. Such is the nature of human things: 'No one sews a piece of unshrunk cloth on an old garment; ... And no one puts new wine into old wine-skins.'[23] Worshipping man says 'Amen', and proceeds to do exactly those things!

'Religion', although admittedly not quite satisfactory, will continue in the meantime as the available, manageable term in European or English language which will be used to refer especially to the outward expressions of faith: that is, until another term is found or coined. When that term comes into being, there will be an armistice for a breathing space, and then the battle about words will begin again. Our consent meanwhile to the continued use of 'religion' is not out of a 'zeal for mere age and obscurity': it is a result of a sincere facing of facts.

2. The origin of religion

Alfred E. Garvie[24] has wisely pointed out that the term 'origin' with reference to religion is ambiguous and implies that it is necessary for the scholar to make clear in his own mind what he actually seeks to know as he approaches this baffling and elusively delicate subject. This is a valuable counsel: much of the muddle which has so far bedevilled the study of religion would be at least minimized in that way.

According to Garvie, the word 'origin' may represent the questions: (a) What is the source of, and the reason for, man's being religious in his own nature? (b) What is the source of, and the reason for, man's being religious in the conditions of the world in which he finds himself? (c) What is the earliest form in which religion has appeared, so far as we can trace back its development?

He points out further that a distinction should be made, for the purpose of study, between the *experience* of religion and the *expression* of religion.

In the experience we may assume that there is something universal and permanent, something rooted in, springing out of, human nature; the expression will depend on local and temporary conditions, physical, mental, moral, and social. To ignore or to neglect this difference is to lay hold on the accidental instead of the essential, the contingent instead of the necessary. To explain how and why men conceived the gods in a certain way is not to explain how and why they conceive gods at all; and yet, many theories of the origin of religion, as we shall see, are content with this superficial treatment of the subject, probably because their authors had not made the distinction for themselves.

This last clause – 'probably because their authors had not made the distinction for themselves ...' – explains a great deal about the deficiences of most of the theories about the origin of religion. E. E. Evans-Pritchard's observation is very helpful in elucidating this point:

> The persons whose writings have been most influential have been at the time they wrote agnostics or atheists. Primitive religion was with regard to its validity no different from any other religious faith, an illusion ... Implicit in their thinking were the optimistic convictions of the eighteenth century rationalist philosophers that people are stupid and bad only because they are ignorant and superstitious, and they are ignorant and superstitious because they have been exploited in the name of religion by cunning and avaricious priests and the unscrupulous classes which have supported them. We should, I think, realize what was the intention of many of these scholars if we are to understand their theoretical constructions ... If primitive religion could be explained away as an intellectual aberration, as a mirage induced by emotional stress, or by its social function, it was implied that the higher religions could be discredited and disposed of in the same way.[25]

A warning is necessary here at the outset: in considering theories propounded by others, we must be careful not to fall into the same mistake that we criticize in them, particularly the mistake of pre-conceived notions or of refusal to see the points of view of others, especially where they are right.

We may now look briefly at some of such theories – *briefly* only in order to fill a gap that would otherwise be left open in this work: there are several books – ancient and modern – on the subject; there is therefore no need to repeat here all that can be read in full in the works of the inventors of 'origins' or in the works of those who have commented adequately on them. We are only, therefore, choosing a few representative theories for comment.

The suggestion that religion is a mere invention more or less for convenience of man or society has always had its advocates, as there have been ancient – very ancient – as well as modern rationalists.

J. Estlin Carpenter has written:

A wide-spread view ... presented [religion] as a mere instrument of policy, devised to overawe the intractable.

The diversity of religions seemed to support this view. Plato's Athenian in one of his latest works, the *Laws*, mentions the teaching of the Sophists who averred that the gods existed not by nature but by art, and by the laws of States which are different in different places, according to the agreement of those who make them. In a fragment of a drama of Sisyphus ascribed to Critias, the friend of Alcibiades, it was alleged that in the primeval age of disorder and violence laws might strike crimes committed in open day, but could not touch secret sins, hidden in the gloomy depths of conscience. A sage advised that to moralise men they must be made afraid. Let them invent gods who could see and hear all things, cognisant not only of all human actions but also of men's inmost thoughts and purposes. They were accordingly connected with the source of the most terrifying and most beneficent phenomena, the sky, the home alike of thunder and lightning, of the shining sun and fertilising rain, seat of divine powers helpful and hurtful to mankind.[26]

This sentiment is not peculiar to the ancient world, or to any other period in the history of the world. Only, in consequence of secularism it is becoming more pronounced. The sages of the Yoruba have always admitted that there are certain apparatus or aspects of religion which were originally no more than inventions of priestcraft either for the purpose of serving political or civic ends for the 'good' of the community or to make people behave in the way that would leave the authorities free to run the community according to their own wishes, or inventions merely to provide a priestly hold on the people as well as ensure the priestly means of livelihood.[27] There is, however, a difference between saying that religion has been adulterated with deliberately arranged accessories, and saying that the whole of religion is an invention.

The Greek Euhemerus has acquired, by academic accident, more reputation than actually belonged to him as a person and a thinker. He is usually listed as a forerunner of the rationalistic school of thought with reference to the origin of religion, and has given his name to the theory known as *euhemerism*. There is no doubt, however, but that he subscribed actively to the Greek scepticism of his time: he was said, in fact, to be a member of the Cyrenaic school, which taught that what is pleasant is the only good.

The *Encyclopaedia of Religion and Ethics*[28] makes a well-documented, convincing case to prove that Euhemerus wrote under the influence of certain early writers, particularly that of Hecataeus, who 'attempted to explain the general belief in the existence of divine beings by the theory that the gods of Egypt were but deified benefactors of mankind' and that the gods of Greece were of Egyptian origin, and similar to their parent stock. An essential feature of the work of Euhemerus, written c. 280 BC, was an account of an imaginary journey during which he pretended to have discovered some Happy Isles. On these imaginary isles, he claimed, he discovered a temple in which was a pillar of gold on which Zeus had recorded in sacred script his own deeds and those of Uranos and Kronos. This somehow became the basis of a 'theology' or theogony by which Zeus, Uranos, and Kronos were seen to have been originally mortals, human beings. Zeus was thus interpreted as 'no more than a ruler who had given a powerful impetus to civilization.' From this, Euhemerus went on to assert that these original heroes, men among their fellow-men, were deified, and that such deification had been going on in the history of religion – heroes and benefactors being deified after their death, and some of them raising themselves to divine status even before their death. It all came to the same thing.

The work of Euhemerus, whatever its value, presented a basic thesis which served a certain intellectual (or spiritual?) tendency in his time. Even though the theory was 'generally rejected by Greek writers of the more earnest type, and especially, of course, by such as had engaged in research', it was popularized in Rome and in that way he was promoted to the rank of the leader of atheistic scepticism. It should be observed, however, that the question raised by euhemerism is not really that of the origin of religion : it only comes to that by inference. Its fundamental bearing is with regard to Deity. And this has been an agelong question, raised by a certain type of mind in every age, every generation, and every community of the human race. Attempts to meet the question have taken one of three ways. First, 'I do not know and cannot know; therefore I let the matter rest at that.' From that point this first way branches in two directions. One takes the direction that Deity and his ways cannot be known except in so far as he vouches himself to man : 'Can you find out the deep things of God? Can you find out the limit of the Almighty? It is higher than heaven – what can you do? Deeper than Sheol – what can you know?'²⁹ Or, 'Truly, thou art a God who hidest thyself, O God of Israel, the Saviour.'³⁰ This is the direction of faith, which is the reverent acceptance of that which is, or may be, inexplicable, but is sure to the eye of faith. The other direction is ⑴ one of rejection on the grounds of the impossibility of positivistic, demonstrable knowledge about God. Curiously, this second way is the one followed by the few, while the first one is acceptable to the majority of mankind.

Secondly, there is the route of 'I know because I have experienced'. ⑵ Men and women of ardent, sure, dynamic faith are the ones who follow this route. And this is an aspect of the essential person which no wise man should try to prove or disprove, except that it is not impossible that 'You will know them by their fruits.'[31]

Thirdly, there is the main path of outright rejection. This says ⑶ categorically, 'There is no God and there is an end.' This, as we have already observed, is trodden by those who either feel genuinely that they have no need of Deity to carry on with life – the atheistic-secularists, or those who, like ostriches, are trying for moral reasons to bury their heads in the sand of self-deception.

But the question raised in what is now being summed up as euhemerism does not only relate to theogony or the origin of religion. It calls also, by implication, for an investigation into the origin of the human inhabitants of the earth. Genesis 6.1-4 states that 'the sons of God came in to the daughters of men, and they bore children to them. These were the mighty men that were of old, the men of renown.' The story of hybrids resulting from contacts between divinities and humans is persistent in ancient mythologies. The Yoruba of Nigeria (and, in fact, other peoples in Africa) think that it is not improbable that the original inhabitants of the earth were divinities who, as they withdrew from the earth in visible form, left behind offspring who became what we now know as human beings. I must correct here my former observation that 'This theory makes the divinities no more than deified ancestors ...'[32] I see now that this is forcing an alien meaning into the theory: it need not mean more than it says.

There is no doubt but that there are historical supports for euhemerism. Certain Roman Emperors were deified after death, some proclaimed themselves divine during their life time; and did not one of them 'deify' even a beloved horse? Before the Romans, the Egyptians had led the way. In any culture where kings or emperors are believed to be direct descendants of Deity, assumptions of divinity or later deifications are very easy. So also is this true of cases where rulers are believed to be derivatively divine because their sceptres

are believed to belong to Deity on behalf of whom they rule the
people. The deification of ancestors is not alien to African belief,
especially in places where the cults of ancestors have become predominant. On this ground one must tread warily, however, as it
has become irritatingly easy for certain investigators to rush to the
conclusion that all is 'ancestor worship' in Africa simply because
of the fact of the cults of ancestors. Research into certain cases reveals
that among the Yoruba, for example, an ancestor 'became' a divinity
only by absorbing the attributes of an earlier, original divinity.
Especially is this so where the ancestor had been a priest-king, or a
powerful priest. The process usually began with the divinity being
called (instead of his proper name) 'the divinity of ... (the priest's
name)'; as gradually 'the divinity of ...' drops out, the name or the
principal title of the ancestor remains. Thus, 'Where the ancestor
has been the priest of the tutelary divinity and has also been a
person of very strong character, it is not unusual that the divinity
and the ancestor become so closely associated that (eventually) the
distinction between them is blurred or disappears'[33] some time after
the death of the ancestor. It is possible that this may be general
throughout Africa; it certainly occurs in several places in Nigeria.

Thus, we come to the crucial question with regard to euhemerism:
'Whence did the men who made the claim to be gods derive the conception of gods, among whom they include themselves?'[34] The basis
of this question borders precariously on that of the old ontological
argument and it is possible that a Kant may answer it from the
Kantian vein. It is obvious, anyway, that while euhemerism may
offer a partial explanation of something about religion, it does not
really account for religion, especially as it fails to tell us how men
came to the idea of the divine.

Next, we shall look at the psychological theory of the origin of
religion as represented in the Freudian school.

Freud

One of Sigmund Freud's books bears the intriguing title and sub-
title of *Totem and Taboo: Some Points of Agreement between the
Mental Lives of Savages and Neurotics.*[35] The interesting point for
scholarship here is that Freud must undoubtedly have seen plenty
of neurotics in his clinics or in other connections, but it is certain
that he never set eyes on any of his so-called 'savages'. He was a
veritable stay-at-home investigator with regard to the world outside
Europe; and it is no wonder that he had to draw very heavily on
the fantastic 'yarns' of Frazer's *Golden Bough* and on Robertson

Smith's *Religion of the Semites*, which were principal among his
source-books. The following quotations from the book, taken as
samples, are illuminating:

> It may be as well, however, to warn the reader, in advance, of the
> difficulties with which any statements on the subject have to contend. In
> the first place, those who collect the observations are not the same as
> those who examine and discuss them. The former are travellers and
> missionaries while the latter are students who may never have set eyes on
> the objects of their researches ...[36]

This admission supports what we have already said about Freud's
researches.

> Psycho-analysis has revealed that the totem animal is in reality a sub-
> stitute for the father; and this tallies with the contradictory fact that,
> though the killing of an animal is as a rule forbidden, yet its killing is a
> festive occasion ...[37]

Now, what or who has been psycho-analysed? – a theory, no doubt,
since Freud and 'primitive' men had never met, and no 'primitive'
man ever entered his clinic.

> Such is the highly remarkable theory put forward by Atkinson. In its
> essential feature it is in agreement with my own ... The lack of precision
> in what I have written in the text above, its abbreviation of the time
> factor and its compression of the whole subject-matter, may be attributed to
> the reserve necessitated by the nature of the topic. It would be as foolish to
> aim at exactitude in such questions as it would be unfair to insist upon
> certainty.[38]

What else should be expected in a situation where research is made
up of traveller's tales and unrestrained imagination?
   Freud's writings are full of many such admissions, implicit or
expressed, of the fact that he was writing on a subject about which
he had no first-hand evidence and was therefore playing the role of
a clever theorist who was dragging in distorted facts or attractive
falsehoods to fit his theory.
   Freud's theory of the origin of religion is firmly based on 'totem-
ism' with emphasis on 'the theme of the totemic sacrifice and the
relation of son to father'.[39] He somehow finds the basis of the father-
son relationship in a mental illness.

> The model upon which paranoiacs base their delusions of persecution
> is the relation of a child to his father ... When a paranoiac turns the
> figure of one of his associates into a 'persecutor', he is raising him to the

rank of a father: he is putting him into a position in which he can blame him for all his misfortunes. Thus this second analogy between savages and neurotics gives us a glimpse of the truth that much of a savage's attitude to his ruler is derived from a child's infantile attitude to his father.[40]

Thus, Freud builds the foundation for his theories of the father-complex, and of *projection* – a 'special psychical mechanism known in psycho-analysis', a means of ejection of 'internal perception and intellective processes' into the external world.

Projection created demons out of the hostility which the savage feels towards his ruler, which is the same as the hostility which a son feels towards his father, in consequence of the father's 'severity, his love of power, his unfairness, or whatever else may form the background of even the tenderest of human relationships'.[41] His sons began by rejoicing over the father's death, then mourned for him, then turned him 'into a wicked demon ready to gloat over their misfortunes and eager to kill them'. In this way, primitive man built up a view of the universe which could be summed up in the term *animism*. From the theory 'that the first-born spirits were *evil* spirits', the notion is reached that projection created spirits and demons in general; by man's turning of 'his emotional cathexes into persons, he peoples the world with them and meets his internal mental processes again outside himself' – man's first theoretical achievement was the creation of spirits.[42]

Freud thought that the 'god', to begin with, was a stranger to the situation; before long, however, 'the concept of God had emerged – from some unknown source – and had taken control of the whole of religious life'.[43] And yet, before the book had progressed barely a few lines after expressing that, he had discovered 'the unknown source':

The psycho-analysis of individual beings [of his own imagination!], however, teaches us with quite special instances that the god of each of them is formed in the likeness of his father, that his personal relation to God depends on his relation to his father in the flesh and oscillates and changes along with that relation, and that at bottom God is nothing other than an exalted father ... We are relieved from the necessity for further discussion by the consideration that the totem is nothing other than a surrogate of the father ...; the god will be a later one, in which the father has regained his human shape.[44]

Thus, he concludes:

I should like to insist ... that the beginnings of religion, morals, society and art converge in the Oedipus complex. This is in complete agreement with the psycho-analytic finding that the same complex constitutes the nucleus of all neuroses, so far as our present knowledge goes.[45]

In the book under review, Freud does not disguise the fact that his material, by its very nature, was intractable and that again and again he was forced into difficult and doubtful conclusions.

Before I bring my remarks to a close, however, I must find room to point out that though my arguments have led to a high degree of convergence upon a single comprehensive nexus of ideas, this fact cannot blind us to uncertainties of my premises or the difficulties involved in my conclusions.[46]

It is commendable that Freud is so sincere in his declarations that he was in difficulty with his theory in consequence of the admitted uncertainties of his premises. How one would wish that those who invoke him as an infallible oracle in support of psychological theories would be as sincere!

Freud did not stop with the father-son relation as the emotive factor of religion. He proceeds further in *The Future of an Illusion* to find religion originating in consequence of man's helplessness in face of the formidable odds of life and man's effort to find help outside himself to overcome these odds.

There are the elements, which seem to mock at all human control ... there are diseases, which we have only recently recognized as attacks by other organisms; and finally there is the painful riddle of death, against which no medicine has yet been found, nor probably will be. With these forces nature rises up against us, majestic, cruel, and inexorable; she brings to our mind once more our weakness and helplessness ... For the individual too, life is hard to bear, just as it is for mankind in general ... Man's self-regard, seriously menaced, calls for consolation; life and the universe must be robbed of their terrors ... We can apply the same methods against these violent supermen outside that we employ in our own society; we can try to adjure them, to appease them, to bribe them, and by so influencing them, we may rob them of a part of their power ... This situation is not new. For once before one has found oneself in a similar state of helplessness: as a small child, in relation to one's parents.[47]

Freud maintains that man, finding himself in this position, resorted to projection, by the aid of which he gives the forces of nature the character of a father and turns them into gods for the threefold purpose of exorcising the terrors of nature, reconciling men to the cruelty of Fate, and compensating them for the sufferings and privations of life.[48]

Thus religion is only a result of powerful wishful thinking on the part of weak, intellectually immature man. Religious ideas 'are illusions, fulfilments of the oldest, strongest and most urgent wishes of mankind'.[49] It is this wishful thinking which created God for man 'in the blue field of nothing'. God here is an illusory object which man can both fear and love, on which man could displace his own will, in which the 'transfiguration of the cultural prohibition' called morality becomes a thing of special solemnity.[50]

But religion, 'comparable to a childhood neurosis', will be overcome just as infantile neuroses are overcome spontaneously in the course of growing up; whatever remains of them can be cleared by psycho-analysis. The end of religion as an illusion will come when intellect comes fully to its own; and education and science will surely hasten the day of the primacy of the intellect.[51]

Thus, the sum total of Freud's concept of the origin of religion is that God is an illusion. As Father, he is a mere creation of wishful thinking: a child needs a father because of his helplessness; he needs a father who will be faithful, not subject to weakness, that cannot be frustrated by death; and man, as an intellectual and psychological infant, by the aid of indefatigable projection, produced this Father for himself. Man's psychological ailment which results in religion may thus be called either 'childhood neurosis' or 'father-complex'. And just as a healthy, mature man outgrows childish things, so also will healthy-minded man, the intellectual man, outgrow the illusion which brought about religion.

The usefulness in Freud's theory is that he discerns clearly that, wittingly or unwittingly, hard-pressed man is often given to imaginary thinking, wishful thinking, and day-dreaming. Every person knows those moments when in consequence of difficulties and frustrations he has had to take imaginary wings and fly to a dream world where all is well, for the best, smooth-sailing, and everlastingly beautiful. In Aldous Huxley's *Brave New World*, every person in the 'new world' is adequately provisioned with a hallucinatory drug called *soma*, which is to be taken in moments of difficulties and which will send the person to a peaceful, sweet-dreamland of 'eternity' for as long as he wishes to keep away from the disturbing facts of real life, depending on how much of the drug he takes.

Man is also an adept builder of 'castles in the air'. This happens to everyone, whether it happens 'spontaneously' by a trick of the mind or by deliberate inducement.

With regard to religion, there is no doubt but that false gods have come into being from time to time in consequence of priestcraft and human cunning, and that they are perpetuated by ignorance and fear, or by the pressure of the heavy hand of authority.

Freud's theory of 'child neurosis' or 'father-complex' boils down to the 'search for security'. It is true that security is the earnest, sincere desire of every person: the urge towards self-preservation is so strong in man; the bodily appetites are always clamouring for satisfaction and should be legitimately satisfied; and there is the yearning for joy, and for victory over apparently numberless, unpredictable enemies of man's well-being. Nevertheless, how could it be correct to say that the origin of religion is simply the 'search for security'? How could this be correct with the facts of history before us, showing us unmistakably the ever-recurring element in religion which enables man to say with conviction, 'Though he slay me, yet will I trust him ...',[52] or 'Who shall separate us from the love of Christ? Shall tribulation, or distress, or persecution, or famine, or nakedness, or peril, or sword? ... No, in all these things we are more than conquerors through him who loved us.'[53] Or, 'O God! If I worship Thee for fear of hell, burn me in hell; if I worship Thee in hope of Paradise, exclude me thence; but if I worship Thee for Thine own sake, withhold not from me Thine everlasting beauty!'[54]

One further point about Freud. If the root of religion is a disease of the mind, how comes it that the disease virus is so universally potent and so utterly invincible? For religion is persistent as the most stubborn of human activities. It is vital to life. Suppressed or repudiated or rejected in one form, it presents itself in another and yet another, and goes on with its organic life.

It is not unfair to say that Freud assumes too readily a complete knowledge of human nature, and this alone is enough to open his theory to suspicion. Because of this pretence to knowledge he has an explanation that is too neat and too simple for the hunger and yearnings of the human heart for the living God.

The school of thought represented in Emile Durkheim also came into being for the purpose of explaining away religion. To this school religion is merely a sociological tool. Durkheim maintains that the reality which religious thought expresses is society:

In a general way it is unquestionable that a society has all that is necessary to arouse the sensation of the divine in minds, merely by the power it has over them; for its members it is what a god is to his worshippers.[55]

In summary, he asserts that 'Religion is altogether a social phenomenon' and 'religious beliefs are those which carry with them social
obligations'.[56]

Thus, Durkheim explains religion simply in terms of a sociological
function :

> Now the ways of action to which society is strongly enough attached to
> impose them upon its members, are, by that very fact, marked with a dis-
> tinctive sign provocative of respect ... It is society who speaks through the
> mouths of those who affirm them in our presence; it is society whom we
> hear in hearing them; and the voice of all has an accent which that of one
> alone could never have ... But social action follows ways that are too
> circuitous and obscure, and employs psychical mechanisms that are too
> complex to allow the ordinary observer to see whence it comes ... Men
> know well that they are acted upon, but they do not know by whom. So
> they must invent for themselves the idea of these powers with which they
> feel themselves in connection ... Social action does not confine itself to
> demanding sacrifices, privations and efforts from us. For the collective force
> is not entirely outside of us; it does not act upon us wholly from without:
> but rather, since society cannot exist except in and through individual
> consciousness, this force must also penetrate us and organize itself within
> us; it thus becomes an integral part of our being and by that very fact this
> is elevated and magnified ... This stimulating action of society ... produces,
> as it were, a perpetual sustenance for our moral nature ... So we ordinarily
> think of it under the form of a moral power which, though immanent in
> us, represents within us something not ourselves; this is moral conscience,
> of which, by the way, men have never made even a slightly distinct
> representation except by the aid of religious symbols.[57]

In simple terms the meaning of this is that Deity is an illusion
created by the very fact of the demanding, moulding factor of society.
The individual person belongs to society, having been born, brought
up, nurtured, and trained, with provisions made for his whole living,
by society. But man could not be left to run his life without adequate
safeguards to make sure that his personal choices would not jeopard-
ize the very being of society itself. Society, therefore, had to devise
or invent a means of keeping rebellion-prone man in check so that
its machinery may run undisturbed. The means was achieved by the
invention of certain codes of behaviour : these codes crystallized into
a principle in consequence of which each person finds himself im-
pelled, compelled, or constrained to live in conformity with a norm
laid down by society. This artificial principle – 'a complex of residual
habit' operating in man – is what has been mistaken as, or misnamed,
'conscience' or the divine imperative. The fact is, *vox populi vox dei*

means that there is nothing like 'a divine imperative'; that which speaks in man is only the collective 'voice' of society.

Sociologists who repudiate any kind of faith in Deity have found this theory in its several forms and variations handy; and the theory has its appeal for a certain type of mind. Why?

The reason is that this theory recognizes certain truths about human nature with regard to religion and makes use of them. H. H. Farmer[58] has adequately outlined these basic facts. First:

> The sociological explanation of religion fully recognizes that the aware-ness of being confronted with absolute demands, or sacred values, which are not to be put into the balance with anything else whatsoever, but are to be obeyed if need be even at the cost of life itself, is quite central in, and distinctive of, religion. It does not in the least seek to minimize the power and significance of religion in this respect in human affairs.

The sociological theory admits this; but goes on to say that there is no need to bring Deity in to explain its source. For the absolute demand, sacred values, or the unconditional imperative, there is no other source or origin than the tremendous pressure of the group which has been built into the very texture of the individual person's being. Farmer summarizes Bergson's simile of the individual person as an ant in an ant-hill. 'Its whole life, its whole activity, is domin-ated down to the last detail by the requirements of the ant-group, of the close-knit organic whole of which it is but a single cell.' There is *always* 'the irresistible pressure' – consciously recognized or not, 'of the social organism on its psychical being in the form of a categorical imperative' so that its automatic response as actualized in its life may be aptly described as 'the somnambulism of instinctive be-haviour'.

Secondly, the sociological theory recognizes the fact that man is always in need of, and seeking for, support and refuge. It is not necessary, however, it stipulates, to seek an illusory refuge and support called Deity. All the support and refuge needed by the individual person is provided by society: the sense of being one with society, of having society's powerful reinforcement and pro-tection, gives all the needed satisfaction. All that religious exercises and their results do is to get the individual soaked in social stimuli and encouragements 'in an unusually concentrated form'.

Thirdly, the theory recognizes the awareness by man in religion of the mysterious, the supernatural, and of an 'ultimate reality other than and transcending himself, the source of his being and having the disposal of his life'. It says, however, that something of Bergson's ant-hill simile would explain this. There are only the social forces moving and actuating the individual person; but because of a kind of remote control – society-radio control! – they seem to each person, as he 'becomes aware of their effects in himself and in his neighbours, to come from some mysterious, all-encompassing reality other than himself and his neighbours, transcending all that he is able empirically to observe in their everyday life, and outlasting the brief span of their years ... Thus ... society provides him with the raw stuff of the idea of God.'

What have we to say to all this?

Objections ①

First, there is a fundamental truth in the saying of Durkheim that 'religion is ... a social phenomenon' (we leave out his 'altogether'), as also in 'religious beliefs are those which carry with them social obligations'. In every religion, the emphasis of ethics is that of harmony and well-being of the individual person *within* society. The Hebrew concept of *shalom* = 'total well-being' comprehends every aspect of life for man in his total being as related to personal, domestic, societal, and national issues. Every religion aims at making the individual person so 'unselfish' that he shall be a member who by his life and behaviour positively promotes such harmony and well-being and negatively desists from anything that may disrupt or prevent it. Every religion essentially seeks, therefore, to be an instrument of cohesion in the community; and all religions which claim universality have the mission of establishing an order in which 'The wolf shall dwell with the lamb, and the leopard shall lie down with the kid, and the calf and the lion and the fatling together ... The cow and the bear shall feed ... The sucking child shall play over the hole of the asp ... They shall not hurt or destroy ...'[59] It is not by accident that each epistle in the New Testament, after the doctrinal expositions, ends with a practical application to the end 'that there may be no schism in the body ...'

Society and individual persons are involved in each other, and there is a sense in which one gives meaning and a sense of purpose to the other. But whereas there can be an individual person apart from society, even though he be 'solitary, nasty, and brutish', there is no way by which society can have existence without individual persons. There is no abstract entity called society: whatever society there is, is a society of persons, of living, human beings. It is only in this sense that we agree with Cooley when he says:

A separate individual is an abstraction unknown to experience, and so likewise is society when regarded as something apart from individuals. The real thing is Human Life, which may be considered either in an individual aspect or in a social ... but is always, as a matter of fact, both individual and general.[60]

But here the weakness of the sociological theory becomes manifest: it is saying that the individual person is made for society, thus reducing each living person to a mere cog in the wheel of the societal machine, to a mere particle in a mass, or a drop of water in an ocean which is the community – a thing that is moving only as actuated by a force over which it has little control. Thus, personal freedom is reduced to a sham and man's sense of responsibility a delusion.

Carlyle Marney in *The Structures of Prejudice* observes in the chapter on 'Limitations of Materialism' that 'Canon Streeter archly inquired about ... this functionless shadow with the curious "impotency" of thinking, knowing, self-consciousness. It is odd, said he, that the universe of Automaton should give birth to little automata alive enough to know that they are but an illusion!'[61]

The argument about self-preservation and sense of value inherent in society, which is communicated to the individual person, breaks down on its own premise. If the individual person forming society is only a somnambulist ant in an ant-hill, and society itself has no existence apart from individual persons (which cannot be strictly true conversely), whence does society derive its own consciousness of values in the first instance?

We should have thought that a soul-less machine cannot anticipate its own breakdown! What is it that gave society its own 'sense' of value? And to what end is this value being preserved? Why does society not allow (to follow the argument of the theory) its every member to go on eating and drinking and being merry in the way that whims dictate, and then die any tomorrow?[62]

With regard to conscience, one must admit that it is largely a social thing, informed, developed, guided, warped, distorted, or retarded by the social system and the impingement of social pressure. But what is it that makes conscience so essentially and ultimately individual? This is a question that is still waiting for a satisfactory sociological explanation. The indisputable fact is that conscience is of the personal autonomy and will and, although it often suffers paralysis when the will and the sense of autonomy are paralysed, it is so essentially and ultimately individual that it creates constant rebellion against violations of man's inalienable rights; sooner or later, a person in his right mind refuses to bow down before the golden image of a threatening Nebuchadnezzar and chooses instead to burn in a fiery furnace, if need be, in defence of his personal conviction. In fact, the truth is that, according to the testimony of history, the easiest way for society to cause disaffection, disharmony, or even the destruction of its machinery, is by the suppression of personal autonomy and conscience. Where society (of individual, living persons) ministers to the needs of persons according to the consent (in varying forms of enlightenment and development) of the persons concerned, such persons obey the *will* of society which is, in fact, their own collective will; but where some machinery within society tries to treat persons as impersonal and arrogates to itself the rule of oppression and suppression, individual rebellions begin to manifest themselves, and mass rebellion is only a matter of time.

This is true also for the argument about the need of man for support and refuge. Whereas the promise of comfort, promotion, or favour may lead man to consent to slavery and bondage for a while, there awakens in him sooner or later the fact that he is not a fed beast to be 'kept down' by the hope of reward or fear of punishment. The story of Daniel and that of the three Hebrews, popularly known as Shadrach, Meshach, and Abednego, are significant for the essential noble nature for which man is made and the inalienable right which he claims either always or eventually.

For our part, we hold that it is idle to seek in any of the ways outlined above the origin of that which happened long ago, in the very dim or dark past of the beginnings of man. If we take Alfred Garvie's unscrambling of the ambiguity in the meaning of the word 'origin', this fact will become forcibly clear to us. Man's investigation into 'origin' often results in such an absurdity as that of a miracle-play in which Adam was made to walk across the stage on his way to be created! So much is man anxious to show that he knows everything about how things came to be.

Garvie's meaning (*a*) fixes upon human nature. Everything begins here and ends here. The psychologists and the humanists have made this their happy hunting-round in a bid to debunk religion altogether or to establish a 'religion without revelation'. This was the sports-field of Julian Huxley as of Freud: both started with the same material, human nature; one sees 'religion' as an essential biological function which should be cured of morbid growths and reharnessed correctly, the other sees it as a symptom of a psychical disease which should be purged permanently from the human system. Julian Huxley and his followers accept religion as an inevitable biological necessity, that is, only as inevitable as eating and drinking; whereas the Freudian school interprets it as a sense of need which has been wrongly satisfied and therefore has never really been satisfied.

Garvie's meaning (b) was adopted by the Durkheim brand of sociologists. It has always been clear to man that, left to himself, his life would disintegrate along the line of least resistance. Therefore, a kind of order, or better still, a kind of cohesive force, is needed to maintain order and save man from destroying himself, or the world from destroying itself.

Apart from the fact of the ever-threatening proneness of things to disintegration, there is also the fact that the universe has always presented man with a riddle – a hydra-headed riddle which frightens him, confronts him with the notion that there is more to the universe than the visible and tangible, and urges him on to find solutions to each dimension of the riddle as often and as quickly as it presents itself. Where man takes fright, he flees, but where? Where he accepts that there is more to the universe than meets the eye, he either bows down and worships – but what? Or, he may try to leave well alone – but can he? Where he is urged to find a solution to the riddle, he often discovers secrets which are for his benefit, in which case he is grateful to the benefactor – but who or what is this? And he often confuses himself the more by creating situations which get rapidly out of hand.

Garvie's meaning (c) has always had its basis resting on the 'myth' of the primitive man. The term 'primitive' we have already discussed and shall discuss further. It is only necessary here to under-line the fact that the theorists assume too much, arrogant knowledge of 'the primitive man', or of the beginnings of life. As Evans-Pritchard puts it:

I think that most anthropologists would today agree that it is useless to seek for a *primordium* in religion. Schleiter says truly, 'all evolutionary schemes of religion, without exception, in the determination of the prim-ordium and the serial stages of alleged development, proceed upon a purely arbitrary and uncontrolled basis' ... In these theories, it was assumed, taken for granted, that we were at one end of the scale of human progress and the so-called savages were at the other end, and that because primitive men were on a rather low technical level, their thought and custom must in all respects be the antithesis of ours ... Primitive man was thus represented as childish, crude, prodigal, and comparable to animals and imbeciles ... Needless to say, it was held that primitive peoples must have the crudest religious conceptions.[63]

'Primitive', even as used in this passage which we quote with approval, is questionable. The person whose faith is being studied today is not the primitive man; he is the contemporary man, wherever he is located. The reason for the stubborn use of this most inappropriate term with regard to 'origin' is that it is handy as a tool for erudite guesswork. It is an easy aid for the academically (?) sharpened imagination that

> ... bodies forth
> The forms of things unknown

We should look further at Evans-Pritchard's admirable work on this topic. Perhaps he hopes too much, however, when he says in the quotation above, 'I think that most anthropologists would today agree ...' The field still swarms with unconverted anthropologists and other 'anthropologists'; appearances are still being taken too much for reality: what happens in a tiny corner of a continent is still being recorded as the general fact for a whole continent, often after a misinterpretation, misrepresentation, or distortion.

'Primitive religion' is in fact a reasoning backwards imaginatively and comparatively, from data built up with elements from Western cultures combined with observations or hearsay evidence about certain non-Westerns: from this we are presented with a hypothetical 'religion' qualified with the emotional epithet 'primitive'.

The warning should be heeded 'that it is not sound scientific method to seek for origins, especially when they cannot be found'.[64] This is true especially when, as we have observed, the search is directed not as a matter of objective interest, seeking 'origins' for the sake of objective science or scholarship, but as a weapon to fight 'religion' or as a palliative to soothe an accusing mind. There is, however, a sense in which the matter could be pursued reverently and humbly, as long as we tread warily in a delicate situation. And this concerns the topic of our next section.

3. Revelation

We may begin here with the substance of Alfred E. Garvie's warning:

> In trying to discover the origin [of religion] we must recall the distinction ... between *experience* and the *expression* of religion. In the experience we may assume that there is something universal and permanent, something rooted in, springing up out of, human nature; the expression will depend on local and temporary conditions, physical, mental, moral, and social. To ignore or to neglect this difference is to lay hold on the accidental instead of the essential, the contingent instead of the necessary.[65]

The point that is made here is significant. The expression of religion is something phenomenological, something observable and interpreted correctly or incorrectly. Several writers on religion have fixed on this observable aspect as if it constitutes all that religion really is. They often appear to know everything about religion, to have a kind of precision (or imprecision) instrument which records the working of the dynamism of faith in the believer; whereas their whole interpretation is based upon appearances. In consequence, the interpretation of faith by the believer or one who knows the religion from the inside is ever at variance with its interpretation by a mere observer who thinks that the interpretation of religion is a mere matter of ratiocination, or a matter of intellectual juggling with mere accumulation of data. This difference of outlook is inevitable because

> How should I tell, or how can ye receive it?
> How, till He bringeth you where I have been?[66]

One important virtue of Garvie's warning is that it is a call to recognize the fact that reality comes before thought, experience comes before expression, and fact comes before theory. First the apple fell from the tree to the ground, and then Isaac Newton began to wonder why it fell and in the direction that it did! But while with Garvie we could admit that it is important to recognize the distinction between experience and expression, we would rather emphasize more the fact of the correlation between the two. In religion, experience is the inward thing, something that happens within the being of man and evokes a response, and the expression is a manifestation of the fact that the depth of being has been so touched. Experience, like smoke, finds its own outlet, a way of manifesting the fact that it has occurred.

Now, the question of what experience resulted in religion has been approached in several ways. Here I wish briefly to look at it under its causative factor of revelation, bearing in mind that

> It is only our experience that can interpret what theologians have called revelation, and test its validity. Much as we may wish to, we can no more eliminate experience than we can jump out of our skins.[67]

Revelation in the context of religion is a theological word. In this sense, it means self-disclosure: there is an agent who reveals and there is a mind which apprehends the revelation. Thus, revelation by definition means divine self-disclosure.

Rudolf Otto's thesis[68] on this subject is well known. He describes as *numen praesens* the 'something' which occurs to a man's experience, as a result of which he realizes that there is something 'Wholly Other' than himself, which transcends his world of ordinariness, something 'objective and outside the self', which leads him to the self-evaluation which evokes in him a feeling of self-abasement and dependence. The 'numinous' combines the attributes of that which causes a sense of awesomeness, eeriness, daunting self-abasement and inadequacy with that of attractive, often irresistible magnetism. To this total occurrence he gives the conceptual name of *mysterium tremendum et fascinans*.

Those who live close to nature and are still sensitive to its influence know what this means, having experienced it in

> The flashing of the lightning free,
> The whirling of wind's tempestuous shocks;

or in the paralysing-attractive situation created in animal relationships.

> Wherever the cobra lies in wait, there its prey will reach it. We often see a proof of this when a squirrel approaches the lair of a cobra. As soon as it approaches near enough, the awareness of a terrible presence is communicated to it; and as soon as that registers, the squirrel immediately utters shrieks of vexation, fear, and agony, shrieks which rend the air and broadcast to the world at large its presentiment of grave danger. Notwithstanding, it moves towards the cobra as if tied to the end of a string by means of which it is drawn slowly but surely and inexorably.[69]

In the world of human experience this is not unknown. Charismatic persons have been able to cause such experience in persons of lesser calibre. In the film *Caesar and Cleopatra* shown in England about 1945-6, Caesar appeared as a complete riddle to Cleopatra whose hitherto potent wiles failed to entrap him. When Caesar was leaving Egypt, Cleopatra accompanied him to his boat, and as he went up the gangway, she looked at him and shook her head, shedding tears. Then someone asked her whether she did not want him to leave. Her reply was to the effect that 'I want him to go; I do not want him to go.'

'Numinous uneasiness'[70] would seem to be the main cause of H. G. Wells' *Mind at the End of its Tether.* H. G. Wells was helplessly aware that the being whom he called the Antagonist, whom he had been trying to evade all his life, was moving upon him, catching up with him, inexorably, inescapably, and surely. He wished to escape; he tried to escape; he could not escape. He confessed his helplessness; he admitted defeat; he capitulated.

Mircea Eliade[71] records concrete illustrations of man's experience of the 'numinous' through the created order. 'For religious man,' he says, 'the world always presents a supernatural valence, that is, reveals a modality of the sacred. Every cosmic fragment is transparent; its own mode of existence shows a particular structure of being, and hence of the sacred.' Earlier in the book, he has asserted that: 'The sacred always manifests itself as a reality of a wholly different order from "natural" realities.' '... Man becomes aware of the sacred because it manifests itself, shows itself, as something wholly different from the profane.' Eliade describes the manifestation of the sacred with the word 'hierophany'.

We see that both Otto and Eliade tend to refer to the sacred in terms which may be construed as impersonal. Neither 'the numinous' nor 'hierophany' need necessarily signify impersonality; nevertheless, either could signify that. The question then is, can one speak strictly of 'the numinous' or the sacred *manifesting* or *revealing* itself unless one implies a living Being as the agent of manifestation? Manifestation or revelation presupposes an agent with a conscious will causing a situation by which the manifestation could be apprehended. Thus, it also implies purpose. 'Showing oneself' and 'appearing' could have the same connotation, depending upon the context; but, strictly, there could be a world of difference between the two expressions. If we say, 'The moon shows itself in the sky', we are only using a figure of speech and personalizing the moon; whereas 'The moon appears in the sky' would be a normal expression. If, however, we say, 'The actor appears on the stage', we have presupposed that a person with a will goes to the stage to show himself in a purposeful performance.

'Numinous awe' or 'hierophany' unqualified could lead to the notion of an impersonal, all-pervasive force. Somehow imbued with the will and purpose to make its presence known to man. No religious person speaks in such terms; and to read Otto and Eliade with understanding is to know that their references are to the actual presence in the world of the living Spirit who in the world of situations makes his being known. Thus, the word 'theophany' will be appropriate in expressing the mind of the religious man, as every religion has its basic reference to the transcendental Being who, notwithstanding his numinous transcendence, is yet a present, living, urgent reality in the world and to man.

Emil Brunner declares the mind of the religious man when he says that 'God's essence is the will to self-communication'.[72] The same fact is emphasized by L. Harold DeWolf when he says, 'It is God who is directly made known, rather than ideas about him'.[73]

Thus, we come by another route to consider the question of how man came by his religion in the first instance. We are realizing now that at the awakening of consciousness and in living experience, man encountered that which is 'other than' himself or his fellow men, that which is totally different from the commonplace, that which is the 'Wholly Other'. The 'Wholly Other' is not impersonal but real and living, and it is the 'Wholly Other' who reveals himself. We have seen, according to Otto and Eliade, that the sacred manifests itself in, within, and through the created order. We have seen also that what happens in such a manifestation is a theophany, the self-disclosure of the divine Being.

We shall now consider two principal media of revelation: the created order and man's inner link with God.

The author of the first chapter of Genesis describes the pre-cosmic situation as dark chaos indescribable: he presents us with a picture of non-existence. Then appears the Spirit of God: God in creative activity. The Spirit like a mother-bird sat upon the dark chaos and, in consequence of God's creative energy, there was cohesion, order, life, and meaning. Thus, from the point of creation, in the very act of creation, the seal of the Maker, the seal of God's self-disclosure, has been stamped all over the face of the created order. In Eliade's words, 'Every cosmic fragment is transparent; its mode of existence shows a particular structure of being; and hence of the sacred.'

The author of Genesis goes further. In 1.26f. he says that 'God *2) inner link with God* made man in his own image', and in 2.7: 'Then the Lord God formed man of dust from the ground, and breathed into his nostrils the breath of life; and man became a living being.' This is to say that man is made a rational being, intelligent, equipped with will and a sense of purpose; there is something of the divine in him which makes him addressable and responsible (= capable of response) and, therefore, there exists in him the possibility of his spirit being in communion with the Divine Spirit. This same fact is expressed in several African concepts of man. For example, the Yoruba believe that whereas an archdivinity may be commissioned to mould man's physical parts, only Deity has the eternal prerogative of 'putting' the essence of being into man. In Igbo as well as in Yoruba, the designations of the essence of being, *ori* and *chi*, derive directly from the name of Deity: ORIȘẸ (Ori-șẹ̀), CHUKWU (Chi-ukwu); and this by implication means that the essence of man's being derives directly from Deity.

The significant point here is that revelation presupposes personal communication between the living Being who reveals and the living person to whom revelation is made. It would appear that man is a necessity in this situation; for, without a personal mind to appreciate and apprehend revelation, the whole process would be futile. Hence it has been said:

> God may create a universe *ex nihilo*, but he cannot reveal himself *ad nihilum* ... We may say that apart from the actual communion with God there is no worthy and complete human personality ... apart from some incipient degree of personality, there would be nothing for God to communicate with.[74]

L. Harold DeWolf asserts, 'A revelation must be made to a rational being.'[75] H. H. Farmer is also precise on this point:

> Living, essential religion we shall take to be God's personal encounter with man; being personal, the encounter involves activity on both sides, on the one hand a divine initiative of self-disclosure towards man, and on the other hand, man's self-conscious apprehension of, and response to, that approach.[76]

Thus, from two points of reference, the created order and man's inner link with Deity, revelation or theophany is evidenced. Throughout the Bible, we find that the ways in which God is described are linked with the fact of revelation as apprehended through natural phenomena or through man's inner experience.

And it is through the fact of God's revelation – the fact that God does make himself or his truth known to man – that we have any clue at all to certain fundamental issues of life. Paul Tillich says:

> Natural knowledge about self and world ... can lead to the question of the ground of being ... the question asked by reason, but reason cannot answer it. Revelation can answer it.[77]

We find that in every age and generation, there is a direct contact of God with the human soul, the personal awareness of God on the part of man through God's own initiative. What man knows of God, what he discovers about God, comes as a result of this self-disclosure. Man may, of course, by his own rational mind interpret what is revealed to him and he may rationalize it. But first of all, he has the truth revealed to him in ways which he may be able to describe or not. As John Baillie says:

> Our conclusion must therefore be that such moral and spiritual knowledge as may in any one period of human history seem to have become an inherent part of human nature, and so to be an unaided natural knowledge, is actually the blessed fruit of God's personal and historical dealings with man's soul, and so in the last resort also a revealed knowledge.[78]

In the Yoruba oral traditions, we have the saying, 'Orunmila (the oracle divinity) leaned back and gazed contemptuously; then he said, "You who travel by sea, you who travel by land, surely you perceive that the works of Olodumare are mighty"' (i.e. incomparable).[79] This implies the interpretation of the signs of the universe by man's rational mind.

There are those who will argue that religion could be divided into two categories: the religion based on God's climactic revelation in Jesus Christ, and what they call man-made religion, i.e. other religions besides Christianity. This, of course, is a deliberate or unwitting flying in the face of truth. If revelation indeed means God's self-disclosure, if he has left his mark upon the created order and his witness within man – every man – then it follows that revelation cannot be limited in scope and that it is meant for all mankind, all rational beings, irrespective of race or colour.

St Paul's words are to be taken seriously in this connection: 'Ever since the creation of the world, his invisible nature, namely, his eternal power and deity, has been clearly perceived in the things that have been made.'[80] And it is not an accident that it is recorded that

God 'made from one every nation of men to live on all the face of the earth, having determined allotted periods and the boundaries of their habitation, that they should seek God, in the hope that they might feel after him and find him. Yet he is not far from each one of us; Paul quotes with approval from 'some of your poets': 'In him we live and move and have our being'; ... 'For we are indeed his offspring.'[81]

In every part of the world, therefore, what in general terms is known as worship is a result of one central impulse – that of 'one divine personal will seeking all the time to make itself known'.

The one personal God ... making Himself known, keeping a grip on men ... this implicit sense of the one Living God ... when it became explicit, did so in a form conditioned by the general mental level ... of ideas. ... In this also, we can see the self-disclosure of God in a form appropriate to man's stage of development and historical situation. Belief in the High God was the primitive man's way of apprehending, and responding to, and expressing, the self-revealing pressure upon him of the one God.[82]

And this is further emphasized by the observation:

Religion and revelation condition one another; as God by revelation becomes more intelligible, man in religion becomes more intelligent; the objective content further develops the subjective capacity.[83]

For Africans as a part of the human race, the self-disclosure of God is in evidence, as we shall see later on in this book.

We have next to look at the fact of response to revelation. Revelation, we have observed, is made to, and apprehended by, rational beings; to rational beings who are addressable and therefore responsible. Revelation is basically a matter of divine initiative. But this divine initiative presupposes a response on the part of man, if revelation is to be of any value at all.

Rudolf Otto and Mircea Eliade have reminded us of how the manifestation of the sacred in the universe evokes in man a creaturely feeling, a sense of the fact that there is in the universe a 'Wholly Other' than the creature and the world of ordinariness. In consequence of this awareness, life, places and objects take on new meaning for man and he celebrates or marks off accordingly.

The fugitive Jacob came to a place which in the first instance was ordinary, just a suitable place for a weary traveller to take a night's rest. He slept and had a vivid dream which to him was extraordinary. As a result, the hitherto ordinary spot takes on a new aspect:

Then Jacob awoke from his sleep and said 'Surely, the Lord is in this place; and I did not know it.' And he was afraid, and said, 'How awesome is this place! This is none other than the house of God, and this is the gate of heaven.' So Jacob rose early in the morning, and he took the stone which he had put under his head and set it up for a pillar and poured oil on the top of it. He called the name of the place Bethel; but the name of the city was Luz at first.[84]

The place, the stone, are now not ordinary, but sacred in consequence of a theophany.

Thus, through man's experiences all down the ages – experiences the source of which are mysterious to him, but nevertheless real – he came to make a distinction between the sacred and the ordinary. This does not mean that, originally, he divides life into two disjunctive parts – the sacred and the common. The two are aspects of one and the same life to him, because the common has meaning for him really in terms of the sacred – the sacred informs and gives meaning to the common, and the common is for the sacred a means of self-expression. At any moment, the common may become charged with the sacred presence while the sacred may for man's sake and for the purpose of communication take on a form which is common. But there is no doubt that certain places, certain times, and certain things are marked off *permanently* by man as continuously emblematic of the sacred.

S. F. Nadel observes that the Nupe recognize a distinction between the sacred and the common. They say of an object, a phenomenon, or a type of action, 'that it is, or is not, *nya Soko* – "of God" or "belonging to God"'. He asserts further: 'In a wider context the phrase loses its disjunctive implication; for ultimately everything is "of God", that is, in his creation.' It is doubtful if the Nupe will agree to Nadel's further observation that 'the relationship between God and the created world is once more viewed as a dichotomy ...'[85] Such a view is just un-African.

There is a vital aspect of man's response to revelation which is usually not seen as such and which has led to a gross misinterpretation, especially with particular reference to religion in Africa. This we shall discuss under the following heading.

God in our own image

A very important outcome of man's response to revelation occurs when he reaches the discernment that he has to do, not with sheer numinous force or with an undiscriminatingly blighting sacred; that he has to do, in fact, with the living Being whom he could best conceive in the best term known to him, that is, as one who has the attributes of active, purposive livingness, attributes of a living, 'personal' being. This has led to what is generally described as anthropomorphism.

Anthropomorphism, in simple terms, means that man is thinking of Deity in his own image, even though that image may be conceived in superlative, supernormal terms.

Anthropomorphism has always been a concomitant of religion, all religions, every faith. In the purest religion that human heart can conceive, there can be no way of avoiding anthropomorphism. We can only console ourselves by speaking of degrees or levels of anthropomorphism when comparing religions. In religion, there is always that which forbids man to think of the Ineffable in mundane terms; and yet as the necessity is laid upon man to express his adoration of, or his faith in, the Transcendent, he inevitably falls back upon the only terms (maybe at their best) that he knows, terms of personal attributes and human relations, even terms of human anatomy. It is because of this inevitability of anthropomorphism that we run easily into apparent paradoxes in religious language: we call Deity 'the Ineffable' and immediately proceed to describe him. The prophet Isaiah asked the questions 'To whom then will you liken God, or what likeness will you compare with him? – questions which imply the answers 'Nothing' and 'None'; but he nevertheless proceeds to describe him as '... he who sits above the circle of the earth ... who stretches out the heavens like a curtain, and spreads them like a tent to dwell in ...'[86] Later, in the same book we read: 'Behold, the Lord's hand is not shortened, that it cannot save, or his ear dull, that it cannot hear ...'[87] Certain figures used for God in the Bible, like shepherd or husband, are due to this fact that man must find a way of thinking and speaking of Deity. The fact is, the living Spirit in entering into personal relations with man refuses to be thought of, spoken of, or addressed, in abstract, impersonal terms, especially as he brings man into relationship with himself. As man realizes that a hierophany implies a theophany, he discerns at the same time that here is Something which meets him in an I-Thou encounter, confrontation, or communion:

Life begins with twofold intuition that there is an essence to the universe which forbids relationship beyond itself, and that between that essence and the individual self, there is capable of being developed a quasi-personal relationship which would be impossible unless this essence were discovered to possess the quality of responsiveness.[88]

A. C. Bouquet tells of the American chapel-deacon who said (unhappily) that he mentally visualized Deity as 'an oblong blur', and of the Englishman who protested that his modernist vicar was always inviting him to worship 'a Scotch mist'.[89] The point of these illustrations is that man's spirit can never be satisfied in worship and communion with anything less than itself. And to balance this up, we have the statement by Emil Brunner that '... the warm, intimate, personal, often inevitably anthropomorphically conceived God as depicted in the Bible will not fit into a philosophical mould'. The same may be said about the inevitable incidence of anthropomorphism in African traditional religion, whether we think of Deity or of the divinities.

One of the reasons why certain people are scared about anthropomorphism is that erroneous notions have been peddled about it rather effectively in the anthropological market. Anthropomorphism, we are told, 'originated in children and savages; it is the puerile projection of the self into the external world'. There is no doubt that in anthropomorphism there is an element of projection. This we have already admitted by implication. It will be, however, correct to say that anthropomorphism began with the dawn of religion, rather than to say abusively that it originated with children and savages.

There is, of course, the constant danger that anthropomorphism may, and does, degenerate into a state in which Deity and divinities are conceived to be indeed 'of like passion' with men, the numinous character and wholly-other-ness of the Transcendent having been ignored by man's imagination. But so much has been made of this danger that the whole vital truth about the place of legitimate anthropomorphism in religion has been set aside.

The point that we wish to emphasize here is that anthropomorphism is not the monopoly of religion anywhere in the world. It is patently incorrect to predicate it as a thing peculiar to religion in Africa. It is inevitable as an element in religion anywhere, everywhere, at all levels:

> The growth of religion would have been impossible if there had not been at least one fact – the personality of God – which it not merely started from, but to which it constantly returns and in which, properly understood, it finds its constant touchstone of truth.[90]

Under this heading of 'God in our own image', I wish to examine two heresies which, in fact, belong to the realm of anthropomorphism, although they are rarely recognized as such. These are the 'high god' heresy and the heresy of 'the withdrawn god'.

(*a*) The 'high god' notion issued out of the current intellectual dilemma in which Western scholars and investigators find themselves with regard to the so-called religion of the 'primitive peoples'. It is as a result of their effort to resolve the dilemma that the 'high gods of primitive peoples' emerged as an intellectual creation. The question at issue, which brings about the dilemma, is discussed fully below.[91] It is briefly this: 'Do primitive peoples have any concept or knowledge of God?' And since that question can no longer be answered in the negative, how do we answer the supporting question of 'What or which God, their own God or the real God?' The heresy began precisely at the point where the question was answered explicitly or implicitly, unequivocally, that it must be 'their own god', that is, a god other than the supreme God as known in the personal experiences, theology, or religio-cultural conception of the Western world. The mind of the Western scholar, or investigator, or, still more to the point, theorist, has played a trick on him: he has rejected on the ground of prejudice and emotional resistance to truth the fact that the same God who is Lord of the universe is the one whose revelation is apprehended universally and therefore by 'the primitive peoples' in their own way, and he immediately falls, consequently, into the trap of *making* God in his own image by thinking that, 'I look down upon these people as an offensive scum of humanity: it follows, therefore, that the God whom I worship or, at least, who is regarded as the God of my glorious and incomparable culture, must be of the same mind as I – He can have no time for an excrescence of their kind!'

Thus, the world has been treated to meaningless terms like 'the high gods of primitive peoples' or '... wherever you go among these people, there is a supreme god'. It would seem that the authors of this heresy have been so absorbed in the task of proving the difference between 'their own God' and 'the high gods of primitive peoples' that they have failed to see the glaring conclusion of their own premise, i.e. an artificial supreme god for each nation and a consequent artificial, universal polytheism. The reason for the racial confusion and injustice and unrelieved suffering throughout the world today is that there is a plurality of imagined, racially egocentric gods who are independent of one another and each of whom is seeking at the earliest opportunity to champion the cause of his own racial protégés in undoing other gods and their protégés. There is an Ewe proverb which says, 'There is no beast so wild that it cannot become a prey to another wild beast.' A refusal to recognize the fact that the whole world belongs to the same God thus results in a refusal to accept justice and fair play equally for all, and injustice meted out to others has a way of coming back in retribution upon its perpetrators.

The 'high god', as I have said elsewhere,[92] is an offspring of the union of ignorance and prejudice, a union in which prejudice – blind prejudice – is the dominant partner. It exists only in the minds of its creators; it is 'an academic invention, an intellectual marionette whose behaviour is regulated by the mental [or moral] partiality of its creators. Therefore ... he could be made to be just everything that would preclude the slightest suspicion of a revelation from the one true, living God.'

It is obviously going to take some time yet for a change of heart to take place with regard to this heresy. In a recent article,[93] J. K. Parratt suggests that a fuller examination of the characteristics of the high god supports the view that God in Yoruba belief is a typical high god and that he is 'far removed from the "Father of our Lord Jesus Christ and ..." equally far from the Allah of the Qur'an ...'. This invention of an equidistant god by Parratt should not be surprising, as he can only see even the 'Father of Jesus Christ' or 'the Allah of the Qur'an' as merely 'a supreme God' – both being two separate gods: 'These religions (Islam and Christianity) have *a* (italics mine) supreme God ...' Perhaps a suggestion which may help our foreign friends is that they should make it clear to themselves what they are actually about – whether they are comparing abstract religious concepts, *actual* beliefs, or comparing gods!

It is not certain if sophisticated Africans themselves have yet made up their minds quite clearly on the subject of whether God as known to their forbears in the traditional religion is the same God of the whole universe or a God abjectly different from the superior, white-man God. Not long ago, one of our universities in Nigeria brought people from all over the world, of course at very great expense, to a conference for the purpose of discussing the barren and useless topic of the 'high god'. So far as one could gather, there were brilliant academic presentations on the topic – which should not be too difficult since it is only abstract and academic, after all – but there was

Dogma!

not a voice raised to point out <u>the dangerous heresy implied in the</u> <u>topic or to denounce the abusive connotation of the term</u>. It would appear that the Africans who were at the conference were little more than interested or bewildered onlookers!

(b) <u>The 'withdrawn god' or *deus otiosus*. Here again, we have an</u> <u>intellectual abstraction, and no more</u>. This is so whether it is pro- pounded as a theory by 'the competent authorities' on the beliefs of the 'primitive peoples' or falsely declared to be a result of information from 'the natives'. It is a notion which has been credited to African belief without due regard to all the facts.

A. B. Ellis was certainly drawing heavily upon his own imagina- tion when he said:

> The native says that he (Olodumare) enjoys a life of complete idleness and repose ... and passes his time dozing or sleeping. Since he is too lazy or too indifferent to exercise any control over earthly affairs, man on his side does not waste time in endeavouring to propitiate him, but reserves his worship and sacrifice for more active agents.[94]

Leo Frobenius saw a practical fulfilment of his classical education in this regard: To him, Olodumare 'leads an entirely platonic, mytho- logical existence'.[95]

A careful and scholarly article on this subject by the Reverend Father James O'Connell deserves our attention.[96] Father O'Connell examines K. L. Little's description of Deity according to Mende belief, which he quotes as follows:

> In the beginning there was *Leve*, spoken of nowadays as *Ngewo*, which may be directly translated as (Supreme) God. All life and activity, in both a material and non-material sense, derives from him. *Ngewo* created the world and everything in it, including not only human beings, animals, plants and so on, but spirits also. In addition, he invested the whole Universe with a certain non-material kind of power or influence, which manifests itself in various ways and on specific occasions in human beings and animals, and even in natural phenomena, such as lightning, waterfalls, and mountains. He is the ultimate source and symbol of that power and influence, but though all-powerful, he is not an immanent being. Like most African Supreme Gods,[97] having made the world, he retired far into the sky ... Little is known about the exact nature of *Ngewo*, because no one has ever seen Him. He is not entirely unapproachable, however, and sometimes a prayer may be addressed directly to Him. Indeed, it is custom- ary to end most supplications with the expression *Ngewo lawa* – 'God willing'.

Father O'Connell seems to have accepted this description as

accurate before he proceeds to find explanation for 'the withdrawal of the high god and his neglect in ritual'.

He then goes on to look at the explanation given by Mircea Eliade and Raffaelle Pettazzoni. Eliade's explanation he sums up in these words:

Eliade stresses the exclusively abstract character of the sky god and suggests that this character allows him to be pushed aside in practice by divine forms that meet men's need of sensory contact and tangible imagery. [He quotes from Eliade] 'Every substitution marks a victory for the dynamic, dramatic forms, so rich in mythological meaning, over the Supreme Being of the sky who is exalted, but passively remote ... the supreme divinities of the sky are constantly pushed to the periphery of religious life where they are almost ignored; other sacred forces, nearer to man, fill the leading role.' Pettazzoni [Father O'Connell continues] prefers to move away from the kind of explanation propounded by Eliade to an explanation that does not depend on man's proclivity to find concrete powers more effectively real than more abstractly conceived creative omnipotence but that depends on this creative omnipotence itself. [He quotes Pettazzoni as saying] 'It may however be the case that *otiositas* itself belongs to the essential nature of creative Beings, and is in a way the complement of their creative activity. The world once made and the cosmos established, the Creator's work is as good as done. Any further intervention on his part would be not only superfluous but possibly dangerous, since any change in the cosmos might allow it to fall back into chaos ... The *otiositas* of the creative Being ... is the most favourable condition and the one naturally best suited to maintain the status quo. This, I think, is what the idleness of creative Supreme Beings[98] signifies; it is due not so much to their character as Supreme Beings as to their being Creators.'

Father O'Connell chooses to comment first on Pettazzoni's explanation, with particular reference to the concept of God in West Africa. He asserts that according to general West African concepts, the 'high god' is not completely withdrawn. This fact is supported by the following factors: the ultimate sanctioning of the ethical order is his prerogative; he is the final succour in cases of extreme distress; and the gods are only the expressions of his power. Thus, he concludes, 'Pettazzoni's explanation consequently proves too much – for it to be correct he should be completely withdrawn ever since creation.'

Eliade's explanation he treats by saying:

While the lesser gods loom large *psychologically* in people's minds, people are none the less conscious of the limitations of the gods ... Eliade's explanation would at most account for a *preoccupation with the gods* of human crafts and environment. It does not account for the careful handing on of the myths of beginning and creation ... The lesser gods come forward not because they manage to push the high god into the background but because he himself withdraws and leaves the scene to these beings whose natures are known and whose interventions can be predicted.

Father O'Connell adds another reason for the 'withdrawal': the fact that people were uneasy about the all-purity of the high god in addition to their uneasiness about his all-powerfulness.

We see from the explanations above that there have been brilliant attempts to solve the problem of 'the withdrawal of the high god'. But, how did the problem come about in the first instance? It came about because man created it – man who created god in his own image imaginatively and makes his creation behave like himself. The problem began when for some reason, Western scholars created an 'inferior' god or 'inferior' gods for the (to them) 'inferior' races of the world. It became complicated when he 'created' not just two gods – one for his race, and one for the collective batch of 'the primitives': he retained his own one god and gave his imagination the rein to overrun the world of 'the primitives' with 'high gods' of all descriptions. One should have thought that all those who accept the fact that we are in a universe, whether they are philosophers or theologians or scientists, should have discovered the rank absurdity of such an intellectualist's creation.

When one looks closely at the explanations outlined by Father O'Connell, it is easy to see that they are at best the approach of a brilliant intellectualist who stands outside the garden walls and pronounces on what is happening inside only by the aid of imagination. If one should speak of 'projection' with reference to religion and religious studies, here we have a veritable illustration: the intellectual man is constructing for himself a scene in which Deity and divinities are involved in a *coup d'état* whereby Deity is the loser, but is somehow allowed a consolation status of being approached or addressed on rare occasions if he behaves himself and keeps away and does not seek by his all-power to disrupt the machinery of the universe, which is firmly in the hands of the divinities. *[margin note: Emotional re-statement]*

We admit that the notion of the apparent withdrawal of God from the African scene is not entirely the fault of foreigners; but there is no doubt that they either misunderstand, or are deliberately exaggerating, what is no more than an illustration of a fragment of the whole truth, thereby making it the whole truth. The myth according to African belief is that once the *skyey heaven* was close to the earth, so close that human beings could stretch up their hands and reach it or touch it. Then something happened through man's fault, the Lord of heaven was angry, and the *skyey heaven removed itself* far away from the earth. Those who have learnt not to press an illustration at every point should see that the 'withdrawing' of the *skyey heaven* from its former close-to-earth location does not *necessarily* mean the withdrawal of Deity from divine activity in connection with the earth. I do not know any version of the myth which even as much as gives that impression.

Father O'Connell makes a correct point when he says that the 'withdrawal' was due to man's uneasiness about the all-purity of Deity. Andrew Lang makes the same point when he points to the fact of 'the moral pre-eminence of God who could not be bribed'. One of the oldest stories that we have on the topic of man's estrangement from God puts the situation quite clearly. In Genesis 3 and 4, it is man who has to leave the presence of God either by being driven away or by moving away. This is a fact that will bear close examination.

For example, a young woman and I were travelling on the train somewhere in England. For some time during the course of the journey, I saw that the sun was on our right. Later on, I saw that it was on our left and mentioned the fact. Then the young woman breathed a sigh of relief, with the remark: 'Well, I am glad that you also see it; I thought I was going mad!' What happened is quite obvious: while we were busy engaging each other's attention in discussion, the train had turned a horse-shoe, with the result that it turned our right side to where our left was in relation to the fixed position of the sun. But as far as we were immediately aware, our impression was that it was the sun that had moved from our right to our left. This is all of a piece with the habit of mind which persists universally in *making* the sun 'rise' in the East and 'set' in the West, in spite of the *fact* that it is our earth that is rotating and creating the appearance. A train journey further illustrates how the human mind, in an idle moment, will often *make* trees and houses and huts flee away in consequence of the movement of the train in which one is travelling.

The point that we are making here is that in speaking of 'the withdrawn god' the intellectualist is only allowing his mind to play an academic trick on him; and unfortunately, he reaches the stage when rationalization imperceptibly slips into self-delusion and he comes to believe that he has reached an easy answer to one of

the most urgent problems of life. But, of course, one has to make
up one's mind whether one is thinking of the God who is, or an
intellectualist's god who is only a result of the projection of an
academic mind. If one is thinking of the living God who is, there is
a limit to how much one is allowed to use the apparatus of imagination in arranging the theocratic affairs of the universe, allocating
to him what should be his defined role. If one is thinking of an
academic invention, then, of course, there is a wide latitude for one
to juggle with one's own self-created situation. It is thus possible
to divorce God's 'character as Supreme Being' from his being as
'Creator'. But whatever may be the position taken by the foreigner,
it is but fair that in researching into the theocratic world of 'the
primitives', he should in all honesty endeavour to represent that
world accurately with due regard to the truth of the actual minds
of 'the primitives'. Here we remember, however, the typical boast of
the Elderly Gentleman in Bernard Shaw's *Back to Methuselah*:

> I am an experienced traveller. I know that what the traveller observes
> must really exist, or he could not have observed it. But what the natives
> tell him is invariably pure fiction![99]

M. J. Herskovits is right when, after speaking of 'the question
repeatedly raised by students of West African religion, whether or
not the Creator, having made the world, left it to its own devices and
the pleasure of inferior gods', continues:

> The assertion of the existence of such a belief is found so often in the
> literature that it must be viewed as defining the traditional European
> approach to African religions.[100]

What is happening, in fact, is that Western philosophers and theo-
logicians have abandoned the deistic theory which was once
dear to them; but rather than let it pass into the limbo of forgotten
things and exploded theories, they have somehow found a way of
keeping it going by bequeathing it to Africa, along with the gifts of
cast-off clothes and other discarded apparatus of Western civilization.
Hence their deep concern about installing fugitive supreme gods in
Africa.

One factor which has always bedevilled the study of religion is
that there are those who are loath to admit that 'the poor reach of
our minds is totally inadequate for the task of requiring an exhaustive knowledge of the Divine Majesty', even when they entertain a
belief in God at all. Where they think that they do not, then the

mind is closed altogether.

As we shall discuss and substantiate below,[101] the notion of the supreme god who has relinquished his right in the theocratic government of the world, in consequence of embarrassing pressure, is alien to African thought. Also, it will be seen that Africans do not think in terms of a plurality of supreme gods.[102] When in each locality they think or speak of the supreme god, they speak of him in terms of the all-embracing, all-controlling *ho theos* – the God.

We may find an answer to what is happening in Africa today with reference to the concept of God, as it is happening everywhere else throughout the world in varying degrees, in the observation of Paul Tillich that the original revelation could be exhausted or suspended.[103] We are still largely in the dark about the history of origins in Africa, and it is therefore difficult for us to say precisely how sharp and definite the statements about the concept of Deity have been. And matters are complicated by the fact that we have to depend on oral tradition for our knowledge of what things have been and what they are.[104] Add to this the fact that the religion is largely a priestly affair, and we have a clue to the reason why an investigator is easily led astray. Moreover, in these days, in addition to the complications inherent in the African situation, we are being overtaken by the events of secularism and technology and are finding ourselves in the situation where the clamours of things are bringing us into the situation where 'the word of the Lord was rare in those days; there was no frequent vision': men are simply deafened and blinded spiritually. There is enough, however, to show that God in African thought is not the withdrawn God of European deism. And, here also, the right word has been pronounced: the 'character of a concept may change or blur, but the same concept still becomes the point of reference, even though its origin may have been forgotten or it may have gathered accretions during the course of history'. This has the support of Alfred E. Garvie's words:

... religion involves revelation; *where religion is sincere, there revelation is real* ... even in the crudest conceptions and the rudest worship we must recognize the divine presence, often tragically obscured as to its real nature not only by human limitations, but also by human errors and sins.[105]

Thus, to argue or suggest that God in African thought is other than the God who is 'The Lord ... the everlasting God, the Creator of the ends of the earth' is patent nonsense. There are factors which make for incomplete or even faded or distorted pictures of God; but the original picture is his, nevertheless. Incompleteness or distortion in the picture of God is a universal fact which should not be palmed on Africa by means of academic shrewdness.

4. *Definition of religion*

By now, everybody who is seriously engaged in the study of religion has been convinced that to attempt a definition of religion is an almost impossible, if not altogether impossible, task; and every serious scholar is on the verge of giving up the task.

J. B. Pratt reports:

Professor Leuba enumerates forty-eight definitions of religion from as many great men (and elsewhere adds two of his own, apparently to fill out the even half-hundred). But the striking thing about these definitions is that, persuasive as many of them are, each learned doctor seems quite unpersuaded by any but his own. And when doctors disagree what are the rest of us going to do?[106]

H. Fielding Hall listed twenty definitions,[107] with or without the authors' names, setting the tone of his collection with the warning by Anon.:

The difficulty of framing a correct definition of religion is very great. Such a definition should apply to nothing but religion, and should differentiate religion from anything else – as for example, from imaginative idealization, art, morality, philosophy. It should apply to everything which is naturally and commonly called religion: to religion as a subjective spiritual state, and to all religions, high or low, true or false, which have obtained objective historical realization.

J. B. Pratt and Anon. are telling us, in fact, that we must be very careful how we attempt this task, if we are not ready to abandon the attempt altogether. If, for example, one has to fulfil all the conditions laid down in Anon.'s warning or avoid all the pitfalls that he enumerates, one is bound to give up the attempt as altogether impossible. Also, it is certain, as careful writers on this subject have pointed out, that the majority of those who are mentioning the word 'religion' do not necessarily have any particular definition in mind; they in fact use the word loosely with little regard to what it might mean, partly because it is enough for them that they see religion in existence and in practice, and partly because they have an immunity from the academic curiosity that bothers about definition.

One important problem about the definition of religion is that, by and large, authors of definitions do not make their positions with regard to religious or philosophical convictions clear. For the position taken by an author is bound to reflect itself in his definition. It is also worth remarking that a definition reached out of a personal experience of religion may be different in quality from that reached through mere academic deduction by someone who has not been spiritually or emotionally involved in religion, or one whose purpose is to debunk religion. We must keep reminding ourselves that the adherents of religions practise their religion without bothering themselves about definitions. It is the academic busy-bodies, or those who are seeking a convenient handle for the purpose of discussion, who have a concern about definitions. Thus, there are several possible points of departure from which definitions of religion emerge and, inevitably, the various positions usually bring about disagreements, although this need not necessarily be so: a careful study may show that the several definitions are supplementary to one another, provided the author of each definition does not make the usual mistake of asserting that his own definition is the only possible definition and the last word on the subject.

If these points are borne in mind, it will be seen that many of the definitions that we have so far have, each in its own way, make a supplementary contribution in answer to one of life's most difficult questions. We may substantiate our point by looking at a few definitions as illustrations.[108]

At first glance, the definition by Max Müller is attractive. Religion, he says, 'is a perception of the Infinite'. It is attractive because it can (a) imply a psychic activity of the whole person, and (b) signify an object of perception which is real. But on second, careful thought, it appears to be vague. 'The Infinite' needs to be clearly defined; and perception may suggest subjectivity and passivity rather than objectivity and activity. One is not just religious by merely 'perceiving' and not doing something purposeful and with intelligence about 'what' is perceived. Also, there is the danger that the 'object' of perception may be something which exists in consequence only of the projection of a mental image.

Immanuel Kant defines religion as 'a recognition of our duties as divine commands'.

> Religion is the belief which sets what is essential in all adoration of God in human morality ... Religion is the *law* in us, in so far as it obtains

emphasis from a law giver and judge over us. It is a morality, directed to the recognition of God.

This is all of a piece with, or a corollary to, Kant's theory that the conception of the Godhead arose from the consciousness of the moral law – the Divine Imperative in man. Here also, we have a definition based upon certain <u>fundamental truth about religion. Religion is</u> <u>usually based upon a relationship, which is usually covenantal</u> : this *A fundamental truth about religion* is well illustrated in the Old Testament as in the New. It is the same in African traditional religion. This implies that the moral element is a vital factor in every religion. But what the covenant relationship implies is that morality is an offspring of religion and is not the same as religion. More important still is that man must first recognize the Determiner of destiny before he accepts the Law-giver in him. 'I am the Lord your God ... You shall ...' It is only when this is the regular order of things that moral demands can be appreciated and moral duties rightly fulfilled.

'<u>A feeling of absolute dependence, of pure and entire passiveness</u>' *Schleiermacher* <u>is Schleiermacher's interpretation of religion</u>. He asserts :

> The Universe is an uninterrupted activity, and at every moment reveals itself to us ... It is religion to take up into our life, and to allow ourselves to be moved in these influences ... The one thing and everything in religion is to feel all that moves us in our feeling ...

<u>The truth in Schleiermacher's definition, I believe, is that the key-</u> <u>note of every religion is that man should let God be God and accept</u> <u>his own creatureliness</u>. The source of man's trouble in the world is connected intimately with his egocentricity and self-assertiveness in forgetfulness of the fact that he is a dependent being. It is also a fact that emotion enters markedly into man's experience and prac-tice of religion, as it does into any human thing, whatever it may be.

Schleiermacher has been criticized on the ground that religion to him is bound up with only one element of man's psychic make-up, that of feeling; but it would appear that Schleiermacher was reacting here against mere intellectualist, or other, limitations with regard to the definition of religion and was thus carried away to another ex-treme. Moreover, it is often not very certain whether he is confusing God and the world, whether he is thinking of a self-directing force within the universe, or whether (which is most likely his position) he is saying that God's creative and redemptive activity is offered to man through the created order.

We should consider, however, the interpretation of Schleiermacher by Paul Tillich, especially on the matter of 'feeling' and 'dependence':

> When he defined religion as the 'feeling of absolute dependence', 'feeling' meant the immediate awareness of something unconditional in the sense of the Augustinian-Franciscan tradition ... 'Feeling', in this tradition, referred not to a psychological function but to the awareness of that which transcends intellect and will, subject and object. 'Dependence', in Schleiermacher's definition, was, on the Christian level, 'teleological' dependence – a dependence which has moral character, which includes freedom and excludes a pantheistic and deterministic interpretation of the experience of the unconditional. Schleiermacher's 'feeling of absolute dependence' was rather near to what is called in the present system 'ultimate concern about the ground and meaning of our being'. Understood in this way, it lies beyond much of the usual criticism directed against it.[109]

J. B. Pratt, who has put a great deal of consideration into this matter, advises that we can get to an acceptable definition of religion only when we appreciate the fact that 'religion' is not a doctrine, or a law, or a hypothesis; that 'religion is not a matter of any one "department" of man's psychic make-up but involves the whole man'. It includes what there was of truth in the historical attempts to identify religion with feeling, belief, or will. And he draws attention to the fact that religion is immediately subjective, and yet points to the other fact that religion involves and presupposes the acceptance of an objective.

> Religion is the attitude of a self toward an object in which the self genuinely believes ... The definition which I propose is the following: Religion is the serious and social attitude of individuals or communities towards the power or powers which they conceive as having ultimate control over their interest and destinies. ... The religious attitude towards the Determiner of Destiny must not be 'mechanical' ... nor coldly intellectual. It must have some faint touch of that social quality which we feel in our relations towards anything that can make response to us.[110]

J. B. Pratt is aware that his definition may be considered arbitrary or probably too wide, and he deliberately avoids a kind of definition narrowed down in consequence of a particular theological belief. He wishes to stick to his persuasion as a psychologist and have a definition which would embrace everyone who has developed the 'attitude' which according to his definition may be called 'religion'. Thus, he avoids those terms connected with religion which may narrow down a psychologist's approach to the study of religion, even though they are implied in his definition. On the whole, he would stick to 'attitude' and the subjective aspect of religion, and avoid, or be guarded about, any suggestion of an external revelation.

A. C. Bouquet declares:

> For most Europeans, at any rate, 'religion' has come to mean a fixed relationship between the human self and some non-human entity, the Sacred, the Supernatural, the Self-Existent, the Absolute, or simply, 'God'. From Suez eastward, however, such a relationship seems as often as not to be described or describable in terms of movement, as a 'Way'. Thus we have the *hodos*, or way, of the Pharisees. Early Christianity in the Book of Acts is called 'that Way'; Buddhism is described as 'the noble eightfold Path'; and Japanese ... religion is called Shinto, 'the Way of the Gods'. ... Confucius' message is called by him 'The Way'. ... Let us recall that a 'way' is not simply meandering, but implies direction, and therefore relation to a goal or purpose.[111]

For our part, we take the following position:

(a) Many theories of religion appear to come to grief either from the limitation imposed by their authors' positions declared or unavowed, or because their critics will not take the trouble to see the element of truth that may be in them.

(b) Religion is an ultimate fact of human nature; therefore it is the whole person that is involved in it: it is the whole person who receives the stimulus of a spiritual communication, and it is the whole person that responds to that stimulus. The danger of thinking that man can be treated separately as a thinking or willing or knowing machine as occasion warrants is incalculable, especially when this concerns his position with reference to the ultimate issues of life. For academic purposes, it may be temporarily permissible to treat man analytically as a physical body, a mind, and a spirit; or his psychic make-up as thinking, willing, and feeling. But we run into danger if we do not even in such a 'scientific', academic approach know that the reality of a person is the whole person. A person does not say 'My foot is sick' or 'My head is not well' or 'My stomach needs to be filled' in consequence of a sore foot, or a headache, or hunger. It is the whole person that is sick or hungry, and if any of these signs is not respected and treated accordingly the whole person may be eventually out of action or perish. It is so – even more so – in spiritual (and emotional) matters. As H. H. Farmer observes, 'Religion is ... a response of the whole personality ... It is the personality grasping, intuiting, something through its own profound interest in its own fullest realization.'[112]

(*c*)   We have to respect the fact that every religion[113] claims a transcendental origin. If we are defining religion we have to consider this vital fact with regard to what the religion says about itself. Paul Tillich has a statement to which we should give a consideration at this point. He records his agreement with Anselm, who links the certainty about God to man's self-consciousness, and then proceeds to say, 'In a religious statement ... where God is not the *prius* of everything, he can never be reached ... If you don't start with him, you cannot reach him.'[114]

(*d*)   Thus, from our own point of view, man is important to religion. We shall go so far as stating the obvious fact that without man, there can be no religion, at least in the sense that we know it in its current essential and phenomenological dimensions. But to begin our definition with man is to overlook the fact that religion is as old as man, that is, as far as we know; it is as old as the dawn of consciousness when man came to an encounter with the fact of his environments which confronted him with something more than the physical world of things, when he became aware of a supersensible world and of a power 'Wholly Other' than himself. Theories have been propounded on 'the dawn of religion' to explain away, to give a name (even if the name is no more than 'Illusion' or 'Nothing'), to the Something the awareness of which gripped man and transmuted life for him in the long-ago. Whatever has been said or left unsaid about the situation, it is generally known now that religion has always been an inescapable, inevitable, concomitant of human life as we know it today. It is therefore questionable to think that, somehow, man himself invented something which, as it were, apprehended him at the very point of his recognition of himself as a being-in-relation. There is also the fact of the universality of religion which cannot be honestly denied. There has been no nation or people for whom religion has not had something to do with the formation of the basis of culture or racial life. Even if religion is a result of mental sickness, still, an invincible cosmic virus which is capable of causing such a universal, chronic epidemic is worthy of our close attention. We may remember that there have always been, all the way down the corridor of history, prophets of the doom or end of religion; and all that they have for their trouble so far is that they are still prophesying!

Furthermore, to begin our definition with man is to try to perpetuate man's harmful, exaggerated notion of himself – that things exist only in consequence of man and only to serve man's selfish end, his whims and caprices, his convenience. This is the notion which has imaginarily created an anthropocentric universe, with the result which we all experience today – chaos in every sphere of human life and undertaking.

(e) Thus, I have proposed the following definition of religion :

Religion results from man's spontaneous awareness of, and spontaneous reaction to, his immediate awareness of a Living Power, 'Wholly Other' and infinitely greater than himself; a Power mysterious because unseen, yet a present and urgent Reality, seeking to bring man into communion with Himself. This awareness includes that of something reaching out from the depths of man's being for close communion with, and vital relationship to, this Power as a source of real life.

Man thus realizes from the beginning that he has a dual nature: his commonplace life is here on earth; but there is a living Being to whom he is linked by reason of his essential personality. In short, man is so [constituted and] conditioned that he must be dependent upon God if his life is to be real, full, and harmonious. His life is really worthwhile only in accordance as it is controlled and sustained by God.

Religion in its essence is the means by which God as Spirit and man's essential self communicate. It is something resulting from the relationship which God established from the beginning of (human) life between himself and man . . .[115]

III

The Study of
African Traditional Religion

Africa, in a way corresponding to her vital statistics on the map of
the world, carries a question mark in her heart. This is a question
within herself, and a question about her to the rest of the world.

The reason for the question is that Africa is just now passing
through the birth-throes of a new life. She has been a centuries-long
sufferer: her illness has been written off as chronic, her sickness as
sickness unto death or, at best, something that would leave her more
dead than alive.

She has suffered so much because she has been callously and frequently raped and despoiled by the strong ones of the world who
are adepts in the art of benevolent exploitation and civilized savagery. Even now there are organs of her body which are under torture
and cruel assault and, consequently, she is still more or less a sick
personality.

Nevertheless, she is not without friends. There have been those
who have given their lives, their time, or of their substance
in order to heal her 'open sore' which has various manifestations.
Such friends are still few and far between, and the quality of friendship is often a baffling question. There are those who have *graciously*
given her a place in the newly imagined 'Third World' which stands
in sharp contradistinction to the 'First World' of Europe and the
'Second World' of America. Even these are divided in their attitude
to her: should she be accorded the status of a corporate personality,
worthy in her own right to stand on equal footing with any other
continent? Is she not still too immature or crude to be recognized
fully as a full sister continent? And her sons and daughters, what-

ever their education, achievements, or status, would they ever be admitted across the subtle but palpable line of demarcation which separates the elder (the stronger of the world) from the younger (the weaker, 'coloured' ones)? One thing that is certain is that while there are die-hard enemies of her life (because they think that her death or chronic infantilism is of benefit to them), she has an unfailing fund of condescending paternalism and generous patronage. Where she behaves herself according to prescription and accepts an inferior position, benevolence which becomes her 'poverty' is assured, and for this she shows herself deeply and humbly grateful. If for any reason she takes it into her head to be self-assertive and claim a footing of equality, then she brings upon herself a frown; she is called names; she is persecuted openly or by indirect means; she is helped to be divided against herself.

Africa is giddy and uncertain yet of what she really is or is to be. She is giddy and vague as a victim of a serious accident, or as one heavily drugged, who is just at the threshold of a return to consciousness. In her precarious state she gropes, she reaches or strikes out in this direction or that, like someone who is trying to make sure whether she is really alive or not, like someone who pinches herself to make sure that she is not dead: she is experimenting with the delicate, spiritual thing called racial life.

Africa is emerging; she is awaking. However painful this may be, however slow and confused the process, there is no turning back the hand of the clock for her. Those who have raped and assaulted her; those who are raping and assaulting her; those who are sincerely helping her to stand on her feet as a healthy personality (and these are rather few); and those who are half-heartedly assisting her (and these are greater in number because their interests – racial or economic – are at stake); these are all eagerly watching her struggling for life – watching her as one watches a victim who somehow is developing unexpected power and resilience which might be a threat to the erstwhile strong; watching her as a doctor who is genuinely concerned about the life of a patient, or as a friend with deep concern for the welfare of a friend; watching her as a scientist whose only concern is the result of an experiment which would acquire him merit; watching her as a businessman who watches anxiously the precarious fortunes of the Exchange.

Africa is constantly in the news. An academic aberration known as 'Africanists' has come into being. Brain-products on Africa have increasingly become a marketable commodity; and so everyone wishes to be an author on Africa – as long as he writes something for a gullible public.

Here indeed is a confused situation. Anyone who wishes really to understand or interpret Africa must pray for the grace of patience, painstaking ability, and honest sincerity. The past is rather confused, as we shall explain presently; the measurable present is in a flux; the future, one can only hope, would be the only adequate interpreter of both.

1. *Natural difficulties besetting the study*

Geography

The geography of Africa, internal and *vis-à-vis* other continents of the world, appears to be her first disadvantage which won her the derogatory appellation of 'The Dark Continent'. The unknown is usually the mysterious and is usually surrounded with dread. Imagination, aided by travellers' tales and fabrications, is ever ready to fill in the blank. And so, most of what has been written and said about Africa in the past and even now is either mostly or partially untrue, or exaggerated and distorted from various motives. Here we have the first basis of *mis*understanding about Africa.

Africa is large in size. It is necessary to emphasize and underline this. Even in spite of all the communication and information media with which the world is so amply blessed, the generality of the Western world still finds it difficult to comprehend this fact. That is why when an African is on a visit to Europe he is asked, 'Where do you come from?', and when he answers, for example, 'Nigeria', the next question is in the nature of: 'Oh, did you happen to see Albert Schweitzer recently on the edge of the primeval forest?' But ignorance is ignorance everywhere and perhaps one should not blame a people for not being 'educated'. It becomes very questionable, however, when those who call themselves scholars or researchers and should know better convey back to their own world the misleading impression that having visited Tanzania or Ghana or lived for a few days in Kano, they have not only seen and known the whole of Africa but have also become authorities on her overall nature – physical, moral, spiritual, and economic.

It is foolhardy to generalize on Africa. If it must be done, the author of such a generalization should attach a clear 'N.B.' to say that this is a generalization and indicate from what specific data, which should also be clearly explained.

Further, certain things which belong to the painful history of the past in Africa make it very difficult to say precisely what are the aboriginal cultures and beliefs in very many areas of the Continent. Laurens van der Post's *The Lost World of the Kalahari* seems written as an act of penance for one of the many acts of violation to the personality of Africa. On the inside of the cover we have these words:

> In this enthralling book, a distinguished explorer and writer describes his rediscovery of the Bushmen, outcast survivors from Stone Age Africa. Laurens van der Post was fascinated and appalled at the fate of this remarkable people, who seemed to him a reminder of our own 'legitimate beginnings'. Attacked by all the races that came after them in Africa, the last of the Bushmen have in modern times been driven deep into the Kalahari Desert. It was there, in the scorching heat of an African August, that Colonel van der Post led his famous expedition. His search for these small, hardy aboriginals, with their physical peculiarities, their cave art, and their joyful music-making, provides the author with material for a dramatic and compassionate book.

Van der Post himself writes towards the very end of the book:

> 'But these old people, how will they get on?,' I asked, pointing to the ancient couple I had met the first morning, now slowly following in the wake of the others.
> 'They'll go as far as they can,' Ben answered. 'But a day will come when they can't go on. Then, weeping bitterly, all will gather round them. They'll give them all the food and water they can spare. They'll build a thick shelter of thorn to protect them against wild animals. Still weeping, the rest of the band, like the life that asks it of them, will move on. Sooner or later, probably before their water or food is finished, a leopard, but more commonly a hyena, will break through and eat them. It's always been like that, they tell me, for those who survive the hazards of the desert to grow truly old. But they'll do it without a whimper'[1]

(because perforce they have reconciled themselves to what they accept as an unalterable fate!).

This is a painful illustration of happenings which make a study of African cultures and beliefs difficult. There are parts of Africa where in consequence of European settlements the aboriginal peoples have been wiped out and the racial memory obliterated; there are areas where, in consequence of displacements by stronger peoples, the aboriginals have been forced to be on the move for over a long period and then, of course, scatter, several of them dying, and the rest settling among, and merging with other peoples, with the result that their identities have now been lost or at least confused with those of the peoples with whom they have merged: in which case the racial memory is as lost or as confused as the people themselves. Inter-racial or inter-clan warfares, aggravated by the dislocating and devastating factor of the slave trade, took a hand in the matter: whole peoples were either exterminated or reduced to insignificance – whatever the case, the racial memory is grossly disrupted.

In this connection, the observation of David Tait is apposite:

> Unlike many peoples Konkomba have no signs of a developed cosmogony. This is no doubt partly the result of their expulsion from their original territory by the Dagomba four centuries ago. Primitive cosmogonies tend to trace an unbroken connexion between the living, the land and the first messengers from the Creator. This is impossible for Konkomba.[2]

Direct or indirect colonial indoctrination has been so effective in many areas that the aboriginals have come to see themselves as grasshoppers in their own eyes and have become so mentally, despising whole-heartedly their own native cultures and religious values, and ultimately abandoning them and forgetting their basic tenets and practices.

In 1963, when I was lecturing for a month at an 'Institute for teachers of theology in Africa' at Salisbury, Rhodesia, a local archpriest of a traditional cult was invited to the 'institute' to give information about the beliefs of his people. He and his followers came in tattered European dress. It was sad to some of us at the institute, amusing to some, and a matter of racial triumph to some, to see what a lamentably pathetic figure the archpriest cut: it was clear that not only was he ill-informed about his own cult and its traditions, but also that he was doing his best to show how much he admired the white man and his ways and would rather forget that he was an African, and become a European. This he declared by speech and by attitude. And the limit was reached when he pronounced in connection with his belief in reincarnation: 'If a person is wicked, after death, he will reincarnate as a black man; if he is good, he will reincarnate as a white man!'

Where the colonial policy of assimilation has given the impressionable African the notion that he has become a European in all but the colour of his skin, which he should 'never mind', and that he could in fact become the President of France tomorrow, *if elected*, the temptation to live up to the dignity of whatever he imagines that he has become is so great that foreign ideas and cultures become to him the only way of real life. Consequently, his own native traditions suffer adversely. In 1967, I met a French-speaking African during the course of a meeting somewhere in Europe. Naturally, I spoke to him in English since he had something of English and I had nothing of French or of his own African language. Tolerantly, he answered me, with the prefacing remark: 'I am speaking to you in English because of my respect for you. If it were someone else, I would not have answered him at all. Anybody who wants to speak to me must address me in my own language' – i.e. French ! !

There are areas where, fortunately, the cultures and traditions are still preserved to a great extent in consequence of the protection afforded by the natural armour of sunshine and mosquitoes: when anti-malaria remedies and prophylactics were discovered, it was already too late for foreign settlers to take domicile and destroy the soul of the people. Nevertheless, even here foreign exploitations have left their detrimental marks on the cultures of the people of the area.

There is the inevitable, ever-operative factor of death. Death carries away from time to time those who are custodians of the cultural and religious traditions, persons who bear their charges in their persons and in their memories. As one generation of these passes away after another, so the traditions become remembered in lesser and lesser details and, naturally, dislocations, distortions, and gaps occur. This is where the weakness of the traditional religion as a thing dominated by priesthood, with little element of *prophecy*, is most manifest. For example, the Ndazo, priest of Gunnu among the Nupe, is known as a 'rare man': he must be a man born 'with a tuft of hair on the top of his head'. S. F. Nadel records that during his stay in Nupeland, 'only one village in the whole country had a true Ndazo'. About fifteen years after, when I visited Nupeland, I met one who was getting on in years, very likely the same one whom Nadel had seen in the same village (Doko). I was told then that there were only three of them in the whole of Nupeland and that the third one was a little boy. In the event that a true Ndazo is not available in any area, the cult of Gunnu gradually and eventually dies out in the particular area. And if this should be the case throughout Nupeland or over most of the land, it would mean the extinction of the cult, unless there is a deliberate twist in the tradition.

The influence of other cultures and religions has its part to play. As generation after generation of Africans come under the influence of other cultures or embrace new faiths, they either cut away completely from the old faith, in which case they gradually forget its traditions and consequently leave nothing of it for their descendants; or (as is more usual) they practise both complementarily, and in the ensuing syncretism, the old religion in its conservative form becomes a thing of the past.

Western education, civil or mercantile service, and travelling for various other purposes, somehow alienate people from their own culture, not infrequently taking them away for a long time from their homeland, with the result that they lose touch with their native traditions. If such persons return home and become chiefs or heads of traditional cults, they are usually rather wanting in the requisite knowledge of the traditions connected with their offices. The result is that, usually, they are not helpful as informants: they will either pretend to know and deliberately give out false information, or declare their ignorance with the dignified nonchalance of assumed sophistication.

And, finally, there is the bewildering situation of myriads of languages and innumerable dialects. In Nigeria there are at least two hundred and fifty languages – languages, not dialects; while in each language area there are several dialects some of which are *almost* distinct, different languages.

Thus, we have in Africa a continent of multitudes of nations, myriads of peoples, countless languages or dialects, and peoples of various levels of cultures. Africa is a confluence – which often turns to a whirlpool – of intermingled races and cultures, the origins of most of which are obscure partly because of the reasons already enumerated above and partly because there is no recorded history of the ancient past of Africa by Africans. Researches are still going on slowly and painfully so that the riddles posed by certain ancient cultures or institutions may be unravelled. Zimbabwe in Rhodesia remains still a mystery, even though there are exploratory books on it; the commingled culture of Ile-Ife in Nigeria is still being disentangled; these are just two examples. The question of the origins of many of the African peoples is still to be settled.

This complex situation makes Africa still a dark continent: dark in the sense that its cultural resources and religious traditions are largely still to be explored, studied with carefulness and understanding, and the results recorded without prejudice.

This is also to say that the cultures of Africa are not simple but complex; so are the systems of beliefs and practices. In the past this complexity has led would-be scholars on Africa to take refuge in meaningless or insulting terms like 'amorphous', 'savage', 'barbarous', or 'primitive' in describing what they did not really understand.[3]

One of the greatest obstacles in the way of the study of African traditional religion is, of course, the lack of written records by Africans of their ancient past. All that we have from indigenous Africa are the oral traditions. And these, as we have observed, have been affected adversely in very many ways, with the result that it is not an easy task now to bring them together and form a systematic documentation. More often than not, fragments of one and the same 'tradition' will have to be collected and pieced together in order to get the whole story. Here is a pitfall ready for the unwary who could be easily excited by the attractive and daunted by the apparently dull and difficult: one can easily imagine that two sherds of the same tradition are independent, contradictory accounts and conclude by choosing one and rejecting the other. Thus, careless, convenient or inadvertent suppression of evidence is a frequent occurrence.

2. Sources

In *Olodumare: God In Yoruba Belief*, I have made a list of the oral traditions according to Yoruba culture.[4] The same pattern, more or less, will obtain throughout Africa. Whatever may be our difficulty in handling this delicate material, it is all that we have; and we have to make the best of it. This is, in fact, why it has been said that 'imaginative sympathy and (where possible) experiential participation' should be part of the equipment of the scholar who is researching into any religion. An understanding of the oral traditions will enable the scholar to see and know the religion from the inside. Africa, in her every locality, is rich in mythology and folktales. Records of these have been made from time to time; but in most cases, their value for religious studies is still to be appreciated.

There is, of course, the 'problem' of correct interpretation of these traditions. First, it is necessary in this regard to listen carefully and get at the inner meaning of each of them. Secondly, it is also necessary to remember that the African situation is one in which life is not divided artificially into the sacred and the secular; that it is one in which reality is regarded as one, and in which the things of earth (material things and man's daily doings and involvements) have meaning only in terms of the heavenly (the spiritual, reckoning with the Transcendent and that part of man which has link with the supersensible world). Thirdly, a doctrine is not necessarily unhistorical or *merely* imaginary simply because it is mythological. *The Pocket Oxford Dictionary* is rather misleading in this connection. It defines 'myth' as 'primitive tale imaginatively describing or accounting for natural phenomena ... tale of gods or demi-gods, old wives' tale, prevalent but false belief, person or things falsely supposed to exist'; and 'mythical' as 'imaginary, not really existent'. This meaning attached to 'myth' is of a later development. Originally, *muthos* is 'anything delivered by word of mouth', 'speech', 'conversation implying the subject of the conversation', 'the matter itself'.[5] Our use of the word as an element of the oral traditions must necessarily bear this original meaning, although the fact of imagination (properly defined) must be given due regard. A myth is a vehicle for conveying a certain fact or a certain basic truth about man's experiences in his encounter with the created order and with regard to man's relation to the supersensible world. It endeavours to probe and answer questions about origins and meanings and purposes. These answers are naturally clothed in stories which serve as means of keeping them in the memory as well as handing them down from generation to generation.

Liturgy Every cult has its set liturgy. Liturgy consists of the pattern as well as the subject-matter of worship. It is here in fact that 'experiential participation' will be of immense benefit to the researcher. In an unwritten liturgy (or any liturgy), the thing does not sound the same when recited outside the context of actual worship. In fact, experience shows that very often it is either inaccurately said or stumblingly said. Liturgy may be defined as the means of communication and communion with Deity within the setting of worship. For the purpose of study the following elements in liturgy should be taken into account: (a) The invocation: during this a rattle or an instrument of the same import is sounded and the libation is poured; the divine being is called by names and attributes and summoned to attend worship. (b) Prayers: In these, the needs of the worshippers are expressed and the divine Being besought to satisfy them. Thus, from the liturgies of African traditional religion we learn the names and the attributes of Deity or the divinities, the confidence and hopes of the people, the capability believed to belong to Deity, and the fact of the general relationship between Deity and man.

There is usually a certain body of systematic recitals connected with the cult of the oracle divinity. I am not certain if such is to be found everywhere in Africa. I have pointed to the existence and value of these in the Yoruba oral traditions.[6] Wherever a body of cultic recitals of this nature is in existence, it will be of immense value to make a careful study of it. That is because it usually enshrines the philosophy, theology, and often something of the history of the people.

We have the songs. These constitute a rich heritage of all Africa. Africans are always singing; and in their singing and poetry, they express *themselves*: all the joys and sorrows of their hearts, and their hopes and fears about the future, find outlet. Singing is always a vehicle conveying certain sentiments or truth. When they are connected with rituals, they convey the faith of worshippers from the heart – faith in Deity, belief in and about the divinities, assurance and hopes about the present and with regard to the hereafter. In each people's songs, there is a wealth of material for the scholar who will patiently sift and collate. *[songs]*

And finally, we have those pithy sayings, proverbs and adages, *[proverbs]* which are the *sine qua non* of African speech. These are to be found in abundance everywhere and it can be astonishing how much they alone could teach us about religion in Africa.

These oral traditions constitute the scriptures as well as the breviaries of African traditional religion: therefore, no one can expect to see the religion from the inside unless he proceeds through them. They are, in fact, probably of more value to the student than some printed scriptures and common orders, because they are indeed 'living and active'.

In the past, casual observations about African traditional religion were made by the outsiders – European travellers, explorers, civil servants and missionaries. Then anthropologists and ethnographers became interested in the field, and began to present the Western world with written information about Africa. To almost all of these categories of observers or investigators, religion was just one of the elements in Africa's widely varied range of activities. Naturally

Western investigators, by and large, had looked at the religion of Africa from the general European point of view; and then each investigator or observer according to his own special or specialist's line of interest. The travellers had their tales to tell, and a curious religious habit would naturally lend spice to the tale. If the explorer could add to his reports something about the ritual practices of 'the primitives', it would certainly make his report less boring, especially if he made his descriptions as fantastic as possible. The missionary had no use for the religion which he had pre-judged, before he left home, to be an expression of benightedness, something that he came out to fight and kill; that set the limit to his interest in the religion and, therefore, whatever he said about it was in condemnation.

Nevertheless, it was out of this assortment of investigators that the few and far between who became genuinely interested in the religious traditions and practices of Africa first emerged. These first saw that here was something worth studying for its own sake. There came the time when there were missionaries who began to feel that a knowledge of the Africans from the inside was necessary for the success of their work of evangelism – for how can you speak to a person whom you do not understand and who does not understand you?

3. *Stages hitherto in the study*

In the development of the opinions of investigators on the subject of African traditional religion, we may identify three periods for the purpose of our study. These are the period of ignorance and false certainty, the period of doubt and resisted illumination, and the period of intellectual dilemma. The three periods overlap: that is, an element of each period is manifested in all of them severally, and the first two periods exercise a concerted influence and produce the third one, which is the period through which we are currently passing.

(a) *Period of ignorance and false certainty.* This period is so designated because it is the period when to peoples of the Western world, Africa was such a physically and spiritually dark continent that nothing good could reside in, or come out of, her. To them, indigenous Africa was barren of culture or any form of social organization. If anything in her could be called religion at all, it could only be because in Africa the Devil in all his abysmal, grotesque and forbidden features, blackest of aspect, armed to the teeth and with horns complete, held sway. Naturally then, all rituals had to be propitiatory and of the crudest and most fantastic nature. And, of course, all worshippers of such a power must take after their own 'god' in character and manners of life. Thus, imagination conspired with ignorance and prejudice to furnish the outside world with a false but entertainingly welcome picture of Africa. *Travellers' tales* were also available in abundance and, true to type, they were well seasoned with fanciful stories which might be partly true in substance because they told with characteristic exaggeration and distortion of certain happenings in restricted localities; but more often than not, the stories were at least eighty per cent inventions of idle imaginings.

This period is well illustrated with the Berlin newspaper which Leo Frobenius read before he ever visited Africa. Frobenius records:

A very learned article which appeared in a Berlin newspaper in 1891 began thus: 'With regard to its negro population, Africa, in contemporary opinion, offers no historical enigma which calls for solution, because, from all information supplied by our explorers and ethnologists, the history of civilization proper in this Continent begins, as far as concerns its inhabitants, only with the Mahommedan invasion.

Before the introduction of a genuine faith and a higher standard of culture by the Arabs, the natives had neither political organization (!), nor, strictly spoken, any religion (!), nor any industrial development (!).

Therefore, it is necessary, in examining the pre-Mahommedan conditions of the negro races, to confine ourselves to the description of their crude fetishism, their brutal and often cannibal customs, their vulgar and repulsive idols and their squalid homes.

None but the most primitive instincts determine the lives and conduct of the negroes, who lack every kind of ethical inspiration. Every judicial observer and critic of alleged African culture must, once for all, make up his mind to renounce the charm of poetry, the wizardry of fairy lore, all those things which, in other parts of our globe, remind us of a past fertile in legend and song; that is to say, must bid farewell to the attractions offered by the Beyond of history, by the hope of eventually realizing the tangible and impalpable realm conjured up in the distance which time has veiled with its mists, and by the expectation of ultimately wresting some relics of antiquity every now and again from the lap of the earth.

If the soil of Africa is turned up today by the colonist's plough-share, no ancient weapon will lie in the furrow; if the virgin soil be cut by canal, its excavation will reveal no ancient tomb, and if the axe effects a clearance in the primaeval forests, it will nowhere ring upon the foundations of an old-world palace. Africa is poorer in recorded history than can be imagined. "Black Africa" is a Continent which has nor mystery, nor history![7]

Frobenius places on record the fact that 'the stalwart Anglo-Saxon, <u>Stanley, gave the name of "dark" and "darkest"</u>' to Africa, and promoted the general notion of Africa as a continent

whose children we are accustomed to regard as types of national servility, with no recorded history; mere products of the moment ... where ... there is no rule but that of 'insensible fetish', and where all power is said to degenerate into the reign of brute-force alone, beneath a sun whose rays seem but to scorch and wither the world it shines upon.

He quotes a great light of the church who 'assured us, once, that these "niggers" had no souls and were but the burnt-out husks of men'.[8]

A veritable heir to the opinion so confidently expressed in these quotations, an opinion born of ignorance and false certainty, was <u>Emil Ludwig, modern in date but antiquated in thought, who made</u> <u>the notorious statement, 'How can the untutored Africans conceive</u> <u>God? ... How can this be? ... Deity is a philosophical concept which</u> <u>savages are incapable of framing.'</u>[9]

We have described this as the period of ignorance and false certainty because <u>Africa was to most Europeans a dark continent indeed;</u> <u>but dark only because the Western world was living in complete or</u> <u>almost complete ignorance about her and about what is really</u> <u>obtaining inside her.</u> Unfortunately, this description of the state of things in Africa suited their current taste, especially as it acted as a foil to their own cultural situation. Thus, by and large, it was comforting for them to remain in their unenlightened ignorance. And they were confirmed in this state by the false oracles on the African situations whose inspiration had its source in the unexpurgated, unchecked, 'despatches' from abroad.

(b) *Period of doubt and resisted illumination.* <u>The doubt is in</u> <u>general with regard to the assumed certainty about religion in Africa.</u> As we have observed, among the medley of those who were 'interested' in, and those who were enthusiasts about, the ways of the 'primitive' peoples of the world, <u>there soon began to appear certain</u> <u>investigators whose interests were not those of mere curio-collectors</u> <u>or those who sought with sadistic zeal and relish for the bizarre,</u> <u>the detractive, and the disparaging, but those who were genuinely</u> <u>concerned to find the truth and nothing but the truth, and therefore</u>

approached their task with the interest of faithful scientists. These began to record the results of their researches and reached their conclusion *according to the natural and intellectual tools with which they were equipped.* They showed unmistakably their doubts as to whether there could be any people anywhere in the world who were totally devoid of culture and religion, especially with particular reference to the knowledge of the living God. Some of them reached the clear conclusion after exhaustive researches that there could be no such people: the culture and the concept of God might vary with regard to degree or theological detail, especially where there were no written systematic statements about beliefs, but knowledge and beliefs about God undoubtedly existed.

We may mention three of the names which stand out prominently, even at this time of the day, among those who made their indelible marks on this period; these were Andrew Lang,[10] Archbishop N. Söderblom,[11] and Father W. Schmidt of Vienna.[12]

Andrew Lang's outstanding contribution to the subject is contained in his monumental work, *The Making of Religion*, in which he records his discoveries with particular reference to the nature of the religion of 'primitive' peoples in general. He states with emphasis that there is, in each locality, a definite knowledge of God, which was indigenous to the people. He made the startling declaration that 'certain low savages are as monotheistic as some Christians';[13] that:

this belief cannot have been a development through a polytheistic pantheon, because it exists most clearly among tribes that have never had the social conditions for such a development. 'The maker and ruler of the world, known to these races, cannot be shadow of a king or chief, reflected or magnified on the mists of thought: for chief or king these people have none.'[14]

Father W. Schmidt also maintains the thesis that

the belief in, and worship of, one supreme deity is universal among all really primitive peoples ... The 'high God' is found among them all, not indeed everywhere in the same form or the same vigour, but still everywhere prominently enough to make his dominant position indubitable. He is by no means a late development, or one traceable to Christian missionary influences.[15]

Like Andrew Lang, he discovers in each case a monotheistic religion in which God is believed to be 'eternal, omniscient, beneficent, moral, omnipotent, creative, and satisfying all man's needs – rational, social, moral, and emotional'.

The question here at the moment is not whether or not 'what we find among uncivilized people is ... monotheism in its historically legitimate sense ...'[16] This question we shall have to face later on in this book. The main point of fact is that those investigators who maintained that 'primitive' peoples had religion as well as knowledge (not merely ideas) of Deity succeeded in shaking the foundations of the certainty which the Western world had held for a long time concerning the pre-literate peoples of the world, at least causing them to wonder whether it was proper to give credence, after all, to everything that was contained in the 'despatches' and documentary curios sent from abroad.

The very reaction of certain Western scholars to the researches of these honest investigators from the cosy comfort of the cushioned armchairs of their studies made the period one of resisted illumination. Even though it was no longer possible to be categorical in the denial that pre-literate peoples had *any* concept of Deity (or even *any* religion), there was a wide, seemingly concerted effort to resist the truth, as if there was a racial or an academic fear that the truth might hurt; and would it not be better to persist in either continuing to attribute whatever of value might have been discovered to outside influences, or to admit the fact of the situation with all the possible reservations that could be mustered? Thus we find no end of academic red herrings drawn across the tracks.

John Oman, after examining the works of several scholars with this particular reference, maintains that such monotheism as was found by Lang or Soderblöm is not reflective monotheism; and one of his ways of showing his own resistance is to be found in these words, 'Livingstone, for example, says that wise persons in Central Africa agreed with him about good or evil, one God and a future state. But, first of all, a native, speaking from a standpoint given him by a Christian Missionary, is a very different person from one speaking from his own.'[17] A. C. Bouquet expresses what Oman is trying to say more clearly, in his own case with particular reference to Father Schmidt's work:

> These are obviously very large claims, and their vindication must depend entirely upon the adequacy of the evidence adduced for them. It is plainly impossible for the present writer to investigate every detail of the evidence, and he must therefore content himself with saying that up to the present expert opinion has not been favourable to the theory above outlined. The handling of data has been regarded as tendentious or at any rate lacking in thoroughness ... There would appear to be too many exceptions to the

rule for it to be possible to accept its universal operation. It is very difficult to determine the extent to which an apparently primitive people reproduces the vestiges of a previous contact with some group of monotheists ... Much more minute and wholly impartial sifting of the information collected, with a most careful scrutiny of the credentials of the collectors and of those from whom they derive their information, together with a note of the date when it was obtained and the circumstances of the people concerning whom the information was given – all this is indispensable before we can be satisfied that the so-called 'high god' theory is firmly established beyond dispute.[18]

We shall add H. H. Farmer's comment here:

> Most striking of all (if W. Schmidt's researches and conclusions may be accepted) is the fact that in what is certainly one of the oldest strata of humanity at present known to us, the African pygmies ... there *is* a clear acknowledgement and worship of a supreme being to whom all other supernatural beings are far inferior and invariably subject.[19]

Most of the resistance against truth with reference to Africa had its root in the fact that most of those who commented on the findings of those who were actually on the spot were stay-at-homes. John Oman matches intellectual calculations against David Livingstone's first-hand evidence. A. C. Bouquet is inclined to the contact-from-outside theory; if he is to take Schmidt seriously, he would want to see the *curricula vitae* of investigators as well as those of informants with explanatory notes on methods of research and dates of research, and perhaps with X-ray photographs. H. H. Farmer proceeds to use the evidence, having safeguarded himself with an expressed doubt.

The resistance is not always deliberate. It is just a matter of fixed ideas over against evidence, 'expert opinion' against results of actual research or investigation, theory against facts. The position of the stay-at-home critics is summed up in the words, 'It is impossible for the present writer to investigate every detail of the evidence, and he must therefore content himself with saying that up to the present *expert opinion* (italics mine) has not been favourable to the theory above outlined ...';[20] which, at best, is a mere begging of the question. Any honest scholar today should realize that the question at issue is not of the nature of the monotheism – whether it is 'reflective monotheism', whether it is 'monotheism in its historically legitimate sense', or not. The question at issue is brought out clearly by our third period.

(c) *Period of intellectual dilemma.* As we have observed, even at the time that most Western scholars were writing off Africa as a spiritual desert, there were undoubtedly a few who had the uneasy feeling that the story of a spiritual vacuum for a whole continent of peoples could not be entirely true. We have seen also how resistance to facts was set up because convenient pet theories were being shattered or challenged. This, in fact, brought in the first phase of the dilemma. The urgent question was, and is, can scholars afford to give up their darling theories for concrete evidence? We should note that the scholars under reference have their own cultural pride (natural or acquired) to battle with, and that they are prone to get themselves entangled in the net spun by travellers' tales and thus have their intellectual movements detrimentally restricted or re-tarded. Then there is the second phase of this particular dilemma : if there is an African concept of God, if Africans know God, what or which God? Their own God or 'the real God'?[21] This is precisely the predicament in which scholars currently find themselves. The question 'You mean, his own God? Not the real God?' is put into the mouths of a company of English women who were wandering in Malaya. Those women were not anthropologists or sociologists or theologians; they were 'plain' women from the Western world who were reflecting in that remark the inherited prejudice of their race. In naked, plain, unadorned terms, they only expressed plainly what learned men express more palatably under the sugar-coating of academic terminologies.

In order to meet this predicament, various evasive means have been adopted. The obnoxious title of 'high god'[22] has been invented; 'a supreme God' is another convenient phrase. Any term except that which would identify God in African belief with *the* Supreme God. A. C. Bouquet expresses the Western mind when he says, 'Such a High God hardly differs from the Supreme Being of the eighteenth-century Deists, and it is absurd to equate Him with the Deity of the Lord's prayer.'[23] This is the academic tradition which is be-devilling the study of religion in Africa today.

The question of what is in truth the African concept of God we shall discuss later. Suffice it now to say that the matter of religious studies in Africa must be an on-the-spot task, and those who do it must go into it prepared to learn the truth. There is a proverb in Yoruba to the effect that there is none so difficult to wake as one who is only pretending to be asleep. If a person has made up his mind not to see the truth, nothing can wake him to it.

In the meantime, there have been, and there are, Western scholars and investigators who are genuinely devoted to finding out the truth about religion in Africa. Even here, we have to distinguish between the enthusiastic investigator and the trained scholar. For example, we have a gentleman who has been writing books on the beliefs of the people of a certain part of the continent. Those who suspect him to be an anthropologist or a theologian may wonder why he dabbles so much in medical terms and does not stick to his anthropology or theology; and those who suspect that he might be a medical practitioner may wonder why he does not stick to medicine but must dabble in the study of religion. The fact is that he is a medical practitioner who finds himself in a situation where he is fascinated by the religious practices of the people among whom he lives. Apparently, he feels that there is need to put on record his observations and proceeds to do so; but since he is ill equipped to engage properly in the study of religion, he has been rather confused in his writings.

Then, we have the explorers, anthropologists, missionaries, and theologians, some of them trained researchers and others amateurs; several of them doing their best to be honest and as accurate as they can be in their interpretation of what they observe and what they are told. These have the virtue of having worked in the African scene and come to the recognition that there are concrete values in African beliefs; they have tried to put behind them the flat denials which characterized the writings of their predecessors and several of their contemporaries. Inevitably, we meet in most of these sympathetic authors certain tendencies which should be regarded with understanding sympathy while we point out where they go astray. In some cases, they have been so pleasantly surprised and relieved in regard to what they discovered that they have tended to make more than the reality of the situation; in others, the factors of reading in or reading out are in evidence; and there is the fact that where interpretation becomes difficult, they have forced it or take refuge in a reversion to certain academic types by employing borrowed terminologies which, in the light even of their own researches, should have been counted as outmoded. In almost every case, the understanding and interpretation of ordinary, ritual, and emotional languages have been a very trying, often baffling, often defeating, exercise. It may be that this is inevitable. Even the most careful and most honest study must have its limitations because of man's finitude. Especially must the situation be difficult with regard to investigation into, and interpretation of, something the core of which is intangible and must therefore be the more trying for those who are strangers to the native climate. Moreover, with the best intention in the world, the spirit of the prophet is still subject to the prophet – the prophet who is very much man, faced with the handicaps and barriers which limit the best intentions.

On the whole, we can discern that where the basic aim is search for truth, this becomes unmistakable in the products of research. We shall look at three examples of such honest researches.

The Voice of Africa, in two volumes, by Leo Frobenius, first appeared in English in 1913. There is every evidence that this work bears the stamp of a reaction against certain previous opinions on Africa, especially opinions such as were represented in the person whom he described as 'a great light of the Church' and in the Berlin newspaper of 1891 which he had read before he ever visited Africa.[24] As a result of his visit to Africa and his investigations, he says:

> I have gone to the Atlantic again and again, ... I have traversed the regions south of Sahara, that barrier to the outer world ... But I have failed to find it governed by the 'insensible fetish'. I failed to find power expressed in degenerate bestiality alone ... I discovered the souls of these peoples, and found that they were more than humanity's burnt-out husks ...[25]

His sympathetic approach is more clearly revealed as he says:

> What, however, strikes everyone desiring to observe African nations in the true African spirit as particularly remarkable; that which is so extraordinary among parallel phenomena, is that this people should give evidence of a generalized system; a Theocratic scheme, a well-conceived, perceptible organization, reared in a rhythmically proportioned manner; here – here among the swarming population of West Africa. Who would have believed – nay, who would even have dared to hope for it a few decades ago, since this faculty for grouping, for combining the circle of the Gods into one Divine Being, is essentially lacking in every individual we customarily call 'negro', or let me rather say, is not present in the idea 'negro', as we are accustomed to use it.[26]

As the works of Frobenius show, he actually participated in certain rituals and this gave him an insight into the life and beliefs of the people.

Leo Frobenius appears to have become somewhat sentimental, however; he probably remembered too much of his classical education in his interpretations and so got himself mixed up. In West Africa, with particular reference to Ile-Ifè, the Sacred City and the cradle of the Yoruba, he thought that he discovered 'the Lost Atlantis' and concluded that Africans, especially in this particular area, were the children of that ancient, blissful civilization. Upon this he based the existence of what is of value in African cultures and beliefs, and by it he accounted for certain marks of retrogression. He concludes, therefore:

They no longer obeyed the laws handed down to the sons of the Gods, their sires of bygone days. They remember them still. They still make part of their dreams. These people have only fallen away from the height of human achievement. A glorious ideal of mankind had been thrust into the depths ... Today, the noble features of the children of the Gods, fashioned in terra-cotta and bronze figures, are presented to our gaze in all their pathetic loveliness. The buried treasures of antiquity again revisit the sun. Europe brings up to the surface what sank down with Atlantis.[27]

The Atlantis theory rather disturbs Frobenius' thesis. Atlantis was first seriously considered by Plato in a philosophical romance (*Timaeus*), where it represented a state of earthly perfection, a kind of paradise where all was of the best in the best of all possible worlds. The Greeks had thought about this earthly abode of the blest as a place on earth which could still be discovered. Greek geographers had fixed its probable location in the 'unknown and therefore mysterious, West Africa'. In Plato, however, the place had gone under the sea; nevertheless there is a yearning for its rediscovery: for there the perfection of the life of the gods would be known.

Now, the validity of this theory depends upon whether there was, in fact, an Atlantis which was lost, or became sunk under the sea, and whether, if indeed it existed, its original location was in Nigeria and in a place so far away from the sea. If Plato's Atlantis was only imaginary, then Frobenius has based his theory on no foundation in reality. It must be admitted that the cult of Olokun[28] – the Poseidon of Yoruba conception – is part of his inspiration.

The value of Frobenius' works is undeniable, however. He opened his eyes and mind and allowed Africa to reveal herself to him and yield to him something of her secret. His works bear unmistakable evidence of a reaction against what he considered to be erroneous notions about Africa; and he did not allow himself to be blinded to facts wherever he could correctly discern or interpret them. His mind may be compared to a camera which, according to the power of its lens, records every detail of an object from the side upon which it has been focussed. He rightly discovered that, in Africa, there was an undeniable evidence of certain ancient cultures, and that there was need to find a reason or reasons for the degeneration of most, or total extinction of several, of these. He wisely rejected the notion that there could be a whole continent whose peoples had 'no souls but were mere burnt-out husks of men', a notion which was born of ignorance, racial pride, and prejudice.

Of course, any well-informed person reading the works of Frobenius with a clear mind today will see that he was often tripped up with regard to accuracy of facts and interpretation. Nevertheless, his industry, his earnest desire and painstaking effort to reach the truth, and his honesty, are not to be doubted. He even declared unblushingly again and again that he stole treasures from Africa for the European museums!

P. A. Talbot was a civil servant in the British colonial government of West Africa. We refer here to his four volumes on *The Peoples of Southern Nigeria.* On the whole, these works are still illuminating on the way and wisdom of the people. In Volume II, he deals with religion. He has no hesitation in saying that the religion bears a striking resemblance to the religion of ancient Egypt and the Mediterranean areas generally. He adopts the diffusionist theory in explaining the resembance and concludes that the religion of Nigeria must have been of a higher type which had suffered retrogression – the dense forests which surround the people and their general environment must have caused the impress of Egyptian thought to be lost on their character and culture. He sees, however, that

Nigerians are, as a rule, long past the primitive degree of development ... On the whole, the religion strongly resembles that of ancient Egyptians, who combined a belief in the existence of an omnipotent Supreme God ... with that in multitudes of subordinate deities, mostly personifications of natural phenomena.[29]

The rest of Talbot's thesis we shall consider at relevant points later on. It is enough here to say that he was one of those who show unmistakable perceptiveness in dealing with a very delicate subject. His reference to a resemblance between the Egyptians and Nigerians in belief raises the question which has exercised Nigerians themselves recently, that is, the question of their origins – a delicate question about which there are not enough data yet available for dogmatism. There is no doubt that there are concrete Semitic traits to be found throughout Africa and that with the movements of peoples, the cultures of the river valleys of the Nile and the Euphrates very probably trickled into different areas of the continent. The merit of Talbot's works is that he discerned the nature of the religion as it basically is, and illustrates it as it was in current practice.

We shall mention here two of R. S. Rattray's works: *Ashanti* and *Religion and Art in Ashanti*. In these volumes, the author has striven, according to his vindicated claim, 'to make them [Ashanti religious beliefs] as purely objective as the subject and scope seem to demand'. His works bear the mark of honest recordings of what he actually saw, heard, or learnt of what the Ashanti actually knew and believed. His approach was one of sympathy, openness, respect and reverence throughout. He learnt the language of the people and so could converse directly with the elders, whose wealth of knowledge was thus placed at his disposal. He actually took part in almost all the rites and rituals which he describes, and it is no wonder that he so ably and so lucidly describes them. In spite of travellers' tales and the inevitable difficulties attending researches by foreigners in complex cultural situations, he was able to see the Ashanti as they really were, and in the same way as a predecessor of his in the field had been able to see them over one hundred years before him:

It is a singular thing that these people – the Ashantees – who had never seen a white man nor the sea, were the most civil and well bred I have ever seen in Africa. It is astonishing to see men with such few opportunities so well behaved.[30]

He records his belief that the Ashanti were so culturally adequate, as far as any race whatever could be, that is, that they were so well supplied with all the basic materials for cultural greatness and fulfilment that it would be a tragedy if they fell back upon imitation in order to attain the goal – 'Their ideal should be, not to become pseudo-Europeans, but to aim at progress for their race, based upon what is best in their own institutions, religion, manners and customs; ... they will become better and finer men and women by remaining true Ashanti'.[31] Rattray was also so pleasantly surprised by what he discovered that he thought that the influence of foreign cultures or beliefs had probably not been altogether to the good of the Ashanti:

I sometimes like to think, had these people been left to work out their own salvation, perhaps some day an African Messiah would have arisen and swept their Pantheons clean of the fetish ... West Africa might then have become the cradle of a new creed which acknowledged One Great Spirit, Who, being One, nevertheless manifested Himself in everything around

Him and taught men to hear His voice in the flow of His waters and in the sound of His winds in the trees.[32]

From Rattray all who are researching into African traditional religion may learn respect, caution, and reverence. We have quoted him in chapter I of this book.[33] We shall quote further from his *Religion and Art in Ashanti*:

> I am afraid, although I have endeavoured to make this volume and *Ashanti* as detailed as possible, that many of my descriptions are even now incomplete. When the library of the inquirer has been village, swamp, and forest, and his reference books human beings who have to be handled delicately; when the inquirer is often working under considerable physical discomforts, or physical disabilities, there are bound to be omissions. Serious faults of commission are less excusable, and it is hoped that there are not many in these pages. As a field worker who has endeavoured to investigate and record rapidly disappearing rites and customs ... I have had little opportunity to make deductions or elaborate theories.
>
> Experience has taught me, moreover, that there is sometimes a danger when we have before us a description of a rite which leaves us uncertain of its real meaning or its true *raison d'être*. We may commit the possible error of filling in this gap in our knowledge by construing the custom in terms of our own psychology.[34]

Thus, we give credit to all foreigners who have in the past attempted to systematize African beliefs in writing, in spite of all besetting difficulties. Certainly some of those investigators of yesteryear are more careful than some modern ones who appear to know *too much* theoretical off-the-spot anthropology and sociology, the main sources of which are convenient pickings from the researches of other people.

Nevertheless, we have to face the ultimate fact that the best interpreter of Africa is the African – the African with a disciplined mind and the requisite technical tools. Here, however, we are confronted with an embarrassing situation. For a very long time, as we have seen, researches into African cultures and beliefs have been by Europeans. Almost all that the outside world knew about the continent of Africa was in consequence of the writings and stories and tales by explorers, investigators, colonial government civil servants, and missionaries. During this period and even largely till now, it is the stranger who has the pride or honour of showing the African round in his own home.

It was only comparatively recently that modern Africans (especially south of the Sahara) began to be educated in the Western way. The education has always been by European methods and with

European teaching materials. In consequence, a finished product of this system inevitably becomes a pseudo-European, trying to live and think like a European. His education, especially in mission schools, has directly or indirectly taught him that true dignity lies in being like the European in every way : this includes an attitude of contempt towards his own native custom and religion – for has he not been taught that 'all these are of the devil', empty of values, and incompatible with the status into which Western education has promoted him? Thus, it is usually a struggle for Africans who have been educated in this way to convince themselves that it is worthwhile to know Africa as she really is by undertaking research into her history, cultures, and beliefs, and seeing things not through the eyes of the Europeans but as Africans looking at Africa without prejudice. It is very doubtful whether any African in this category in the passing and present generations could ever be completely weaned from the Western-originated bias which has been so much implanted in him that it has almost become a part of his being.

Further, 'educated' Africans have other handicaps. The first and most embarrassing is that he is a poor person and therefore a beggar – this is so whether he is a university professor or lecturer, or a private investigator. The way that this affects his research is that he has to beg from European foundations or trusts for the financing of his project and, whether he does this through his university or directly, he is never sure whether he is going to receive a favourable reply. If he is honest enough to say that his project is religious studies, it is a foregone conclusion that the answer to his application will be 'nothing doing'. If he could tell a story which would disguise what he is actually doing, then 'something' might be forthcoming. This attitude against religious studies must have stemmed from the erroneous notion that 'religion' is synonymous with Christianity in terms of *missionary* enterprises, or that it is becoming a word which disturbs some minds or consciences : certainly it is not yet appreciated fully that 'religion permeates African life' and that it is, in fact, a vital key to the understanding of Africa.

Secondly, the 'educated' African, when he becomes self-conscious and aware of himself as a person created by God to be autonomous, is apt to display a reaction which has the tinge of inferiority complex. The tendency for him is to want to show 'those Europeans' that 'we Africans' are as good as they are and what they have by way of culture we also can match from our own; whereas his calling is really to show himself and his home as both really are, without the uncalled-for, obnoxious complication of undue self-assertion vis-à-vis the Europeans.

Thirdly, in these days of search for self-identity, there are those who are fascinated by the theory that African culture derived from ancient Egypt or from some other cradle of ancient civilization. The whole edifice of this notion is often raised upon a very doubtful, often impossible and fantastic philological foundation – words which sound nearly or remotely alike are declared emphatically to have derived one from another – the current one, of course, from the ancient or classical one. Edwin Smith's warning on this point should be heeded by all who are working in the field of African studies.

> Etymological methods are not invariably helpful and indeed may easily mislead ... This philological region is the happy hunting-ground of fantastic etymologists. Certain writers seem to be supremely ambitious to find origins outside Africa for African ideas, particularly in Babylonia and Palestine; and they make great play with verbal similarities.[35]

A. C. Bouquet's words are also apposite here:

> Turning to the anthropologist and archaeologist, whose work dovetails, we find that their chief contribution lies in helping us gradually to realize the horizontal diffusion of various religious ideas and practices which are becoming familiar. In the nineteenth century, when travellers found some familiar cultural phenomenon also present in a distant part of Africa or Asia, such as a creation- or flood-story, or sacrificial or sacramental ritual, they were prone to assume that it had got there through European or Christian influence, perhaps at a fairly recent date. We are now beginning to realize that such diffusions ... are not necessarily recent, but may well be of considerable antiquity, and perhaps not even diffusions at all. When we find in fact similar but widely-separated magical and religious practices, these may either be remnants of a widely extended zone of custom which existed in the remote past, or else concurrent developments due to the working of the human intellect in a similar fashion in different places without any borrowing or contact.[36]

The same point is emphasized by Edward B. Tylor:

> In criticising details, moreover, it must not be forgotten how largely the similarities in the religions of different races may be of independent origin, and how closely allied are many ideas in the rude native theology of savages to ideas holding an immemorial place in the religions of their civilized invaders.[37]

Fourthly, the plague of generalization against which we have already warned is a constant threat to African writers: it would appear sometimes that the African writer sees his own native locality as the centre of the African world from which the cultures and religious beliefs of Africa take their norm. If this temptation is not overcome, honest and objective study with reference to Africa as a whole will be impossible.

Fifthly, there is the temptation to suppress evidence. Often, this is not through deliberate falsehood, but more often than not, out of an absorbing zeal to uphold a particular thesis; or because one thinks that a particular piece of evidence which appears contradictory *cannot* be relevant at all.

For example, in my original thesis which eventually became *Olodumare: God In Yoruba Belief*, I mentioned categorically that Oduduwa was a male. By doing this, I had rejected offhand the fact of the persistent tradition that Oduduwa was a female. Later on, when I was preparing the thesis for publication, I discovered that the evidence that I had ignored was so stubborn and so much an integral part of the fact that it could not be dismissed without violence to truth. It was then that I was open-minded enough to see that the two variant traditions must be treated as complementary.

But the case could degenerate tragically into deliberate falsehood, as it has often done in connection with African studies. There is usually an emotional resentment bedevilling the study, and then we have such a situation as is described in Charles Williams' *Descent into Hell*:

> He was finding the answer to Aston Moffatt's last published letter difficult, yet he was determined that Moffatt could not be right. He was beginning to twist the intention of the sentences in his authorities, preferring strange meanings and awkward constructions, adjusting evidence, manipulating words. In defence of his conclusions he was willing to cheat in the evidence – a habit more usual to religious writers than to historical ...[38]

On the other hand, the African scholar meets with what amounts to almost spontaneous resentment from Western scholars generally if in his works of recording and interpreting the cultures and beliefs of his own people it is discovered that what he has written corresponds with certain elements of European philosophy and beliefs. This was, in fact, one of the strong criticisms of even Fr Schmidt's work. E. S. Waterhouse says, 'The attributes which are recorded by Schmidt seem to be interpreted too readily in terms of *our* (italics mine) theology.'[39] How much more when this happens in a book written by Africans! The Western world still has to take to heart in this connection, as in all connections, the words of Placide Tempels that 'Anyone who claims that primitive peoples possess no system of thought, excludes them thereby from the category of men. Those who do so contradict themselves fatally elsewhere.'[40] He is writing about the Bantu.

One can only hope that time will cure those who have made up their minds that certain values are impossible in Africa simply because she is Africa and not Europe. In this connection, we have a rather disturbing example in F. B. Welbourn's review[41] of *Biblical Revelation and African Beliefs*, which was written, even at this time of the day, with a mind set for finding fault with whatever is done by Africans. Welbourn is certainly justified on some points in his criticism; but even the value of such points is densely overshadowed by his glaring prejudice. In his zeal to debunk, he even contradicts himself unwittingly : he condemns Fr Mulango and Professor Mbiti for generalization from particular localities and limited experiences and yet presumes to know enough about the whole of Africa as to say that 'he (Idowu) is *surely* (italics mine) wrong to *imply* (italics mine) all African societies believe in a Supreme Being'. He could not have read my foreword to the book; if he had read it, he would not have accused the participants at the Consultation of African Theologians of wittingly or unwittingly contradicting one another in the published papers of the consultation, or speak of their incapability of being aware of the 'often widely differing African societies', and of 'the aggressive *négritude* of Professor Idowu's introduction'. Here we have a veritable example of the attitude of a certain category of Westerners when evaluating the works of African authors – either they are perfunctory in their reading and yet rush to the press with criticism or condemnation, or they resort to the tactics of blind denial. The 'aggressive *négritude*' of Africans who are prepared to wean themselves intelligently from prefabricated scholarship and made-in-Europe academic tradition is a phrase with which, in its various forms, we are now becoming familiar !

The augury at the moment with regard to African scholarship and research in Africa is that the African scholar will strike the balance by weaning himself from his pseudo-Westernism as well as his resentment and unnecessary self-assertion. Then his work of interpretation will be scientific, objective, and truly scholarly.

4. *African traditional religion?*

The next question which we have to face in this chapter is what is meant by 'African traditional religion' and whether or not one could speak of 'African traditional religion' as a precise term. The question is two-dimensional: can one speak of *one* indigenous religion for the whole of Africa? And what is the significance of the word 'tradition'?

This is not an easy question. As we have observed, the basic obstacles to any study of Africa with reference to cultures and beliefs are the size of the continent, her historical rape and her consequent disruption, racial, social and spiritual. There is also the important fact of the complexity of her cultures and systems of beliefs. All these must be taken into account before one can attempt an answer to the question.

When we look at Africa with reference to beliefs, our first impression is of certain objective phenomena which appear to be made up of systems of beliefs and practices which are unrelated except in so far as they are loosely held together by the factors of common localities and languages. But a careful look, through actual observation and comparative discussions with Africans from various parts of the continent, will show, first and foremost, that there is a common factor which the coined word *négritude* will express aptly. There is a common Africanness about the total culture and religious beliefs and practices of Africa. This common factor may be due either to the fact of diffusion or to the fact that most Africans share common origins with regard to race and customs and religious practices. In certain cases, one could trace specific cultural or religious elements which are common over wide areas which lie proximate to one another; and often there are elements which jump over whole territories to re-appear in several other scattered areas on the continent. With regard to the concept of God, there is a common thread, however tenuous in places, running throughout the continent. Whatever outsiders may say, it is in fact this one factor of the concept, with particular reference to the 'character', of Deity which makes it possible to speak of a religion of Africa.[42] There is, for example, one name of God which appears in various forms in several places according to the native tongue of each locality. The Kulung, Piya, Pero, Tagale, and Waja of Nigeria call it Yamba, and it appears in

the Cameroons and the Congo in the forms of Yambe or Yembe. I
have a strong feeling that the Akan name of God, Onyame or
Nyame, is a variation of the same name.

S. F. Nadel takes up this question with particular reference to
Nupe religion. He begins by anticipating the objector's standpoint
of thinking that the word 'religion' with reference to the Nupe is
only a convenient label. He looks at the whole situation: the Nupe
are internally divided in various ways; their religious beliefs and
practices differ considerably in different parts of the country, with
local cults and forms of worship varying from region to region,
village to village. Yet, he feels justified in using the word 'religion'
to cover the whole of the varying systems in consequence of an
underlying unity; the varieties hang together in relevant respects –
the diverse and separate practices being instances of a common
creed; Nupe themselves will describe it (all) as concerned with Soko
(Deity), not with the divinities; on the whole he uses 'religion' to
cover both that which may be properly so described, and every other
thing that bears on religion.[43]

The most basic concept of Nupe theology, that of the Supreme Being, is
also the widest. In a sense it stands for the whole realm of religion ...[44]

We may support this with Tempels' findings among the Bantu, 'Life
belongs to God. It is he who summons it into being, strengthens
and preserves it.'[45]

We find that in Africa, the real cohesive factor of religion is the
living God and that without this one factor, all things would fall
to pieces.[46] And it is on this ground especially – this identical concept – that we can speak of the religion of Africa in the singular.

Now, the word 'traditional'. We have used this word to mean
'native', 'indigenous', that which is aboriginal or foundational,
handed down from generation to generation, that which continues
to be practised by living men and women of today as the religion
of the forbears, not only as a heritage from the past, but also that
which peoples of today have made theirs by living it and practising
it, that which for them connects the past with the present and upon
which they base the connection between now and eternity with all
that, spiritually, they hope or fear.

Recently, W. Cantwell Smith has questioned the appropriateness
of the phrase 'traditional religion'. 'As I said before,' he says, 'I
learned to refine the concept "religion"; every religion is a new

religion every morning.' One might almost go on to say, the concept 'traditional religion' is a contradiction in terms. A man is not religious if his religion is only traditional – or even primarily traditional. There are groups for whom history, even historical tradition, has been religiously important; but only if, and in so far as, and because, it could introduce the devotee to something beyond history, something here and now, and/or beyond all time. He raises this question because he is very much aware that it is easy in the study of religion to lose sight of 'what is happening to man's religiousness in the flux and turmoil of the modern world'.[47]

This is in line with A. C. Bouquet's warning that in studying religion, one must be careful not to engage oneself in the fruitless task of studying 'fossil religion'.[48] As we have already observed, religion that is worth the name is religion as practised by living men and women, and that means that the phenomena of change must be taken into account. Thus, 'traditional religion' as used for indigenous religion in Africa is religion as it actually is today. But religion as it is today is meaningless unless its basic past is related to the present. It is true that:

> Traditions now extant are deposits of earlier men's faith. At best, they can be the efficient cause of the faith of men of today. Yet, if there is one quality characteristic of our modern age, it is the possibility of dislocation between faith and inherited formulation. An investigation concerned only with formulation, will all too probably miss the heart of the matter.[49]

But the same will be true of an investigation concerned with 'faith' which ignores its history and tradition. 'Faith' does not hang in the air: it is in the hearts of persons for whom it gives meaning to the past, informs the present, and establishes hope in regard to eternity.

One fact of major importance is that to the majority of Africans today, in spite of all the effects of contacts from outside, the indigenous religion remains *the real religion*.

We must admit, however, that the term 'African traditional religion' is tentative: it is the result of a search for a comprehensive title; and it is useful only as long as all the safeguards enumerated above are heeded.

Nevertheless, we have to add at once that African traditional religion with reference to the whole of Africa, as a subject of study, is an impossible proposition, where detailed study and thoroughness are concerned. Some time ago, I began to write a book on *God in West African Belief*. Before long I began to run into difficulty and had to admit that it would be unwise for any one scholar to attempt such a formidable task. Therefore, I limited my scope to *God in Nigerian Belief*. But even here, I was faced with the predicament of at least 250 distinct languages and variations of cults and traditions in bewildering numbers. This is to say that any study of African traditional religion that is to be thorough and academically effective and profitable should be regional or one that covers only a limited area. The more limited the area covered the more effective and honest the study will be. No honest scholar can be quite satisfied with a study done by proxy through research assistants scattered all over the field or by library work, whereas there is no way of avoiding either of these methods where the area covered is large and the scholar himself does not understand more than one or two of the languages. As the study must go on until enough scholars are produced all over Africa to tackle the subject each in his own language area, any study done in such areas where the native tongue is not that of the scholar must be regarded as tentative.

5. *The aim of the study*

In the study of African traditional religion, we do not set out to glorify the dead past of Africa. This is a temptation against which African scholars especially must be on their guard. In these days of vigorous nationalism, of '*négritude*', of 'African personality', there is always the tendency to wish to drag the dead back to life rather than for the living to realize their own intrinsic personalities and make sure of their own bearings for now and for eternity. If there are any values by which the forbears lived and by which the present generations are living, if there is any heritage from the past which is spiritually and morally potent for today, these are the things to be researched into, refined if need be, and preserved for posterity. It is both spiritually and morally wrong to approach our study with the mind that for Africans, whatever had or has been African, practised traditionally by Africans centuries ago, recently or currently, must be good enough. This is to study with prejudice. African scholars need to beware of being so emotionally involved as to lose their scholarly perspective.

The purpose of the study should be to discover what Africans *actually* know, *actually* believe, and *actually* think about Deity and the supersensible world. There is a whole world of difference between this and what any investigators, at home or from abroad, prescribe through preconceived notions that Africans *should* know, believe, and think. It is also to find out how their beliefs have inspired their world-views and moulded cultures in general.

To achieve this end, the scholar must guard against 'reading in' what is not there, and 'reading out'[50] what is there, with regard to African beliefs and practices. This involves the matter of critical judgment and interpretation, which are a great responsibility, especially where one is dealing with a culture that is not one's own or where one is in danger of feeling too much at home. I may give two illustrations:

Once I met an Englishman in Minna, Nigeria. He told me that he was working among the Gwari – 'a very interesting people: they are stone-worshippers!' 'How do you know that they are stone-worshippers?' I asked. 'Oh, one day I was travelling with the boys (his porters and domestic servants); during the afternoon, we stopped to rest near a village. One of the boys sat on a boulder. A woman came out of a hut and was very furious with him and drove him off. That stone, I gathered, was their god; and that was how I knew they were stone-worshippers'!!

Recently, a research student was working in the sacred city of the Yoruba. By his conversation, I discovered that he had been visiting one person, and only one, whom he called possessively 'my informant'. It turned out that 'my informant' was one of the sophisticated sons of the place who had made up his mind long ago about what things should be, drawn his own conclusions, and closed his mind. On being asked whether or not he consulted the priests and the elders of the people, our research student said, 'Oh, no! *my informant* is very knowledgeable, he can tell me all that I want to know!'

I leave these two illustrations to the reader's judgment.

IV

The Nature of
African Traditional Religion

Here we again come to delicate ground, for the same reason that one has to tread warily and be sure of one's perception when discussing religion in Africa. The main factor to watch here is the bewildering variety with which one is confronted within a basically more or less homogeneous system. It is as a result of this, plus the fact of preconceived notions, that all sorts of offhand names have been coined or adopted to describe – what appeared to be indescribable – the essential characteristics of African traditional religion. We shall do well first to examine some of these names, under the following comprehensive heading.

1. Errors of terminology

We may begin with and dispose of a few attributive words which have been abused consistently by writers on Africa. Then we shall deal with abstract substantives.

There are three such adjectives, among others, which call for immediate attention. These are the words 'primitive', 'savage', and 'native'. Really, there should be no need at this time of the day for any dispute about such words, in consequence both of the findings of scholarship hitherto and the lip-service which is being so loudly paid to progress in scientific and open-minded thinking. But we have to deal with the human mind, which has a sure way of addicting itself stubbornly to the obviously incongruous, if only to satisfy personal, racial, ethnic, or political egocentricity.

(a) *Primitive*. *The Concise Oxford Dictionary* defines this word as 'Early, ancient, old-fashioned, simple, rude; original, primary.' It should be obvious that in the light of some of the words in this definition, 'primitive' cannot be appropriate in certain contexts in which it is being currently applied. With reference to any people in the world today, 'early', 'ancient', 'original', or 'primary' does not apply. Primitive man, in the sense conveyed by the words quoted, disappeared from this world thousands of years ago. The peoples who are being so described today are contemporaries of, and as old or as recent in earthly lineage as, the races of those who are so describing them.[1]

The fashion that perpetuates the incongruous use of the word stems from the notion that anything that does not conform to a certain cultural pattern accepted as the norm by the Western investigator is regarded automatically as primitive; that is, that which belongs to the category of those things which have somehow been left behind in the race of cultural sophistication. 'Primitive' in this connection means, categorically, 'backward', 'rude', or 'uncouth'.

The anthropological or sociological use of the word 'primitive' has been defended on the ground that it only refers to that which is adjudged to be nearer in behaviour or pattern to the original with reference to the human race or culture. It is with this excuse that Western writers still persist in applying the word to Africa, and to African beliefs and practices. This follows also the slothful pattern that where a new, adequate term is not conveniently ready to hand for any situation, an old one, however outmoded or unsuitable, is applied without any apology.

Two facts must be conceded here. First, there are peoples in the world today whose manners of life can be described as still closely related to those which are known to history as the ways of their early forbears. In fact, it is possible to find areas where not much has radically changed. 'Dating back to the flood' may here be applied as a relative, loose term. This may be due to the fact that there has not been much contact from outside, or to the stubbornness of cultures which somehow resist the solvent of foreign agents. Education as known to and introduced by the West has not covered the whole world; and it is not everywhere that Western or new ways of life have been adopted as second nature. Secondly, there is an element of the ancient subsisting in every culture. Whatever the stage of development, each culture maintains itself on the antinomous principle of continuity and discontinuity. Even in a new culture (or in reality a medley of cultures) like that of America, there are unmistakable vestiges of the cultural backgrounds of the peoples who are now embraced by the common name of Americans. For example, in the year 1969, Earlham College in Richmond, Indiana, celebrated a very elaborate May Day: an old English pageant was called into being – May poles, May Queens (an adult and a juvenile), the President of the College and his wife appearing 'anciently' as the Lord Chancellor and Queen Elizabeth I. This elaborate celebration occurs at Earlham every fourth year; it is not only to remind the people of their origins; it is also to revitalize in them the basic culture which makes them distinctive even within a new cultural situation of which they are part.

What happens to cultures in general happens also to religions. There are religions which may be more closely related to what is known about their early forms than other religions, depending upon the historical and geographical circumstances of those who practise them. But there is no religion where the principle of continuity and discontinuity is not manifestly in operation, although, unfortunately, there are certain religions about which the leaders are dishonestly trying to suppress the fact of their indebtedness to the past.

Nevertheless, as we have observed earlier in this book, every religion is a new religion every day – that is, as long as it is a religion practised by living people who are being affected by the inevitable factor of change which is the lot of all on this earth. Stagnation is as alien to nature as it is to history. Things may appear stagnant; but sooner or later they will manifest the signs either of progress or retrogression. Thus, strictly, religion in its pristine form is no longer in existence. What we see today is modern and contemporary, wherever its location may be. This is partly admitted by Freud when he says, *inter alia*:

It should not be forgotten that primitive races are not young races but are in fact as old as civilized races. There is no reason to suppose that, for the benefit of our information, they have retained their original ideas and institutions undeveloped and undistorted.[2]

It is especially wrong to speak of the religion of any living people as 'primitive' simply on the ground of racial or ethnic prejudice. 'Primitive' in most Western writings is a derogatory term and therefore obnoxious. Therefore, it is not only inappropriate but also offensive to describe African traditional religion unreservedly as 'primitive'.

(b) *Savage.* Here, in the use of the word 'savage', we meet again the inveterate streak in race-proud man.

On 29 May 1969 (note the year!), I was relaxing in a hotel room in New York City after a hard, hot day's work, looking at the television. An advertisement came on the screen, and with it the words 'Ah, Africa! The Nigerian jungle!! Where kola grows in abundance!!!' It turned out to be an advertisement for coca-cola. The 'civilized' world is constantly indulging in this 'superfluity of naughtiness'. Is it in consequence of the working of a defence mechanism? The underlying notion seems to be unmistakable: anything outside their own countries or cultures, even though from such a situation they derive immense benefit for which they should be grateful, is regarded with disdain. It is only occasionally that one meets the few and far between who genuinely appreciate, try to understand, and seek to enter experientially into, the ways and wisdom other than, and different from, their own.

'Savage' stands at the opposite end of the pole from 'civilized'. The terms are antithetic to each other. Too often, peoples or cultures and religious practices are described as savage through sheer prejudice, lack of sympathy, or understanding.

We must not blink the fact, however. There are wide areas of the world today which are not technologically developed, which for that reason may be aptly described as developing or under-developed, but strictly only for that reason. It is clear that in the technologically developed countries, things are different, with a clean and dazzling difference, from those in the other areas of the world which have less or little technological opportunities. It is an ocular fact that streets are much cleaner, towns and cities are well planned and laid out, and houses are beautiful, well-built and equipped, not only with modern amenities, but also with due regard to health requirements. Also, public manners of life are guarded with regulations called etiquette and, *in public*, everyone tries to conform to these. Whereas in certain other areas of Asia and Africa, by and large, the externals of things are not as 'whited' or as 'gilded'. On the whole, people behave as they really are. Public behaviour and private practices have not yet learnt the art of double life. And there is no doubt that, therefore, it is not an unfair judgment, everything considered, to say that things could be better regulated for the good of all.

There are also situations created by ignorance or lack of knowledge about certain basic facts of nature. But ignorance with its products, however disturbing or unpleasant these may be, should not be made a forced synonym for savagery.

On the whole, man is man everywhere in the world. We have only to see beneath the surface to realize that the differences made possible by cultural and technological climates are not necessarily symptomatic of racial differences between one race and another with regard to human nature. As E. S. Waterhouse observes,

> We are aware of the fact of reversion to 'primitive' type, physically and mentally. Primitive emotion and superstition is not far beneath the surface of civilization. Scratch a Russian and you find a Tartar, scratch a civilized man and you find a savage. Civilized and savage are brothers under their skins.[3]

A few comparative illustrations will illuminate the subject for us. First, capital has been made out of the fact of human sacrifice in Africa. Human sacrifice, we trust, has become or is fast becoming a thing of the past throughout Africa. I have discussed the subject at some length in *Olodumare*.[4] The fundamental principle behind it is that 'it is expedient ... that one man should die for the people, and that the whole nation should not perish'. This substitutionary principle has been put into practice from time immemorial, though, more often than not, its expression has been the perversion which has acquired the name of human sacrifice. What is both interesting and disappointing is that the Western world is putting on blinkers with regard to the perversion of this principle which is daily occurring in its midst. Political murders, euphemistically glorified as 'assassinations', negro lynching resulting in the death of countless numbers of people of African descent in America, the extermination of the aboriginal peoples in America, Australia and New Zealand in order that those who came to acquire their lands forcibly might possess the lands for themselves and for their posterity, the German gas-chambers which, like Moloch, devoured countless numbers of Jews, the wanton and wholesale murders of apartheid South Africa and Rhodesia : these perversions, in each case, are of the same character as ritual human sacrifice, although in these euphemistic instances, the case for it is very much weaker.

Secondly, I have never watched on the television the films on

'Wrestling from Canada' and 'Wrestling from Britain' without being filled with horror at what to me as an African is the sheer 'savagery' of the whole performance. In Yorubaland for instance, wrestling is an art implying artistic movements and beauty of strategy; and when once any part of a contestant's body (apart from the feet) has touched the ground, be it no more than the tip of a finger, that contestant has been defeated and the contest is over. There is nothing of the callous, cruel assault on the contestant, twistings of, or attempts to damage, any organs of the body, or sitting upon a person and buffeting him when he is down.

Thirdly, there are undoubtedly several parts of Africa where feuds *feuds* are settled with matchets and spears, dane guns or arson. The difference between this and such undertakings in the Western world is that weapons have been scientifically perfected – pistols, revolvers, bombs and nuclear appliances are civilized Western counterparts.

<u>Our contention here is that if there is savagery in the world – and there is plenty of it – no race has the right to impose the monopoly of it on any other race</u>. ✓ For example, in Charles Williams' *Shadows of Ecstasy*, the following occurs:

> Philip, looking at him, thought that he wasn't looking very friendly, and that he was looking rather African, in fact rather savage. Savage was a word which might here, in fact, have a stronger meaning than it generally had. Inkamasi's head was thrust forward, his jaw was set; his hand moved, slowly and relentlessly, along his leg to his knee, as if with purpose, and not a pleasant purpose.[5]

And this is quite definite:

> My dear fellow, when you've been out here (in Africa) as long as I have you'll realize that there's no such thing as a civilized native. The dark centuries of savagery are too deeply rooted in the native character, and although a native may live peaceably and behave to all intent and purposes like a white man, you can never be sure that his heritage will not come out in him one day. And that goes for Africa North, South, East, and West.[6]

<u>The innuendo in these quotations is that there is a sense in which savagery is distinctly African; which is patently nonsensica</u>l. There is something for us to learn from this novelist's character:

> 'He (grandfather) was black,' she added tragically, 'I hate the very thought of that blood that runs in my veins, although my memories of *him* are of a noble and kingly person murdered by Englishmen more savage and cruel than any member of my unfortunate grandfather's tribe.'
> 'Quite so,' said Lucien, 'there are degrees of savagery, and nobility can

sit like a crown upon the brow of a black man as well as upon a white. The colour of your skin is not so important as you may believe, my child.'[7]

Savagery is a thing of the unregenerate human nature and is committed to the degree in which the 'old Adam' holds sway or the instruments of man's inhumanity to man have been perfected or refined, with whatever weapons are available to each people. Savagery is wicked and should be one of the elements to be exterminated in order that harmony may dwell in the world. No people should be called savages simply because they are technologically backward or because their own ways of reverting to the raw 'natural' state have not yet acquired scientific justification and technological polish.

(c) *Native.* My wife and I were on a week's holiday, residing at a Quaker Guest House called 'The Blue Idol' somewhere in Sussex. There were other guests staying at the same time in the house. One evening, after supper, several of us sat round a table, playing a game of cards. It was my turn to shuffle the cards and I did it in a way which a British woman considered admirable: for she burst out, 'Oh, how wonderfully you do it! Do all natives do it the same way?' '*Natives* of where – England, Scotland, or Ireland?' I asked her. By the way she was taken aback and by the expression on the faces of the other Europeans in that room, it was patent that they were probably realizing for the first time that they themselves must have been *born* somewhere! The fact is that to her and, by and large, to the peoples of the Western world, the word 'native' has acquired a derogatory nuance and has become one that is reserved for the 'unfortunate', 'backward', non-Western peoples of the world. This is so, thanks to the anthropologists and missionaries, and the stay-at-home investigators who must always find terms of unmistakable distinction between themselves and 'those others'. 'Prayers for native Christians' are still being offered in churches of Europe and America; 'native Christians' being not Christians who are born and are living in Europe and America, but Christians of Africa and Asia and those other 'benighted climes'. This defines the Western mind on the issue beyond doubt:

It was about this time that Damu, quite unknown to himself, developed two minds, or rather his own mind split in two parts. One part was his civilized or white mind, the other his native mind which, gradually submerged by his life in England, had been reawakened by contact with his

present surrounding. It was his native mind that trifled with the idea of
rising against the people he hated, while his white mind laughed at the
fantastic notions. Conversely, it was his white mind that made him curious
about the Leopard cult, for a native would have been terror-stricken at the
very notion of probing into such mysteries.[8]

So also is this:

Oh yes. Abu bin Zaka is a pure European. Not a drop of native blood in
him.[9]

The question is, how has the word 'native', a good word of Latin
origin, come to acquire this obnoxious, abusive connotation? The
aberration must have been of long standing. *The Concise Oxford
Dictionary*, in its usual way of conformity to current usage, brings
itself up-to-date by defining the noun 'native' as 'One born, or whose
parents are domiciled in a place; member of non-European or uncivilized race'; and the adjective as 'Belonging to a person or thing
by nature ...' 'Born in a place (especially of non-Europeans), indigenous'.

It is glaringly obvious that the definition of 'non-European' has
nothing to do with the original meaning of the word. The Latin
word *nativus* from which 'native' is derived has simply the meaning
of 'born', 'come into existence by birth', 'innate, natural'. Thus, the
word 'native' strictly means either 'one who is born' in a particular
place, any particular place anywhere in the world; or '(something)
natural to, inherent in, characteristic of, a person, nation, or situation' – also without discrimination of any kind.

One can only hope that this derogatory use of a good word
will cease and that those who are abusing the word will learn to
appreciate the fact that even they, as anyone else, were born in
the one natural way common to mankind, that the locality of the
habitable world where any people were born and are domiciled
should not be an excuse for restricting to them the use of a word
which is of universal, natural application.

The words of Evans-Pritchard are illuminating with regard to
the three obnoxious adjectives and the inveterate attitude of
Western writers about their use:

A final word: some people today find it embarrassing to hear peoples
described as primitives or natives, and even more so to hear them spoken
of as savages. But I am sometimes obliged to use the designations of my
authors, *who wrote in the robust language of a time when offence to the
peoples they wrote about could scarcely be given* (italics are mine) ... But

the words are used by me in what Weber calls *a value-free sense, and they are etymologically unobjectionable* (italics are mine). In any case, the use of the word 'primitive' to describe people, living in small-scale societies with a simple material culture and lacking literature *is too firmly established to be eliminated* (italics mine). This is unfortunate, because no word has caused greater confusion in anthropological writings ... for it can have a logical and a chronological sense and the two senses have sometimes not been kept distinct, even in the minds of good scholars.[10]

The words italicized speak for themselves.

(d) *Tribe.* The Pocket Oxford Dictionary is quite definite about the derogatory and discriminatory meaning of this word. It is defined as 'Group or people in a primitive or barbarous stage of development acknowledging the authority of a chief and usually regarding themselves as having a common ancestor; ... set of people that can be lumped together (usually contemptuously ...)'. *The Advanced Learner's Dictionary of Current English* improves on this: it has 'Racial group, especially one united by language and customs, living as a community under one or more chiefs; ... (usually contemptuous) group of persons ...'

Whatever may have been the original meaning or connotation of this word, there is no doubt that it has departed from anything decent and honourable and has come to bear exclusively the connotation of a dirty, ragged, disreputable fragment of humanity. And this is why, in spite of every attempt to defend the indefensible, Africans should feel offended when the word is applied to them cheerfully and as a matter of course by people who will not apply it to themselves and will resent it forcibly if seriously applied to them. The word should be abolished from the vocabulary of any references to Africa.

(e) *Paganism.* This is probably the oldest of the names adopted to describe the religion of the so-called primitive or 'uncivilized' peoples of the world. This word has a Latin origin – *paganus* – and means originally a village-dweller or a countryman, a person who lives away from the civilized community. Thus, originally, the word was a sociological term, a mark of distinction between the enlightened, the civilized and the sophisticated, on the one hand and the rustic, the unpolished, and the unsophisticated on the other.

The word must have travelled some curious distance in order to become a term with an exclusively religious connotation. In the world to which it originally belonged, what came under the term now was all the religion that there was. And yet, the *Pocket Oxford Dictionary* appears to be unaware of this when it defines 'pagan' as 'acknowledging neither Jehovah, Christ nor Allah; non-Christian'. The *Encyclopaedia of Religion and Ethics* in a passing reference links the term with 'primitive peoples'.[11]

Franz Cumont describes paganism with reference to Rome as follows:

Let us suppose that in modern Europe the faithful had deserted the Christian churches to worship Allah or Brahma, to follow the precepts of Confucius or Buddha, or to adopt the maxims of the Shinto; let us imagine a great confusion of all the races of the world in which Arabian mullahs, Chinese scholars, Japanese bonzes, Tibetan lamas, and Hindu pundits would be preaching fatalism and predestination, ancestor worship and devotion to a deified sovereign, pessimism and deliverance through annihilation – a confusion in which all priests would erect temples of exotic architecture in our cities and celebrate their disparate rites therein. Such a dream, which the future may perhaps realize, would offer a pretty accurate picture of the religious chaos in which the ancient world was struggling before the reign of Constantine.[12]

Grant Showerman, in his introduction to Cumont's book, summarizes Cumont's conclusion on Roman paganism as follows:

The mass of religions at Rome finally became so impregnated by neo-Platonism and Orientalism that paganism may be called a single religion with a fairly distinct theology, whose doctrines were somewhat as follows: adoration of the elements, especially the cosmic bodies; the reign of one God, eternal and omnipotent, with messenger attendants; spiritual interpretation of the gross rites yet surviving from primitive times; assurance of eternal felicity to the faithful; belief that the soul was on the earth to be proved before its final return to the universal spirit, of which it was a spark; the existence of an abysmal abode or the evil, against whom the faithful must keep up an unceasing struggle; the destruction of the universe, the death of the wicked, and the eternal happiness of the good in a reconstructed world.[13]

M. I. Boas says:

The word pagan has little real meaning for most of us (in Europe) today. When we hear it pronounced it affects most of us in a way that has been determined by our schoolbooks, that is, we have a vision of the gods on Olympus, a group of bearded Druids gathered around some woodland altar, or worse – the holocausts to Moloch and the abomination of Ashtoreth ... paganism proves to be something else, with the difference lying not so much in the outer aspects and manifestations as in the essence of the thing. The pagan principle ... proves to be much more deeply seated, more intrinsic in man, a thing timeless, universal.

Pagan, it should be quickly added, is hardly to be limited to what is rude, backward, and unlettered, for the ancient Egyptians, Greeks, and Romans, pagans all, illuminated humanity with the clarity of their thought, the wonders of their art, and the nobility of their ethics and sentiments ... when we call these people pagans we simply mean that their belief was polytheistic in contrast to our own religions which are identified with monotheism, a distinction which is debatable, if not absolutely incorrect ... As a preliminary definition it is better to say that by pagans we mean those who seek to realize the fundamental needs by an appeal to supernaturally ordained codes of law of rituals ... Paganism, we may say, is a primitive way of attaining goals through pre-ordained mechanisms, the hope to realize fundamental needs through the accomplishments of certain well defined and immutable acts.[14]

The following points have emerged so far. First, *paganism* was never, according to its root, meant to be a word used with a religious connotation, except in so far as it might refer to the habits, characteristics, or practices of the country dwellers, which would then *include* religion. Secondly, the word found a passage into the religious context, probably by way of derogatory comparison through those who believed their own religion to be superior to or more meaningful than the religions which they described as paganism. There is still the underlying tone of the crude, the rude, the amorphous, the unpolished. The *Pocket Oxford Dictionary* states categorically that anyone who does not acknowledge Jehovah, Christ, or Allah is automatically a pagan. 'Pagan' it defines further as non-Christian. In this way, the word implies a one-sided value-judgment. Thirdly, from Franz Cumont we are enlightened that the root cause of the later use of the word for the religions which are considered 'lower' was the difficulty of finding a comprehensive name for a religion which appeared to be hydra-headed or made up of a variety of cults. He speaks of 'religious chaos', and even though he discovered that the 'religion' later developed a theological and philosophical homogeneity, he still has to leave it with the name 'paganism'. It seems that this is the fate of religions which are not known to have derived their names from historical founders who could be both their earthly inspirations and the focal points of their tenets. Fourthly, from the definition of M. I. Boas, we see a definition reached after the dissection of a full-grown baby. He would set a distinction between religion and paganism, paganism being according to his description synonymous with, or at least very close to, magic. If, as he maintains, paganism of his definition is the darling sin of every religion ('there should have been truly religious men in pagan times, and pagans aplenty in the world of today'), it means that paganism in this sense has become a universal epidemic which can no longer be regarded as the exclusive 'religion' of any particular localities of the world. Moreover, it does not seem that the Greeks or the Romans would ever call themselves pagans. It is not like the name 'Christian' or 'Methodist' or 'Protestant' which those who were first called so in derision or contempt later adopted and used for themselves because, after all, there is something appropriate about it. 'Paganism' is a derogatory imposition from without; it is an opprobrious term.

With particular reference to African traditional religion, there is no doubt that the word 'paganism', whenever or wherever it is used, carries primarily a mark of racial and social discrimination. Even though the discrimination is now tinged with a religious overtone, the basic implication is sociological. There are varieties of cults in Africa, but one could not speak here of the kind of chaos imagined by Cumont. If we accept his final definition of paganism as it arrives at a theological and philosophical stage, one might say that there is a sense in which the word would apply in Africa. That would be true also if we accept Boas' definition. But while there is something of these elements of variety and magic *in* African traditional religion, there is no honest way of using 'paganism' as *the* name for the religion.

(f) *Heathenism.* M. I. Boas says that ' "pagan" must be distinguished from the common usage which makes it synonymous with "heathen", for "heathen" taken literally also means rude, uncultivated.'[15] Here Boas has failed to see the fundamental correlation between the two words. *Paganus*, as we have said, means a rustic, a country dweller, one who is outside the circle of enlightenment, a yokel. 'Heathen', in fact, came into being as an analogy of *paganus*. It is a word of Germanic root. The suffix -en has the same meaning as the -en in wood*en*; and the heath, originally, was the waste land removed from the outskirts of the town, where outlaws, vagabonds, and brigands had their abode; 'heathen' means a dweller on the heath. Thus, the 'heathen' is, primarily, one who belongs to, or has the habit of, or has the forbidding quality or characteristics of, heath-dwellers. 'Heathenism' means the habit or the characteristics, or the disposition, of heath-dwellers.

The Concise Oxford Dictionary, however, defines 'heathen' as (one who is) 'neither Christian, Jewish, nor Mohammedan; unenlightened persons'. Like the *Pocket Oxford Dictionary*, it makes 'pagan' and 'heathen' synonymous. This agreement about their being synonymous is true to their basic meanings and connotations. But here again, we have to question how a purely sociological term of social distinction became transferred entirely to a religious context.

James Hastings' A *Dictionary of the Bible*[16] gives a prominent heading to the word 'heathen' but does not discuss the word as such. Rather, it takes for granted that the *Authorized Version* of the Bible has rightly translated the Hebrew word *goiim* with the word 'heathen', and proceeds to discuss the former. The *Revised Standard Version* returns to the original meaning of *goiim* when it translates it 'nations' (see e.g. Ps. 2.1,). Both the *Authorized Version* and the *Revised Standard Version* retain the word 'Gentile', following the original Greek or Latin which means simply 'race' or 'descent', as a translation of the Greek *ethnē*, which is of exactly the same meaning and purport as *goiim* (see e.g. Matt. 6.32). Is this because the word 'nations', which without qualification will include all mankind, may cause an embarrassing confusion for those who want *goiim* or *ethnē* to retain its derogatory nuance as a mark of discrimination between the rest of mankind and the exclusive races? *The New English Bible* makes matters worse still by deliberately taking a spiritual step backwards in translating *ethnē* in Matt. 6.32 (for example) as 'heathen'.

'Heathen', like the Hebrew *goiim* or the Greek *ethnē* or *barbaros*, is a word coined specially by races who look down from an Olympian height of superiority upon other races: with the Hebrews, it was from a height of spiritual pride; with the Greeks and Romans, from the height of cultural arrogance. Liddell and Scott define *barbaros* as 'barbarous, not Greek, foreign' and go on to comment as follows:

Plato divides mankind into Barbarians and Hellenes, as the Hebrew gave the name of Gentiles to all but themselves. From the Augustan age, the term was applied by the Romans to all nations except themselves and the Greeks; but the Greeks still affected to look upon the Romans as Barbarians.[17]

It is needless to say, after all that has been discussed so far, that with regard to African traditional religion, the name *heathenism* is most unsuitable and is, in fact, a very obnoxious misnomer. It has nothing to do with religion, basically. It is of all opprobrious labels the most opprobrious, and is culpably inexcusable.

(g) *Idolatry*. This term is based on the recognition of a certain tendency in human nature as well as on a misunderstanding born of prejudice. There is a sense, therefore, in which it is justifiable when used in the context of religion, and a sense in which it could be unfair. When, however, it is used to cover all that is religion in any part of the world, there is invariably no excuse, apart from gross prejudice, for it.

'Idol' is from the Greek *eidōlon*. The history of the word is rather complex. The following occurs in Edward B. Tylor's *Primitive Culture*:

> Now one doctrine which there comes into view is especially associated with the name of Democritus, the philosopher of Abdera, in the fifth century B.C. When Democritus propounded the great problem of metaphysics, 'How do we perceive external things?' ... he put forth, in answer to the question, a theory of thought. He explained the fact of perception by declaring that things are always throwing off images (*eidōla*) of themselves, which images, assimilating to themselves the surrounding air, enter a recipient soul, and are thus perceived.[18]

Eidōla seems to have come eventually to represent the intermediate region 'between sheer non-existence and full reality', an image 'copied from the real thing', a shadow thrown by real existence, a world 'imaging the real world of Forms'.

Eidōlon bears the dictionary meaning of 'a shape, image or phantom'; 'an image in the mind, idea, spectre or phantom'; 'an image in the mind, idea, a vision, a fancy', and from these it developed into a portrait, especially of a god; and later still, 'false god' (following a philosophical bias that *eidōla* may connote a world of false judgment). In logic, it connotes first the form of an idea, the formation of an idea in the mind and, later, 'false mental conception'.

Thus, *eidōlon* seems to have been tossed about between the representation or shadow of that which is fully real and that which is not real or that which, if real at all, is real only as a creation of the human mind.

The *Encyclopaedia of Religion and Ethics* has a useful, though occasionally errant, introduction to the subject under the heading of 'Images and Idols'. Its discussion, especially under the sub-headings of 'Purely representative images' and 'Idols', makes an illuminating contribution to our understanding of the topic. It defines images as

figured representation of beings and objects for a utilitarian or sentimental purpose. This kind of representation implies not only that man reasons about his ocular impressions, but also that he claims the power of exteriorizing them accurately and even of reproducing them after they have disappeared from his vision.

Under 'Purely representative images' it lists:

drawn, carved, sculptured or painted images of a purely commemorative, instructive, or edifying nature. ... The image may be realistic, but interpreted in such a way that it becomes a pure symbol – e.g., among Christian images, the lamb and the dove. ... Every great historical religion except Judaism and Islam has attempted to express its legends and myths in images. These representations may have a commemorative or explanatory intention; but we must remember that certain religions use them especially for the purpose of education and edification. ... No religion can rival Christianity in the multiplicity of its images. ... The desire to be permanently in touch with venerated objects led man to set up his own image in places where everything evoked the memory of his Divine patrons. ... The two aims of having the gods near oneself and being near them were frequently combined by placing religious images on objects of everyday use – jewels, ... weapons and tools, ... and coins ...[19]

'Idols' the encyclopaedia defines as 'a fetish representing the supposed form of the spirit dwelling inside it'.

There is an emphasis that

idolatry is neither a general nor a primitive fact ... idolatry is but a step in religious evolution and ... even represents a comparative advance. From the time of its first appearance onwards, man appeals to art ... to aid him in giving material shape to his religious ideal ... Whatever opinion one may have of the origins of religion, it must be admitted that at a certain period man began to experience the need for representing in concrete and personal form the mysterious forces which he conceived of as being, on the one hand, embodied in certain natural or artificial objects, and, on the other, situated at the very source of the phenomena of nature.[20]

The trouble about most approaches to subjects as delicate as this is that people tend to employ words in current use without due regard to their basic meanings. J. B. Pratt, for example, writes on the assumption that any religion which makes use of visual, material objects in its cultures is idolatry, or that the very use of such is idolatry. For example, he says, 'No one who has, with any degree of intelligent sympathy, watched *the practice of idolatry* (italics are mine) in its more earnest form, as for example in India, can have failed to recognize the real help which it seems to bring to many of those who make use of it.' He, however, quotes with approval three informants whose words are illuminating on the subject:

①One very unintelligent Hindu whom I met in India showed me his idols and told me they were not images of his gods but the very gods themselves.②Another, rather higher in intellectual scale, said to me, when I asked him about the image of Shiva which he was worshipping, 'The image is not Shiva; Shiva is in heaven. But I want to worship Shiva, so I make a picture or image as like Him in appearance as I can, and then I pray to Shiva in front of it because it helps me to pray.'③By a third Hindu – this one a learned Bengalee Brahmin who gave me a long dissertation on the religion of his country – the subjective aspect of the cult and its retention explicitly for the sake of its psychological effects, was clearly recognized and emphasized. 'The idol,' he said, 'is useful in aiding visualization and concentration. It is a sensuous symbol, just as the word G-O-D is. Both are symbols, one tangible and visible, the other audible; and both are helpful to our finite minds in standing for the Infinite. The man who worships before an idol in effect prays "O God, come and dwell in this image before me for the moment that I may worship thee here concretely!"' '21

Note, various interpretations of various believers

It is important to note that when Pratt is reporting about his second informant, he speaks of 'the image of Shiva which he was worshipping' and the part of the reply which says '... I pray to Shiva in front of it (the image)'. The same significant note is struck in the clause, 'The man who worships before an idol ...' The important difference here is whether the worshipper is actually *worshipping an idol* or is *worshipping before an idol*. And here is a world of difference.

A. C. Bouquet emphasizes this difference when he says:

Yet as often as not the personality is unified around a dominant interest which is purely local. The prophet is inclined to call such a restricted interest an 'idol', in the sense of being an inferior god or 'no-god'. But an 'idol', strictly speaking, is an *eidōlon* or image and symbol, and where the reality is hard to describe, such a symbol, whether mental, verbal, or physical, may be a justifiable aid to concentration, provided that the mind is not content to settle on it, but to see through it and beyond it, and to reckon it as at best inadequate.22

The major question remains to be answered, however. Is the word 'idolatry' appropriate in describing a whole religion – any religion? Is it appropriate with particular reference to religion in Africa?

From the etymology of the word, *eidōlon* does not mean originally what is false, although it has acquired this meaning with the progress of time. In consequence of the current derogatory and contemptuous nuance of the word, 'idol' should not be used for any emblem of religion, or any cult-object which is only a representation or symbol of the being to whom worship is offered. Such an object, strictly, is not an end in itself but a means to an end. As its function is symbolic, it has a meaning beyond itself.

In *Olódùmarè: God In Yoruba Belief,*[23] I have discussed the matter of symbolic representation at some length. The main purpose of such a symbol is to aid man's perception, concentration, and to be a constant reminder of the divine presence. This has been age-long in the history of religion.

[handwritten margin note: Yet, other interpretations]

Thus, a religion is not necessarily idolatry simply because it uses material representations of the cult-objects. And one is here in full sympathy with Marett in his outburst:

> Would that it were in my power to banish once for all from the pages of anthropology the pernicious fallacy that, in primitive, or any other, forms of religion, the use of material symbols is bound to imply a materialistic outlook.[24]

[handwritten margin note: A corruption]

And yet, there is a sense in which symbols of any kind or material representations do constitute a grave danger to religion – any religion. Man's mind in its weakness, especially where it is exploited by priestcraft, very easily ignores the delicate line of demarcation between the reality represented and what is primarily only a symbol.

> There has, of course, been a grave risk attending the use of images and symbols in worship. What is designed to be a means to en end could easily become an end in itself. We know too well how these emblems can become heavy weights tied to the wings of the soul, thus making earth-bound a thing meant for heaven. This is where idolatry comes in. ... For it is quite possible and does happen that men can become 'fools' who *actually* bow down to wood and stone. This is a sin which in its crude or refined form constantly besets religion at every step of its development. It is in the light of this that we should understand why the Old Testament prophets called idols 'vanity' or 'nonentity' and roundly condemned idolatry.[25]

Specifically with reference to African traditional religion, the word idolatry does not apply technically; as also the word 'idol' in its popular connotation does not apply unreservedly to a cult-object. Edward B. Tylor has a glimpse of the truth as he says:

> The idols are not, as Bosman thinks, deputies of the gods, but merely objects in which the god loves to place himself, and which at the same time display him in sensible presence to his adorers. The god is also by no means bound fast to his dwelling in the image, he goes out and in, or rather is present in it sometimes with more and sometimes with less intensity.[26]

This is put better, and its erroneous notions and exaggerations corrected, by P. A. Talbot when he says, with reference to the religion of Southern Nigeria:

> ... their rough idols are never believed actually to represent the bodies of the gods; they are even beyond the stage in which the divinities were thought to fly to their images, when their help was implored.[27]

The fact about the use of material emblems is that to Africans, the material has no meaning apart from the spiritual; it is the spiritual that informs the material and gives it whatever quality and meaning it has. The material therefore can only be, at best, technically, a symbol. It is the divine entity that is represented by the material object to whom worship is rendered The material symbol can rot away, become destroyed, be carried away, and be replaced, but not so the divine being. Symbols may change, Deity or his ministers remain.

To call African traditional religion 'idolatry' is to be grossly unfair to it and to do violence to its essence. Nevertheless, there is the constant tendency towards idolatry in it, especially in consequence of its inherent weakness as almost entirely a priestly affair.

(h) Fetishism. This is another word which has made a curious departure from its original meaning.

The *Encyclopaedia of Religion and Ethics* says:

> Central Africa is the promised land of fetishism; yet the negro, according to a statement made by Albert Reville, which seems to be well founded, distinguishes clearly between fetishes, which he believes to be inhabited by a spirit, and amulets, which he wears about his person but does not worship, even when they reproduce the form of a living being ... As a matter of fact, fetishism is a direct antecedent of idolatry, and is everywhere co-existent with it. The fetish and the idol are both conceived as the body of a spirit; they are used for the same purposes and employed under the same conditions ...[28]

Perhaps the author would not have been so confused if he were writing today: from the illustration that he quotes, he does not seem to know the difference between emblems or symbols and fetishes, as any cult-object which has no creaturely shape is to him automatically a fetish.

Edward B. Tylor traces the history of the word from the time when it was first used by the Portuguese with particular reference to West Africa:

> Centuries ago, the Portuguese in West Africa, noticing the veneration paid by the negroes to certain objects, such as trees, fish, plants, idols,

pebbles, claws of beasts, sticks and so forth, very fairly compared these objects to the amulets or talismans with which they themselves were familiar, and called them *feitico* or 'charm', a word derived from Latin *factitius*, in the sense of 'magically artful'. Modern French and English adopted this word from the Portuguese and spelt it *fétiche, fetish*, although curiously enough, both languages had already possessed the word for ages in a different sense, Old French *faitis*, 'well made, beautiful', which Old English adopted as *fetys*, 'well made, neat'.

The word *Fetichisme* was introduced as a general descriptive term for 'the African worship of material and terrestrial objects'; and it passed through Comte's use of it 'to denote a general theory of primitive religion, in which external objects are regarded as animated by a life analogous to man's'.[29]

Tylor dropped 'fetishism' in favour of his own 'animism' and would confine the word

to that subordinate department which it properly belongs to, namely, the doctrine of spirits embodied in, or attached to, or conveying influence through, certain material objects. Fetishism will be taken as including the worship of 'stocks and stones' and thence it passes by an imperceptible graduation into idolatry.

At this time of the day in the progress and development of researches in the study of religion, there should be no need to engage in what may amount to flogging a dead horse by commenting on certain elements in the above quotation. But there is an inveterate streak in most investigators which produces the tendency to persist in the use of certain terms, however outmoded they may have become, perhaps without bothering themselves about their appropriateness or otherwise. The quotation immediately above, and what follows, show a confusion in thinking which, as we have observed earlier, results from inadequate data, ignorance, or prejudice. In the quotation, we have, for example, such phrases as 'the veneration paid by the negroes to certain objects, such as trees ... pebbles, claws of beasts, sticks and so forth'; that the Portuguese *'fairly* compared these objects to their own amulets or talismans'; 'the African worship and terrestrial objects', and 'worship of "stocks and stones"'. All these show inadequate grasp of the fundamentals of African worship, and betray the error of taking appearance for reality, the shadow for the substance. It is, in fact, the reason why in certain minds the frontier between what is sweepingly called 'idolatry' and what is generally designated 'fetishism' is ill-defined, if it is defined at all. There continues to be a succession of heirs to the notion that

Africa is the land 'governed by insensible fetish'. E. Geoffrey Parrinder makes a collection of authors who are addicted to the word
'fetishism' or 'fetish' and their expressions.[30] Old Bosman said 'They
cry out, Let us make Fetiche; by which they express as much as,
let us perform our religious worship.' But one is surprised to find Sir
James Frazer in our century speaking of 'the fetish king of West
Africa', when he means a religious head as distinct from a civil
ruler. And Mary Kingsley ... went on to say, 'When I say Fetish
or Juju, I mean the religion of the natives of West Africa' ... Other
writers are even more careless. Nassau, a missionary writer on
Central Africa, used the word fetish so widely that he even wrote of
a 'fetish prayer'. Monteiro, writing on the Congo, spoke of 'undergoing fetish' as taking an oath. And across the other side of the
continent Roscoe uses fetish of the Baganda emblems of gods, of
medicinal preparations, and of 'a fetish of herbs' used by an army
on the warpath.

In *Ashanti*, R. S. Rattray has attacked the use of the words 'fetish'
and 'fetishism' as they are commonly used to embrace all that is
religion in Africa.[31] In *Religion and Art in Ashanti*, he sets out the
difference between religion and fetish according to African (in particular Ashanti) belief. He states that most of what is usually listed
under fetishes or fetishism will be emphatically repudiated as coming under the category of *suman* (magic) by every African with
any knowledge of his own creed.

If any of these definitions (Tylor's) were to be accepted for Ashanti, then
we should be compelled to accept that unsatisfactory appellation 'fetishism'
to describe also the higher Ashanti religious beliefs ... The cult of the
Supreme Being, when His great spirit manifests itself through some natural
object, would become 'fetishism'; the lesser gods (*abosom*) would be forced
into the distinct category of *suman*; the hallowed bones of the dead kings
and all the fine traits in the worship of ancestors would become 'fetishes'
and 'fetish worship'. Clearly, then, there is something wrong with these
definitions.

Rattray summarizes his statement of the difference between religion (including cult-objects) and 'fetish' as follows:

Fetishes may form part of an emblem of god, but fetish and god are in
themselves distinct, and are so regarded by the Ashanti; the main power, or
the most important spirit in a god comes directly or indirectly from Nyame,
the Supreme God, whereas the power or spirit in a fetish comes from plants
or trees, and sometimes directly or indirectly from fairies, forest monsters,
witches, or from some sort of unholy contact with the dead; a god is the

god of the many, the family, the clan, or the nation. A fetish is generally personal to its owner.[32]

It is important to remember what H. W. Fowler says of the word fetish or fetiche:

> Though it has the air of a mysterious barbarian word, it is in reality the same as *factitious*, and means (like an idol, the work of men's hands) a made thing.[33]

This is in line with its history as outlined by Tylor. Fetishes are 'made things', unlike the Divine Being in whom Africans believe and repose their confidence. Africans are not so naïve as not to know the difference between a thing that is made and the spiritual reality who is the determiner of destiny.

What P. A. Talbot says about Southern Nigeria will apply throughout Africa:

> True fetishism, in which the object of worship is not symbolic but is worshipped for itself and not as connected with, or representing, a deity or spirit, is absent from this country.[34]

'Fetishism' as a general description for religion in Africa results from a misuse or abuse of the word and it is most inappropriate.

(i) *Animism*: Edward B. Tylor popularized this term. In his *Primitive Culture* Vols. I and II, he takes animism as given and defines it as 'the doctrine of souls and other spiritual beings in general'; he sees it as 'this great element of the Philosophy of Religion'; it is 'this essential source ... a minimum definition of Religion, the belief in Spiritual Beings', the key to 'the deep-lying doctrine of Spiritual Beings, which embodies the very essence of Spiritualistic as opposed to Materialistic Philosophy' ... the groundwork of the Philosophy of Religion, from that of savages to that of civilized men'.[35]

In Tylor's words:

> The theory of Animism divides into two great dogmas, forming part of one consistent doctrine; first, concerning souls of individual creatures, capable of continued existence after the death or destruction of the body; second, concerning other spirits, upward to the rank of powerful deities ... Thus Animism, in its full development, includes the belief in souls and in a future state, in controlling deities and subordinate spirits, these doctrines practically resulting in some kind of active worship.[36]

Tylor substantiates and illustrates his theory of 'animism' according to his own definition copiously. He looks at the fact of dreams and visions: he asserts that it was in consequence of dreams by which man thought that, while lying down asleep, his physical being was engaged elsewhere in normal or abnormal activities that he first conceived the idea of a separate spirit or soul, or double. It is in consequence of the same medium that he came to the belief that other souls visited his own soul and became confirmed in the belief of other human souls as separate and separable entities.

It is especially when the body is asleep, that the soul goes out and wanders ... Another part has a place here, the view that human souls come from without to visit the sleeper, who sees them as dreams ... That the apparitional human soul bears the likeness of its fleshy body, is the principle implicitly accepted by all who believe it really and objectively present in dream or vision. My own view is that nothing but dreams and visions could ever put into men's minds such an idea as that of souls being ethereal images of bodies.[37]

He looks at the experience of death: there is something which makes a man a living being; when that something is no longer present in man, the physical frame may remain all complete, but the something that is missing makes all the difference between the living and the dead. What is this something? What becomes of it after *leaving* the body?

The apparition of the disembodied soul has in all ages been thought to bear especial relation to its departure from its body at death ... it is naturally admitted that a man's phantom or 'double' may be seen without portending anything in particular ...

Thus it came to be that

the original conception of the human soul seems to have been that of ethereality, or vaporous materiality ... Departing the body at the time of death, the soul or spirit is considered set free to linger near the tomb, to wander on earth or flit in the air, to travel to the proper region of spirits – the world beyond the grave.[38]

So, funeral rites take their significance and meaning; so also does the whole complement of beliefs about haunting, cults of the dead, ancestral cults, life after death, transmigration, etc.

Then he gives attention to the conception of other souls; that is, souls of animals and of those things which, in general, are called inanimate objects.

The sense of an absolute psychical distinction between man and beast, so prevalent in the civilized world, is hardly to be found among lower races. Men to whom the cries of beasts and birds seem like human language, and their actions guided as it were by human thought, logically enough allow the existence of souls to beasts, birds and reptiles, as to men. ... Plants, partaking with animals the phenomena of life and death, health and sickness, not unnaturally have some kind of soul ascribed to them.[39]

Tylor maintains that it is the doctrine of souls that gave birth to the wider doctrine of spirits and thus transformed itself to a complete philosophy of natural religion. He outlines the stages of the development until he comes to the point at which spirits began to be 'regarded as personal causes of phenomena of the world' for good or for evil. A world of spirits came into being – spirits of every area, aspect, or activity of life. 'To the minds of the lower races it seems that all nature is possessed, pervaded, crowded, with spiritual beings.' These are spiritual beings directly affecting the life and fortune of man, and spirits specially concerned in carrying on the operations of nature. The 'spirits considered directly to affect the life and fortune of Man lie closest to the centre of the animistic scheme' – such spirits include demons, guardian or familiar spirits and nature-spirits.[40]

From these he proceeds to the higher deities of polytheism and spells out the process of either their coming into being or how man came to recognize their existence in their various categories and with their variety of functions:

... as we consider the nature of the great gods of the nations, in whom the vastest functions of the universe are vested, it will still be apparent that these mighty deities are modelled on human souls ... The higher deities of polytheism have their places in the general animistic system of mankind. Among nation after nation it is still clear how, man being the type of deity, human society and government became the model on which divine society and government were shaped. Rudimentary forms of Dualism, the antagonism of a Good and Evil Deity, are well known among the lower races of mankind ... Their crude though earnest speculation has already tried to solve the great mystery which still resists the efforts of moralists and theologians ... Savage belief displays to us the primitive conceptions which, when developed in systematic form and attached to ethical meaning, take place in religious systems of which the Zoroastrian is the type.[41]

From this, Tylor passes on to 'the last object' of his survey:

... those theological beliefs of the lower tribes of mankind which point more or less distinctly towards a doctrine of Monotheism ... For this purpose it is desirable to distinguish the prevalent doctrines of the uncultured world from absolute monotheism. High above the doctrine of souls, of divine *manes*, of local nature-spirits, of the great deities of class and element, there are to be discerned in barbaric theology shadowings, quaint or majestic, of the conception of a Supreme Deity, henceforth to be traced onward in expanding power and brightening glory among the history of religion ... More frequently, it is the nature-worshipper's principle which has prevailed, giving to one of the great nature-deities the precedence of the rest. Here by no recondite speculation, but by plain teaching of nature, the choice has for the most part lain between two mighty visible divinities, the all-animating Sun and the all-encompassing Heaven ... To realize this widest idea, two especial ways are open. The first is to fuse the attributes of the great polytheistic powers into more or less of common personality, thus conceiving that, after all, it is the same Highest Being who holds up the heavens, shines in the sun, smites his foes in the thunder, stands first in the human pedigree as the divine ancestor. The second way is to remove the limit of theological speculation into the region of the indefinite and the inane. An unshaped divine entity looming vast, shadowy, and calm beyond and over the material world, too benevolent or too exalted to need human worship, too huge, too remote, too indifferent, too supine, too merely existent, to concern himself with the petty race of men – this is a mystic form of formlessness in which religion has not seldom pictured the Supreme. Thus, then, it appears that the theology of the lower races already reaches its climax in conceptions of a highest of the gods, and that these conceptions in the savage and barbaric world are no copies stamped from one common type, but outlines widely varying among mankind.[42]

Thus far, we have endeavoured to put together the salient points of Tylor's long and amply illustrated treatise. It is hardly fair to say that reading this condensation alone would tell us everything about how his mind worked with particular reference to the subject or lead us to a full appreciation of his scholarly labour to the end that he might present an objective and exhaustive study. Enough has been indicated, however, for the purpose of our discussion of 'animism with particular reference to African traditional religion.

It should be observed also, that we are avoiding deliberately the fruitless labour of flogging a dead horse with regard to the criticisms that have already been made again and again about Tylor's work on 'animism'. We would only observe that with reference to Africa, he is substantially correct in what he says about dreams and visions, the experience of death, the doctrines of other souls, spirits, higher deities, and monotheism. Very often, he exaggerates wittingly or unwittingly, and the inherited language he uses can be rather gross and obnoxious. Furthermore, the graph which he draws of the process of the spiritual and conceptual development of man is too straight and too smooth – in fact, this is the point at which he becomes too academic and disregards the fact of the complex nature of human experience as something which defies chronological tabulation. ˙

We shall call attention especially to the following points:

(i) Tylor maintains that 'animism' is an attendant factor in every religion, in every culture, at any level of development. He does not confine 'animism' to any particular race or culture. He speaks of 'the animism of savages' and 'the animism of civilized men' and asserts that it is a pattern of doctrine and belief which began from rudimentary, inchoate stages and maintains itself through processes of development into a systematic and progressively narrow and high-level definition.

> Animism characterizes tribes very low in the scale of humanity, and thence ascends, deeply modified in its transmission, but from first to last preserving an unbroken continuity, into the midst of high modern culture ... Animism is, in fact, the groundwork of the Philosophy of Religion, from that of savages up to that of civilized men.[43]

(ii) It is not clear, from Tylor's work, whether he is saying that man 'created' the gods or that Deity existed in an absolute sense before man came to discover the fact through animistic processes. He maintains that the factor of anthropomorphism is predominant in 'animism'. Anthropomorphism is a factor which is, in fact, inevitable if man must think at all – the difference between one culture and another in this regard is not one of the presence or absence of the factor; it is that of the degree or level of anthropomorphism.

At this point, we must observe that most of those who employ the word 'animism' and invoke Tylor as their patron oracle appear to have read perfunctorily the first volume of *Primitive Culture* without seeing the inside of the second volume or, worse still, to have derived their knowledge of Tylor's work from secondary sources. To read Tylor thoroughly and with understanding is to see that he admirably and painstakingly proves that although 'animism' is at a lower level in certain cultures, in that it encompasses the widest area of almost everything animate and inanimate, it is not by any means limited in any culture to the general, contemptible, religious feature-lessness and indefiniteness which is the popularly accepted meaning of the term: in every culture it reaches the conception of the gods and, almost invariably the concept of the Supreme God (although Tylor uses the typical Western terminology of 'a Supreme God'.

(iii) With particular reference to Africa, 'animism' is applicable in the sense that it is a doctrine of Spirit and spirits.

In Africa, there is no doubt that people, as elsewhere, have passed or are passing through the stage of what has been called 'animatism' (depending on the age, physical or mental, of the people concerned); that is, the process of thinking by which inanimate objects are thought to possess the active attributes of life. I remember going with my father, when I was a child, to collect certain herbs. When he was entering a thick bush, he asked me to wait for him at a spot. He disappeared into the bush and, immediately, I became afraid because everything around seemed to be instinct with life and menacing. Particularly, a small anthill, about eighteen inches high, shaped to my imaginative sense roughly like a man (with a hat complete) arrested my attention. I was the more afraid and tried to turn away my eyes; but I *had* to keep looking again and again at it; and each time I looked again, it appeared to have moved nearer to me. Fortunately my father returned to me before I was worked up to the point of screaming. This is a stage through which man everywhere passes in varying degrees and it is not to be considered the absolute monopoly of any particular race; although there are races which are generally closer to it than others.

It is a fact that the African world swarms with spirits which, according to African beliefs, are distinct from material objects, although they reside in material objects or express themselves through material objects. Sacred animals, sacred trees, sacred stones, sacred rivers and sacred spots, abound in Africa. We must, however, be careful at this point. Certain sacred objects are only symbols or emblems and no more than that. Tylor's tendency is to make 'animism' embrace 'animism' (properly defined), fetishism, and magic. There is no doubt but that the element of the prevailing presence and ubiquitousness of spirits is far more pronounced in African beliefs than in those of the regions of the intellectualist, European world. But here again, as compared with the rest of the world, it is a matter of degree. The Western person is given more and more today to spiritualism or occultism. Why is that so? Should we not all admit that man's restless spirit is for ever refusing to be smothered under the weight of intellectualism; that as the needle inevitably turns towards the north, so is man's spirit ever seeking to reach the unseen, the unknown, and establish communion for its own peace?

P. A. Talbot observes with reference to the religion of Southern Nigeria: 'Pure animism can hardly be said to exist, or it is so combined with anthropomorphism that it is difficult to separate the two elements.'[44] Talbot seems to be referring here to the fact that religion has acquired a concrete definition with a definite structure. This he makes clear in his total comments on the religion of the people. And this is the point at which most Western writers on African traditional religion allow themselves to be led astray. They are so concerned with trying to prove that Africa does not know *the* Supreme God as known to their own cultural conception that they apply 'animism' to Africa in the sense of the blindness of worship which addresses itself to wood and stone.

There is a sense in which 'animism' forms a vital element in the make-up of religion in Africa; if 'animism' is properly defined as a recognition of the existence of Spirit or spirits as separate from the material. It is, in fact, a positive denial of the notion that there are people anywhere in the world whose worship is offered to material objects or natural phenomena. We accept 'animism' as applicable to African traditional religion if it is understood in the sense of the recognition of the fact that man's spirit is in communication and communion with the Divine Spirit. In this sense, it refers all worship ultimately to the Divine Spirit, often through ministering spirits; it recognizes that material cult-objects (including buildings) can be dedicated to the Divine Spirit or to spirits and therefore become meet for worship – a place where man beholds the 'mercy-seat' or an object through which the world invisible is viewed, the world intangible touched, the world unknowable known, and the world inapprehensible clutched; it emphasizes the fact that the Divine Spirit and spirits do not depend for their being on the material objects used as cult-objects – the spirits are never bound to the material objects; the destruction of such objects does not affect the being of the Spirit – the Spirit may in fact choose, where man's spirit is not in the right, to declare, 'Behold, your house is forsaken' and act on the declaration.

Thus, 'animism' properly defined cannot be predicated as a monopoly of Africa or of any other race, however 'low in the scale of humanity' (whatever Tylor might mean by that). The being of Christianity as of any religion is grounded on the fact that 'God is Spirit'. 'Animism' can, therefore, be predicated as part-definition of every religion. But it is inappropriate as *the* name for African traditional religion: the derogatory and abusive nomenclature of Africans as 'animists' should cease.

2. *What term to use*

This is the real question. Anyone who has really studied the situation carefully must sympathize with those who have found it rather difficult to find a name that is precisely descriptive of the real nature of the religion, and understand why they either take refuge in definitive terms which are unsuitable, or glibly tack on to it names the only excuse for which is that they have the support of some pet theory or long usage.

P. A. Talbot is faced with this problem with reference to the religion of Southern Nigeria but, wisely, he does not force a solution. Rather, he leaves it at stating the fact as he sees it and no more:

> On the whole, the religion strongly resembles that of the ancient Egyptians, who combined a belief in the existence of an omnipotent and omniscient Supreme God ... with that in multitudes of subordinate deities ...[45]

E. Geoffrey Parrinder also recognizes the problem in his study of religion in Ibadan and is wise enough to leave it at:

> It would be useful to devise a term which would denote religions that have a supreme God and also worship other gods.[46]

S. F. Nadel has been far-reaching and discerning in his approach to the problem. Writing with particular reference to the Nupe, he says:

> Here we might note that the Nupe have no special, collective name for their religion. They have names only for particular conceptions, single practices, local ceremonials. As for the total creed, the Nupe can describe it only circuitously and enumeratively, as being concerned with the God Soko, and not with deities named differently; with such-and-such rituals or 'medicines' and not with others; with spirits, but no anthropomorphous ones. and so forth.

Nadel emphasizes the fact that the Nupe refer everything to God as the one ultimate.[47]

I do not know of any place in Africa where the ultimacy is not accorded to God. That is why, because this is very true of the Yoruba, I conclude that the religion can only be adequately described as monotheistic. I modify this 'monotheism' by the adjective 'diffused', because here we have a monotheism in which there exist other powers which derive from Deity such being and authority that they can be treated, for practical purposes, almost as ends in themselves.[48]

The descriptive phrase 'implicit monotheism' will serve as well as 'diffused monotheism'.

We may compare the system among the Yoruba where we have divinities who appear to be completely autonomous, each with his or her own priesthood and set of rituals. A priest will bear, for example, the title of Osogun (the priest of Ogun) or Olobatala (the priest of Obatala). But the unity of the whole is manifested phenomenologically in that the head of the whole community is the Pontifex Maximus of all the cults together . . Hence the saying, 'Every festival is the king's festival'. And, of course, none of the cults have any meaning apart from Olódùmarè, the Supreme God.[49]

We must heed the observation that, all down the ages, peoples have worshipped without being preoccupied with finding names for their religions. It is the outsider, the observer, the investigator, the curious, the detractor or the busybody, who first supplied labels.[50] The exception is Islam, which came into being with its name. We have undertaken the exercise of supplying an essential name to African traditional religion purely because of the need of a handle for the purpose of study, and this is not an easy task, as the local names for Deity differ from place to place and there is no single common name for Deity known to, and accepted by, all Africans. Thus, for a precise definitive name, apart from 'diffused monotheism', we shall have to employ the local name used for God in each area. The defect in this is that we shall be landed with names rather than a name. Thus we shall have a bewildering number of unwarranted -isms: Olodumareism (for the Yoruba), Chukwuism (for the Igbo of Nigeria), Onyameism (for the Akan), Ngewoism (for the Mende of Sierra Leone) or Imanaism (for the Ruanda-Urundi) as the case may be, if we are anglicizing the term. If we are using the vernacular, we shall have to find, in each case, the composite word which means 'the worship of Deity', using the local name for Deity. For example, in case of the Yoruba, as one of the reviewers of *Olódùmarè* suggested, this would be *Is'Olódùmarè* (i.e. *Isin Olódùmarè*, the service or worship of Olódùmarè).

Thus the German word *Gottesdienst*, which means, literally, 'service or worship of God', and by connotation embraces the inward and outward aspects of religion, will be appropriate as a general name for the religion, as it points to its very essence.

V

The Structure of African Traditional Religion

We shall begin our analysis of the structure of African traditional religion by examining what P. A. Talbot says on this topic with reference to the religion of Southern Nigeria, E. Geoffrey Parrinder's classifications of West African Religion, and R. S. Rattray's analysis of the religion of the Ashanti.

P. A. Talbot says:

> The religion of the inhabitants of Southern Provinces of Nigeria would appear to be compounded of four main elements, viz. polytheism, anthropomorphism, animism, and ancestor worship.[1]

Talbot is very guarded in his statement and is wise enough to imply that the reality might be other than as things appeared to him. Nevertheless, his analysis will bear examination. 'Polytheism' can be accepted with reservation as an element in the structure of the religion, if we are thinking only of the pantheons of the divinities. For it is only in this connection that we can predicate pluralism at all of the religion.[2] Thus Talbot is right in saying that 'polytheism' is a compound part of the whole structure.

'Anthropomorphism' should not be reckoned as a separate component element in the structure. Anthropomorphism is only a way of thinking of, of conceptualizing, the Divine Power and powers. There is, therefore, nothing really 'cultic' about it. It is a prevailing atmosphere of religion at every level, in every place.[3]

'Animism'[4] is acceptable only in the strict sense that it signifies the recognition and acceptance of the existence of spirits, often in an uncharacterized sense, with cults existing in consequence of the recognition and acceptance.

Ancestor worship (in essence) is definitely a component element in the structure, although we have to examine whether the term 'ancestor worship' is appropriate or not.[5]

E. Geoffrey Parrinder proposes a *fourfold classification*, saying:

It has been discovered that there exist, in many West African languages, convenient categories for the consideration of the types of religious belief.

Briefly, we may distinguish: (a) a supreme God or creator, sometimes above other gods, sometimes first among equals – Onyame in Twi-Ashanti, Mawu in Ewe-Fon, Olorun in Yoruba, Chuku in Ibo; (b) the chief divinities, generally non-human spirits, often associated with natural forces ...; (c) the cult of the human but divinized ancestors of the clan ...; (d) the charms and amulets, which some have called 'fetishes' or 'juju'.

Parrinder admits by implication that he is inspired to make these classifications by certain statements, such as that of Edwin W. Smith, who

used to say that a pyramid or triangle was an apt illustration of the order of the spiritual forces. At the apex was the supreme God, on one side of the triangle were the nature gods, and on the other side the ancestors, while at the base were the lower magical powers.[6]

The first thing that strikes us in Parrinder's classifications is that he speaks of 'a supreme God',[7] and describes the 'supreme God' as 'sometimes above other gods, sometimes first among equals ...' It is correct to list belief in the supreme God as a vital element in the structure of the religion as he has done. If, however, he is adhering to Edwin Smith's suggestion of a pyramidal or triangular analogy, or if he is using his own experience as one who has lived in West Africa and studied the religion at first hand, then he cannot at the same time place Deity on the apex and place him also within the rank and file of 'the nature gods' whose place is on the side of the triangle, however close to the apex may be the place he is assigning to him. Moreover, of all the names of God on his list, it is only in the case of Mawu that there can be a question at all about absolute uniqueness and supremacy. And that is because Mawu as the generic name for divine Spirit in general is used without qualification, more often than not, for the supreme Deity. Thus, Mawu who is the Source-Being is often confused with Mawu the offspring-beings. There is also the significant fact of Nana Buluku[8] which must not be overlooked in this context – her supremacy and ultimacy, according to Dahomean belief, is beyond question. Parrinder's classification (b) is in order as also his (d). With regard to his (c), there is another confusion, perhaps with the use of word : it is not every ancestor that is 'divinized'; while there are the few who have become deified, there are the countless ones who retain their status of ancestors in the after-life.

With particular reference to Ashanti, R. S. Rattray speaks simply of 'the African's own distinct classification and divisions of *Nyame*, the supreme God; *abosom*, the gods; *samanfo*, ancestral spirits; and *suman ...*', *inter alia* in his condemnation of the common tendency of bringing everything that is religion in Africa under the term 'fetishism'.[9]

Taking Africa as a whole, there are in reality five component elements that go into the making of African traditional religion. These are belief in God, belief in the divinities, belief in spirits, belief in the ancestors, and the practice of magic and medicine, each with its own consequent, attendant cult.

With regard to these classifications, we agree with Geoffrey Parrinder that 'distinctions should not be made too rigidly', especially where such distinctions may suggest that we are dealing with elements which are unrelated, rather than with those which together form the fabric of one religion. E. E. Evans-Pritchard, having examined the matter of component elements in religion, says:

> All this amounts to saying that we have to account for religious facts in terms of the totality of the culture and society in which they are found, to try to understand them in terms of what the *Gestalt* psychologists called *Kulturganze*, ... They must be seen as a relation of parts to one another within a coherent system, each part making sense only in relation to the others ...[10]

We shall modify this by adding that every other element in our analysis is contingent on the first, while the first exists in its own absolute right.

It must be observed, at the same time, that in Africa, situations are not invariably identical with regard to these component elements. This is because of the factors that we have already enumerated.[11] Certain elements may be more pronounced in certain areas than in others; this is noticeable especially in the case of the divinities: this element obtains very conspicuously over certain wide areas, while in others it obtains rather tenuously, and still in others, *practically* not at all.

1. Belief in God

In discussing revelation, we have remarked that there is no place, age, or generation, which did not receive at some point in its history some form of revelation, and that to deny this fact is either to be deliberately blind to facts or to betray a gross ignorance of facts. With regard to religion in Africa, we have now to examine precisely the core of revelation, and this in connection with the African concept of God.

Let us begin by looking at a few sample observations from previous writers on the subject.

In 1885, a book written by Père Noel Baudin, a Roman Catholic missionary, was published under the title of *Fetishism and Fetish Worshippers*. The salient points of Baudin's observations about African belief in God may be quoted as follows:

> In these religious systems, the idea of a God is fundamental; they believe in the existence of a supreme, primordial being, the lord of the universe, which is his work ... and notwithstanding the abundant testimony of the existence of God, it is practically only a vast pantheism – a participation of all elements of the divine nature which is as it were diffused throughout them all ... Although deeply imbued with polytheism, the blacks have not lost the idea of the true God: yet their idea of him is very confused and obscure ... God alone escapes both androgynism and conjugal association; nor have the blacks any statue or symbol to represent Him. He is considered the supreme primordial being, the author and the father of the gods and genii ... However, notwithstanding all these notions, the idea they have of God is most unworthy of His Divine Majesty. They represent that God, after having commenced the organization of the world, charged Obatala[12] with the completion and government of it, retired and entered into an eternal rest, occupying Himself only with His own happiness: too great to interest Himself in the affairs of this world. He remains like a negro king, in a sleep of idleness ...[13]

In *Africa and Christianity* Diedrich Westermann observes:

> In the centre of African myth stands a creative principle, which in most cases is identical with the high-god ... The high-god is, as a rule, not the object of a religious cult and is of small or almost no significance in practical religion. People acknowledge him, but neither fear nor love nor serve him, the feeling towards him being, at the highest, that of a dim awe or reverence. He is the God of the thoughtful, not of the crowd, of the people whose mature observation, personal experience, and primitive philosophy have led them to postulate a central and ultimate power who is the originator of everything existing and in whose hands the universe is safe: it is in the

sayings of these people that sometimes the figure of God assumes features of a truly personal and purely divine Supreme Being ... More often, however, God is the great unknown power which cannot be comprehended by man. Anything extraordinary or incomprehensible may be given the name of God ... While fully admitting that, as a rule, God does not live in practical religion and that the ideas concerning him are often nebulous, it cannot be overlooked that he is a reality to the African, who will admit that what he knows about God is the purest expression of his religious thinking and, in individual cases, also of his religious experience ... The African's God is a *deus incertus* and a *deus remotus*: there is always an atmosphere of indefiniteness about him ... The Alpha and Omega of a pagan's religion is 'My will be done'.[14]

In *Ashanti*, R. S. Rattray makes this statement:

I had some years ago taken a firm stand against a school of thought ... which denied that the conception of a Supreme Being in the West African mind, and His place in their religion, were due to any cause deeper or more remote than the influence of Christian missionary teachings ... Further research, embodying a much fuller investigation into Ashanti religious beliefs than was before possible, has only served to strengthen the opinion which I formerly expressed ... I am convinced that the conception, in the Ashanti mind, of the Supreme Being has nothing whatever to do with missionary influence ... contact with Christians or even, I believe, with Mohammedans. Surely, those who find it incongruous that the West African 'Negro', who seems so backward in most things, should have so far progressed in religious development, forget that the magnificent conception of a one Supreme Deity was not the prerogative of minds which we commonly consider the greatest of old ... but was a conception of primitive people who lived after the pyramids were built but before the advent of Greece and Rome – the Bedouins of the desert ... In a sense, therefore, it is true that this great Supreme Being, the conception of whom has been innate in the minds of the Ashanti, is the Jehovah of the Israelites. It was He who of old left His own dwelling above the vaulted sky, and entered the tent of dyed skins where was His earthly abode and his shrine, when He came down to protect the Children of Israel in their march to the Promised Land.[15]

Our first two authors are typical of the presumptuous notion that in the Western world, and with the great *monotheistic* religions, the concept of God is clear. This notion is based upon the fact that there are written, systematic statements, backed by scriptures, on the subject; and it is assumed that the presence or the possession of these traditional resources is automatically tantamount to 'clear' knowledge of God. Thus, written statements are taken for granted in forgetfulness of the fact that systematic statements or dogmas have come into being as a result of spiritual and intellectual pilgrimages, that there have been stages in their development, and that, even now, with the shifting scenes in regard to the knowledge of the universe, we are continually finding that established forms of beliefs are undergoing changes either radically or in their formulations.

If we take, for example, the spiritual journey of the Hebrew minds, we shall see the stages which were covered from a henotheism which was deeply tinged with ethnocentricity to the ethical monotheism of Deutero-Isaiah. We also see clearly in that case that the prophetic insight regarding the nature of God has always been far in advance of the general concept held by the generality of the people. As for the matter of *clear* knowledge of God, the Bible is naturally full of warnings, and the experiences of the saints have confirmed the fact, that man cannot 'find out the deep things of God' or 'find out the limit of the Almighty';[16] for he 'dwells in unapproachable light, whom no man has ever seen or can see'.[17]

Islamic tradition gives an implied warning in a story told about Muhammad's visit to Allah for the purpose of receiving the scheme for the daily obligatory prayers. When Muhammad arrived at the outer court of heaven, he saw a very voluminous garment the ends of which – height or breadth – he could not see, because of its infinite extensiveness: it was Allah's garment.[18] When he arrived at the Presence, he was confronted with a most bewildering sight: he saw Allah but could not describe the sight; Allah was not sitting down or standing, reclining or lying down; he was not sleeping or awake; the time of day (if it could be called time) was not morning or noon or evening, twilight or dusk. The angels, seeing his bewilderment, sang out: 'We eagerly expect to see what form of salutation Muhammad will use for the Lord ...' We are apt to think that in Islam, because of the Koran which contains prophetic statements about Allah, all Muslims have a *clear* concept of God because they are taught it by their religion. But in this story, we are warned about the mystery – the inevitable mystery – which surrounds the Holy One. And all down the corridor of Islamic history, Muslim theologians and philosophers have been trying to spell out the implications or the contents of this mystery.

The purport of all that we have said so far is that nowhere is the concept of God as clear as we are apt to think that it is in certain cases. We should know this in consequence of our experience or bafflement whenever we are confronted with certain questions about the nature of God – the doctrine of the Trinity in Christianity.

Concept of God not always clear

for example; or whenever we are faced with certain moral problems, like the problem of suffering, which challenge either our faith or our logic with regard to the reality of God, his relationship to the world, or the purpose of the whole created order. Luther's phrase *deus absconditus et revelatus* is always urging itself upon us – the *absconditus* (hidden) aspect more so than the *revelatus* (revealed).

Those who take one look at other people's religion and assert glibly that such people have no clear concept of God, or no concept of God at all, should first look within themselves and face honestly the question, 'How clear is the concept of God to me? How clear is it to my own people, the generality of them and not the few leading thinkers among them?' If a man is honest, and is not just someone who is merely setting one religion against another in competition, he will concede that there are mysteries here as elsewhere, and that a good deal of ignorance, muddled thinking, and general lack of precise knowledge about the subject is universal; that wherever there have been attempts to probe the unsearchable, each people has only succeeded to the extent which the native capabilities of their prophets, seers, and thinkers could carry them. What we regard loosely as the concept of God with reference to any particular people or race is thus only a *result* attained by the few privileged ones through their spiritual discernment and mental or intellectual efforts, and communicated to the generality of the people. 'The faith once delivered to the saints' is a phrase the individual elements of which are very vital to the understanding of the whole. But what is most relevant to the point that we are making here is the phrase 'to the saints' which signifies a particular category within the community which is capable of receiving or appropriating divine communication, through whom it reaches the generality, and whose 'faith' works as leaven on 'the whole lump'.

In the light of this, let us look again at the various conclusions which our authors have placed before us.

Baudin is right when he says: 'In these religious systems, the idea of a God is fundamental'; but he goes astray when he says that '... notwithstanding the abundant testimony of the existence of God, it is practically only a vast pantheism – a participation of all elements of the divine nature which is as it were diffused throughout them all'. What he has misinterpreted is the fact that to Africans, the material has meaning and purpose only through the spiritual, and that the entire control of the material world is the ultimate

[margin note:] Is it clear to me? Is it clear enough to be considered clear!

prerogative of Deity who at the same time manifests himself through his own works. There is no pantheism in the classical or philosophical sense in Africa.

When he said that '... the blacks have not lost the idea of the true God: yet their idea of Him is very confused and obscure', Baudin was, in the first place, giving the people he described as 'blacks' as much credit as could, in fact, be given to the generality of peoples throughout the world. But he was, at the same time, making what is a universal phenomenon a monopoly of Africans. The only difference between the Western world and Africa is that in one case there is a long tradition of systematic[19] thinking the results of which have been committed to writing, and in the other case a long tradition of systematic thinking which in certain areas remains in the oral tradition of the race and which, in other areas, has unfortunately become confused by historical circumstances.

Further, Baudin says:

> The idea they have of God is most unworthy of His Divine Majesty. They represent that God, after having commenced the organization of the world, charged Ọbatala with the completion and government of it, retired and entered into an eternal rest, occupying Himself only with His own happiness; too great to interest Himself in the affairs of His world, He remains like a negro king, in a sleep of idleness.

About this statement we have two points in criticism. (*a*) It is certain that Baudin has given rein to his imagination as conditioned by his preconceived notions in interpreting the minds of the Africans on this subject. He was here attributing to Africans (the Yoruba in particular in this case) something that is very far from their thought about Deity. (*b*) There is a definite reading in of the Western deistic idea into African belief – here we have the usual preconceived idea of 'a withdrawn God', or *deus otiosus*, in a different dress.[20]

Diedrich Westermann says:

> The high-god is, as a rule, not the object of a religious cult and is of small or almost no significance in practical religion. People acknowledge him, but neither fear nor love nor serve him, the feeling towards him being, at the highest, that of a dim awe or reverence.

Westermann did his writing at a time when he probably had little access to the proper sources of African beliefs and practices, or when he had little more than a chance opportunity of a fleeting glimpse of a vast continent. Those who have looked more carefully into African traditional religion will easily see this as a sweeping statement which cannot now be taken seriously.[21]

Further, he says:

> He is the God of the thoughtful, not of the crowd, of the people whose mature consideration, personal experience, and primitive philosophy have led them to postulate a central and ultimate power who is the originator of all things and in whose hands the universe is safe: it is in the sayings of these people that sometimes the figure of God assumes features of a truly personal and purely divine Supreme Being ...

In saying this and making it apply only to Africa with a depreciating intent, he has only conveniently ignored the whole history of religious doctrines which shows unmistakably that everywhere, and not only in Africa, with every religion, and not only with African traditional religion, the role of the specialist and the role of the community have always had their lines of demarcation, although the former does feed, guide and inform the latter. Because Westermann was writing about Africa, he overlooked the established, universal fact that we have already pointed out, viz. that in every locality the seer or the prophet is ahead of his community in idea and insight; that in every age and generation, the 'thoughtful' – prophets, theologians, philosophers, mystics – are in the minority: this is not an unshared peculiarity of Africa; everywhere it is this minority that conceives and brings forth ideas and concepts in systematic forms. The rest of the community usually accept and practise 'faith' with little questioning or search for explanations. And is it not a fact of general application that it is 'the sayings' (declaration or exhortation written or oral) of these leaders-in-insight that become articles of faith or creeds, which are thus the means of faith-in-expression?

This is a fact which is easily proved. If, for example, one stops a housewife or a businessman in a street in London, or Paris, or Berlin, or Geneva, or Ibadan, or Kampala, or Nairobi, or New York, and confronts such a person with a question about God, one will more likely than not receive back a blank look, a confused stuttering, or nervous rudeness as a reply – confronted with such a question, the generality of persons anywhere else on earth would fare no better than the generality of Africans.

The appearance of certain recent publications under the specious cover of what is called neo-theology constitutes a message about how much confusion there is in the minds of the generality of the peoples of the Western world with regard to the concept of God. *Honest to God*, by Dr John Robinson, with the debates which it stirred up, is a case in point. Whatever may be the merit or demerit of that book and others like it, they at least show unmistakably that with regard to this great subject, things are not what they seem on the surface. There should be no doubt now that the majority of the peoples of the Western world, in spite of the Bible in various versions and books which are available copiously, are devoid of any *clear*, unequivocal concept of God.

Westermann's statement that 'The African God is a *deus incertus* and a *deus remotus*: there is always an atmosphere of indefiniteness about him ...' betrays careless thinking, to say the least. First, there is no being like 'the African God' except in the imagination of those who use the term, be they Africans or Europeans. As we have already observed,[22] there is only one God; and while there may be various concepts of God according to each people's spiritual perception, it is wrong to limit God with an adjective formed from the name of any race. Secondly, the answer that we have already given above to the depreciating inclination that dictates certain conclusions about the African concept of God applies also to the *deus incertus* and the *deus remotus*. *Deus incertus* will apply in a sense everywhere in the world because of the inevitable fact of the *deus absconditus* (hidden God) which must be accepted as man's predicament in his approach to the mystery of the sacred and the transcendent; while *deus remotus* is another way of saying *deus otiosus* or 'a withdrawn God', which, as we have seen, is an intellectual or imaginative reading in and which, unqualified, is most inappropriate. And here again we have the deistic idea in the European mind palmed off on Africa.

The *incertus* or *remotus* notion is one that is ever-recurring in anthropological writings. S. F. Nadel, for example, says with reference to the Nupe belief that 'nothing very definite can be said or is known about God'.[23] If he had said this as a fact of general application, it would have been proper; limited to Africa, it is improper. And, as we have seen under 'revelation',[24] it is not true that in Africa, 'nothing very definite can be said or known about God'. Man knows as much as is given to him to know, and he expresses his belief accordingly.

One finds it difficult not to suspect intellectual dishonesty in those who write about religion in Africa in this vein, because there is evidence that there are those of them who must have been acquainted with the problem of epistemology with particular reference to religion.

'The Alpha and Omega of a pagan's belief is "My will be done".' This is just too much! We have already seen that the word 'pagan' should not be applied to Africans because of their belief: 'paganism' is unsuitable as a descriptive name for African traditional religion. With regard to 'My will be done', Westermann is confusing religion with magic,[25] whereas, although the two commingle, they should not be confused. It would seem that our author is here betraying the fact that he has taken mere appearance for reality and has not been well acquainted with what actually is the situation of things. In stating what the actual situation is we shall use what obtains among the Yoruba as an illustration:

Admittedly, the objective petitionary character of Yoruba prayers shows that the fulfilment of man's desires, rather than the will of Deity, is their esse – 'My will be done', rather than 'Thy will be done'; but that is because all the time the Yoruba are basing prayer on the fundamental notion that the will of Deity is supreme anyway and that His will is the ultimate answer to their prayers. We have noticed that their Àṣẹ – 'May it be sanctioned' or 'May it come to pass' – is an affirmation of their belief that nothing happens unless He permits it. This is a point at which we need carefully to distinguish between religion and magic and, therefore, between prayers and incantations. The Yoruba presents his petitions – the very word shows the attitude of mind which accompanies the prayer – not with the attitude of one who is bringing divine power under control for his own benefit, but as one who asks for a favour the granting of which he knows depends entirely upon the will and pleasure of his 'Determiner of destiny'.[26]

R. S. Rattray does not disguise the fact that he wrote with a mind which was reacting not only against the reading in of Western ideas and preconceived notions into the African scene, but also against erroneous, intentionally or unwittingly mischievous interpretations. Thus, he asserts categorically, not only have Africans a clear concept of God but also precisely 'this great Supreme Being, the conception of whom has been innate in the minds of the Ashanti, is the Jehovah of the Israelites'. I wish that we knew what exactly was in his mind when he made this statement, that is, apart from the fact that the Ashanti had a concept of the one Supreme Deity. It is one thing to say that the Ashanti concept of God is similar to, or identical with the Hebrew concept of God (which statement will need careful examination), and another thing to make the statement as quoted above, which suggests either that the Ashanti and the Israelites both derive their concepts of God from the same source, or that the

Ashanti received their concept of God from the Israelites – which would be in conflict with his own argument against those who deny 'that the conception of a Supreme God in the West African mind, and His place in their religion was due to any cause deeper or more remote than the influence of Christian missionary teachings'. Whatever may be in Rattray's mind, we know that in Africa there is abundant evidence of similarities to Semitic beliefs and practices, and that the factor of diffusionism must have been in operation at some remote past in the history of the continent. But it is a fact also that there is nothing to prevent the Ashanti or any other race in Africa from developing its own concept of God. This is underlined in Rattray's observation that the concept was innate in the mind of the Ashanti. Of course, the various components of the human race cannot be isolated in water-tight cultural compartments: we flow constantly into one another and naturally interact and cross-fertilize one another, spiritually, morally, culturally.

We can speak of a multi-sided concept of God in Africa. That is because in each locality, the concept of God usually takes its emphasis and complexion from the sociological structure and climate. It is therefore necessary to understand the variations in the sociological patterns in order to see clearly the reason for certain emphasis and tendencies. Let us take Nigeria as an example. Among the Yoruba and the Edo, where society is highly organized and carefully graded on a hierarchical basis, Deity is conceived as the supreme king of a theocratic world, with heavenly ministers appointed over each department of his realm. Among the Igbo, on the other hand, the divine ministerial system is not as elaborate because society is not as homogeneous as among the Yoruba. Among the Nupe, the divine ministers are rather few and, except in one or two cases, their nature is not clearly defined; while among the Birom and the Tiv, the ministerial system is almost not in evidence at all.

Also, whereas in most of Africa, God is conceived in masculine terms, there are localities where he is regarded as feminine. Among some Ewe-speaking peoples, Mawu, or in particular, Nana Buluku – 'the ancient Deity' – is thought and spoken of in feminine terms.

The local variations in the African concept of God should be appreciated and given due recognition. But there is no need to exaggerate the fact. For, in spite of the variations, an unmistakable basic pattern stands out, the features of which we shall consider under four main comprehensive attributes.

(a) *God is real to Africans*. Here we have to make up our minds ⓐ whether in African belief we are thinking of the God who *is*, or of a god of the scholar's imagination; the God as he is *actually* known, thought of and spoken of by Africans, or a god cut out specifically to satisfy a preconceived 'conception' of the African concept of God. These two approaches – one definitely correct and honest, and the other definitely false and misleading – will make a world of difference with regard to what we find out and record about African belief.

It will be appropriate to substantiate African belief with regard to the reality of God by looking first at some of the observations made by some previous investigators. In the extract made from Baudin's book, we have the following: 'In these religious systems, the idea of a God is fundamental ...'; there is 'the abundant testimony of the existence of God ...; ... the blacks have not lost the idea of the true God ...' In the same way, Diedrich Westermann says of the 'high god' that

> People acknowledge him ... He is God of the thoughtful ...; in the sayings of these people ... the figure of God assumes features of a truly personal and purely divine Supreme Being ...; it cannot be overlooked that he is a reality to the African, who will admit that what he knows about God is the purest expression of his religious experience ...

It is necessary to point out that these words have been taken out of their contexts, as that is the only way by which the actual evidence can be separated from the investigators' commentaries. This will be more to the point:

> ... There is a primary reference to spiritual persons and beings and commonly to God. The Konkomba word *Uumbwar* can only be translated 'God' ... he is everywhere and enters into all human beings through the *Ungwin* ... that part of a man that God gives.[27]

—names

In Africa, each people has a local name for God. Invariably there are other names besides the principal name. God's principal name may be the generic name for deity in general; in which case, there is a qualifying suffix or qualifying word to distinguish between the Supreme Deity and the divinities; and then the generic name plus the suffix or qualifying word belong uniquely to God. There are cases where, emphatically, the name for the Supreme Deity is uniquely his, and no part of it is shared by any other being. It should be pointed out that where the divinities share the basic generic name with Deity, it only serves to emphasize the fact that the divinities derive their being and nature from him.

The names by which Deity is called in Africa are descriptive of his character and emphatic of the fact that he is a reality and that he is not an abstract concept. The names denote that, as Westermann observes, 'he is a reality to the Africans' and convey 'the purest expression of' their 'religious thinking' and of their 'religious experience'.

The Yoruba name, Olódùmaré, is an illustration of a name which is unique to Deity; the Igbo name, Chukwu, illustrates the name of Deity which adds a suffix to the generic name for deity in general: it is made up of *Chi*, and *-ukwu*, *Chi* meaning Source-Being or spirit, and *-ukwu* meaning great, immense, or undimensional; while the Efik name Abasi Ibom (Abasi = God + Ibom = above) will illustrate the name of Deity which is made up of the generic name for deity in general plus a qualifying word to distinguish the Deity from the divinities.

It is true that several of the African names of Deity have not yet yielded themselves to satisfactory etymological analysis, principally in consequence of their antiquity and because ancient Africans have not left us written records of their theology. But such of them as have been analysed and the meanings of which are thus known, show that the names of God are not mere labels, but are descriptive of his nature, the experience of Africans about him, and their belief in him. The theophorous proper names that people bear all over Africa are a further evidence of how real God is to Africans: Oghenedjakpokohwo – 'God directs the person' (Urhobo), Ebere-Chukwu – 'God's mercy' (Igbo), Olútóóke – 'The Lord deserves to be glorified' (Yoruba), Gatkwoth – 'Son of God' (Nuer), Mawunyo – 'God is just' or 'God is kind' (Ewe) are a few such names which signify what God means to Africans in their various situations.

Beside the names, Africa is very rich in attributes of God which show unmistakably that to them Deity is the Living One who is the ever-present, ever-active, and ever-acting reality in the world.[28] The Nuer know God as 'Spirit of the sky' or 'Spirit who is in the sky'. To them he is so real that he is thought of in terms of 'a living person', never in the sense that he has a human form, but because he 'sees and hears all that happens and can be angry and can love'. They address him as 'father' in the sense of 'Our Father who art in heaven'; and as 'friend' implying intimate friendship. He is thus known as 'God who walks with you', that is, who is present with you. He is the friend of men who helps them in their trouble.

The Nuer habit of making short supplications to God outside formal and ritual occasions also suggests an awareness of a protective presence, as does the affirmation one hears every day among the Nuer ... 'God is present' ... The phrase does not mean 'there is a God'. That would be for Nuer a pointless remark. God's existence is taken for granted by everybody ... *Kwoth a thin* means that God is present in the sense of being in a place or enterprise, ... When Nuer use the phrase they are saying that they do not know what to do but God is here with them and will help them. He is with them because He is Spirit and being like wind or air is everywhere, and, being everywhere, is here and now.[29]

One question which has raised a controversy about God in African belief is the question of direct approach to him or of his worship. Certain investigators have rushed to the conclusion that God in African belief is not approached or worshipped directly, often because they are generalizing from one particular piece of evidence which they do not altogether understand, or because they are being deliberately blind to truth. For example, as we have already quoted, Westermann said that in Africa, 'God does not live in practical religion.' Against this we may set the evidence collected by other investigators. R. S. Rattray discovered that Onyame is worshipped by the Akan, with shrines and priests dedicated to him. Godfrey Lienhardt found that 'Nhialic is addressed and referred to as "creator" and "my father", and prayers are offered to it.'[30] The Lugbara recognize God as active in the world and in human affairs: God is distinguished very clearly from the ancestors, as far as sacrifice and offerings are concerned. 'Offering is made to God to remove meningitis and drought ...'[31] The Gogo believe that *Mulungu* governs

the destiny of man sending to him rain and storm, well-being and famine, health or disease, peace or war. He is *the* Healer. Note the prayers, 'I pray *Mulungu*, my child, I pray that it may be healed'; '*Mulungu*, now heal my body, may it be healed.'[32]

Alice Werner is emphatic in her statement in this connection:

It is often stated that Africans in general neither pray to the High God nor offer sacrifices to him, nor in fact, notice him at all, beyond recognizing his existence. This is certainly not true in the case of the Baila, and we have evidence to the same effect from various quarters. The Bapedi (a branch of the Basuto living in the Transvaal) say that their High God ... is called Huveane, and they pray to him for rain ... Mr Hobley distinctly states that the Akamba tribe, in Kenya Colony, pray to the God whom they call Engai ... Gutmann speaks of sacrifices offered to God ... by the Wachaga, which are clearly distinguished from offerings made to the ancestral spirits ... The Ngonde (Konde) people ... pray to Kyala ... and other instances may be cited.[33]

> The Meru regard *Iruva* as *the* Protector. The blessing '(Go), may *Iruva* go before you' signifies protection from every form of journeying adversity, [as also does] 'Let us be put well asleep by Iruva' = 'Let us sleep well in Iruva's protection'. ... In their morning-prayer the Meru thank God for the peaceful rest of the night.[34]

In fact a whole book should be written on this misunderstood point alone.

Even the erroneous assertion that Deity in African religion is approached only in times of distress and as a last resort when other helps have failed, only proves rather than disproves the fact that to Africans, he is there to be approached even at such times, and that can only mean that he is real to them.

(b) *God is unique.* In Edo mythology, there is a story that Olokun (the archdivinity) who is the beloved son of Osanobwa (the Supreme God) and was, therefore, vested with all the attributes and glory due to his position, once challenged his Father to a display of splendour and majesty. In accordance with African practice, he chose an open market-place for the display. When the appointed day arrived, the Father sent his messenger to tell Olokun that he was ready and that Olokun should meet him at once at the appointed venue. Olokun dressed himself in what he considered to be an excellent regalia and came out of his room. Imagine his chagrin when he saw that the Father's messenger was dressed identically as he! 'This will not do,' he thought. He therefore went back into the room and changed his regalia. When he came out again, he found that the messenger had changed identically as he. In the long run, he made a total of seven trials of regalia in order to go out and meet his Father; but each time he was frustrated because the messenger of the Father was identically dressed as he. In the end, he had to give up the attempt, admitting that it was impossible for him to go out and compete with his Father since he could not beat even his messenger in such a display. The Father's messenger was Chameleon!

This is a way of saying that Deity is unique, incomparable. The uniqueness of Deity is one reason why there are no images – graven or in drawing or in painting – of him in Africa. Symbols there are copiously, but no images. The African concept of God in this regard is an emphatic 'No one' and 'None' to the question, 'To whom then will you liken God, or what likeness compare with him?'[35]

The fact of Deity's uniqueness implies his transcendence; and the *transcendent* strong emphasis which African belief places on this is one of the major reasons why investigators have mistakenly rushed to the conclusion that God in African belief is *otiosus*.[36]

The conception of Deity as King, *the* King with absolute supremacy, emphasizes his uniqueness. One of the Yoruba names for him has the connotation of one who wears the unique crown in addition to his superlative attributes.[37] He is the only Deity: he is not of the rank and file of the divinities; he is not a person in the sense that human beings are. John Middleton saw this fact, and put it clearly, in connection with Lugbara belief:

> He is said not to be a 'person', but this is because since he created 'persons' he can hardly be one himself: 'Did he not put Gborogboro and Meme (the first beings) in the world? How then can he be a person? ...' 'The power of God is outside men and outside society, since it created men ...'[38]

Leza is known as 'the one who does what no other can do'.[39] There is a Ruanda proverb which says that 'There is none to equal Imana'.[40] The Nuer speak 'of themselves as *cok*, small black ants, particularly in their hymns ... that is, they are God's ants or, in other words, what a tiny ant is to man, so man is to God'; 'We, all of us, have the nature of ants in that we are very tiny in respect to God'.[41] And the Meru have the saying, 'No matter how great you are, *Iruva* is greater'; and another one translated, 'Every mountain grows less, but *Iruva* does not diminish'.[42]

In this connection it is necessary to guard ourselves against two constant sources of confusion. The first is the tendency to confuse Deity with the divinities, and the second is the tendency to confuse him with either the skyey heaven or a natural phenomenon in consequence of the ambiguous use of the name by which he is called in certain localities. We have already touched on these two points above. We shall only add that such confusion can only come as a result of confusion in thought or as a result of sheer misunderstanding. With regard to the first point, several authors on African belief have now come to the realization that Deity is not to be confused with the divinities or spirits. Alice Werner observes:

> Spirits, as a rule, are not placed in the personal class of nouns, but yet not in the same class as Imana. Mulungu would have the plural *milungu* ..., but I must say I have never come across it in the plural, except where there was reason to suspect European influence. ... Leza, the name used

for the High God by the Baila, Botanga, and several other tribes of Northern Rhodesia [Zambia] and the adjoining territories, also, in one language at least, means 'rain'. 'But,' says E. W. Smith, 'it is not plain that they regard rain and God as one and the same'; rather they speak of Leza as 'the rain-giver', 'the giver of thunder and much rain' ... So, too, the Wachaga, who call ... God 'Iruwa', use the same word for the sun, but insist that the sun is not the same thing as God.[43]

But then she registers her reservation about the distinction. Raimo Harjula writes without hesitation:

The often suggested identification of God and the sun seems mainly to be based on verbal similarities, i.e. the same term is used for the Supreme Being and the sun, or observations which are not interpreted with the total reference or in the light of the whole concept of God in question. ... For the purpose of this study it is more important to note that in everyday speech the two meanings of the word *iruva* are clearly differentiated by using different prefixes in connection with accompanying verbs. When this word means the sun in the sky the verb takes *li*-prefix: *iruva likeikwiimboo* – 'the sun is appearing' (sunrise) ... When the word *iruva* refers to God, the accompanying verb takes the personal class prefix *a* – : *Iruva amanyaa* – 'God knows' ...[41]

And Evans-Pritchard is quite definite:

The Nuer word we translate 'God' is *kwoth*, Spirit ... We may certainly say that the Nuer do not regard the sky or any celestial phenomenon as God, and this is clearly known in the distinction made between God and the sky in the expression 'Spirit of the sky' and 'Spirit who is in the sky'. Moreover, it would even be a mistake to interpret 'of the sky' and 'in the sky' too literally ... They may address the moon, but it is God to whom they speak through it, for the moon is not regarded, as such, as Spirit or as a person. Though God is not [sky, moon, rain, and so forth], ... he reveals himself through them.

It should be appreciated that Africans, like any other race in the world, are capable of finding tentative names for the Ineffable and the Nameless. And there are cases when the name of a suitable phenomenon is given to the Living Reality who causes and whose Being gives being to, the phenomenon. No one should blame the Yoruba for sometimes saying, Ọlọrun sú – 'God is overcast' for 'The sky is overcast', just as we do not blame the Europeans for saying, 'Heaven knows', when they mean, 'God knows'. Thus, there is no need for Nadel to think that Soko (God in Nupe belief) should be translated as God-the-Sky. The name implies by etymology and connotation the skyey heaven as also One who is greater and beyond or behind (in the sense of giving being to) the skyey heaven. Wherever there is any doubt about the meaning of names with regard to distinction between Deity and natural phenomena, the investigator *should* listen to what Africans have to say in explanation; and their explanation will be found easily in the attributes of God, in their songs and proverbs, and in their liturgy.

(c) *God is the absolute controller of the universe.* This is the focal ©️ point at which the fact of the reality and uniqueness of God in the African concept is brought home to us. In a way, the fact of God's control of the universe embraces all that we have said and implied under (a) and (b) immediately above. It also shows up the falsity of the notion of 'the withdrawn God'.

K. Little asserts with reference to the belief of the Mende of Sierra Leone:

> In the beginning, there was *Leve*, spoken of nowadays as *Ngewo*. Leve, or Ngewo, may be directly translated as (supreme) God. All life and activity, in both a material and non-material sense, derives from him. Ngewo created the world and everything in it, including not only human beings, animals, plants, and so on, but spirits also. In addition, he invested the whole universe with a certain non-material kind of power or influence which manifests itself in various ways and on specific occasions in human beings and animals, and even in natural phenomena, such as lightning, water falls and mountains. He is the ultimate source and symbol of that power and influence, but though all-powerful, he is not an immanent being ...[46]

Those who are studying African beliefs with carefulness, open-mindedness, and honesty are now coming to see that ideas like K. Little's of a world created, equipped, and set going with a self-charging and self-directing power is alien to African belief. Africans do not think or speak like this. In fact, they are rather anthropomorphic about their concept of God in this connection; they do not think or speak of 'a certain non-material kind of power or influence' with which God has invested the world so that he could go and abide unmolested in the repose of eternity. Neither do they know of the God who 'is not an immanent being'. They do imply that God is far away (transcendent), but at the same time that he is near and active in the universe, as we shall see later on.

Placide Tempels wrote a book which was aimed at correcting the Western world in its denial that Africa had spiritual and moral values. In his effort, however, he got himself entrapped somewhere between an abstract philosophical world-view and the Bantu world-view. Like K. Little, he postulates for Africans a computer-world in which something called 'Vital Force' appears to be the ruler and governor. 'Force is the nature of being, force is being, being is force', he maintains. He tries to extricate himself from the trap by saying that 'It would be a misuse of words to call the Bantu "dynamists" or "energists", as if the universe were animated by some universal force, a sort of magical power encompassing all existence'; but he continues to maintain, 'God is force, possessing all energy in himself, the mover of all other forces.' It seems that one of the difficulties with which he has to battle is language. It is one thing to say that God is the source of all power and another to equate his attribute with him. It is permissible, for example, to speak loosely in terms of 'God is power', 'God is wisdom' or God is love'; but it is always implied in that case that power, wisdom, or love is an attribute of God who is its source and from whom it becomes the 'property' of other beings. While it is clear that Tempels has mixed himself up, it is my conviction, on reading through his book, that it is not his intention to confuse the source with the outflow, the author with his work. His essential thesis is, in fact, very useful to our understanding of the African concept about the control of all that is:

It is a metaphysical causality which binds the creature to the Creator. The relationship of the creature to the Creator is a constant ... the creature is by his nature permanently dependent upon his Creator for existence and means of survival ... The sage 'par excellence' is God, Who knows every being, Who comprehends the nature and quality of the energy of each ... God is Force, possessing energy in himself, the mover of all other forces. He knows all forces, their ordering, their dependence, their potential and their mutual interactions. He knows, therefore, the cause of every event.[47]

The absolute control of the universe and of all beings is due, in African thought, basically to the fact that all other beings exist in consequence of him; and that whatever power or authority there may be exists in consequence of him; because it derives from him and because he permits it. God 'is the ultimate fountain-head of all power and authority, of all sanctions for orderly relations between men.'[48] Both Evans-Pritchard and Raimo Harjula lay particular stress on the 'concept of creation' in the areas of their study of creation as *ex nihilo* in consequence of the special words in which the idea is conveyed. Evans-Pritchard refers to the word *cak* and observes *inter alia*, 'As a verb "to create" it signifies creation *ex nihilo*, and when speaking of things can therefore only be used of God ...'[49] Raimo Harjula refers to the noun *Mutana* (Creator) which comes from the verb *itana*, 'to do'. Although the verb is commonly used, it in fact 'carries the idea of bringing into existence something

which was not there earlier, not just transforming something'.[50]
John Middleton says:

Lugbara see God as being the ultimate source of all power and of the
moral order ... The elders are nearer to God than are other people, and if
they are rainmakers they also have powers known to come directly from
God ... Lugbara conceive ... changes as being due to the intervention of
God. God then re-creates the structure of Lugbara society so that the changes
are incorporated into it.[51]

Godfrey Lienhardt found the same belief about God among the
Dinka.

Nhialic is figured sometimes as a Being, a personal supreme Being even,
and sometimes as a *kind* of being and activity which sums up the activities of
a multiplicity of beings ... When they say that he fashioned men, ... the
implication is that Man belonged to Divinity to do as he liked with, as
those things which a man makes with his own hands in Dinka society
belong fully to him ... Divinity, as father, is needed to look after, or
bring up, his people ... The Dinka speak of themselves as being resigned
in the same way to the 'word' – that is, decision or will – of their fathers,
and to the will of Divinity ... The transcendent fatherhood represented in
Divinity reinforces the position and authority of the actual human father ...
The Dinka are in a universe which is largely beyond their control, and
where events may contradict the most reasonable human expectation. The
Divinity who is sometimes a kindly father is also the Divinity which is
manifested in the non-rational forces of nature and hence has non-rational
as well as rational and moral attributes.[52]

It is precisely this same belief that is expressed among the Bantu:
'Shikakunamo sits on the back of every one of us, and we cannot
shake him off.' Shikakunamo is explained as 'one of the names sometimes used by the Baila for Leza; it means "the besetting one", the
one who will never let you alone.'[53] This features also in the Ruanda
proverbs 'Imana gives you – it is not a thing bought' (i.e. his gifts are
free); 'He who has received a gift from Imana is not stripped of it
by the wind'; 'Imana has long arms'.[54] The Nuer believe that Kwoth
is the Creator and Mover of all things. He is the very Spirit of the
universe. The universe is his: this fact occurs frequently in their
thought and prayers and determines their attitude to life and all its
issues. Of the universe they say 'It is thine, it is thy universe'; 'He
created the world, it is his word'. Evans-Pritchard lays particular
stress at this point on the Nuer conception of God's will. When they
say 'It is his word', they mean that everything is in being and
continues in being by the supernatural prerogative of the Almighty.
Thus, although Kwoth is in the sky, he is at the same time on

earth and this resolves for the Nuer the paradox of his transcendence-immanence as one who is far away and at the same time
actively and effectively rules the universe and governs human
affairs. He is the giver and, naturally, the sustainer of life. He
instituted the social order and is its guardian. Kwoth is always and
ever good; but he acts according to his own will and the Nuer accepts
whatever he does without complaint, and even sees blessings in
adversities. It is God who makes even a curse operative.[55] The Ashanti summarize this by saying of Onyame that he is the 'Supreme
Being, upon whom men lean and do not fall'.[56]

Whereas Margaret Read as a stranger thinks that Cibambo, an
Ngoni, was 'using his Christian beliefs to rationalize the ancestor
cult, particularly in relating it to the concept of a High God', there
is no doubt that the statement of Cibambo about the Ngoni concept
of God is consonant with the general African pattern. The appel-
lations of God as 'The Great Deviser', 'The Original Source', 'The
Greatest of all', 'The Owner of All Things' can be matched elsewhere all over Africa. Margaret Read herself admitted that 'UM-
kulumgango, the Great Spirit, the originator of all creation, possessed
more power than any other being ...', and that the Great Spirit is
approached through the ancestors, 'spirits of dead Paramounts', for
the ultimate sanction of requests or deliverance from troubles;
further:

> The Ngoni undoubtedly had the idea of a creator, remote and unapproach-
> able by man, as his title implied, but nevertheless referred to as the sender
> of rain, sickness, and other benefits and disasters for the country as a
> whole.[57]

The Meru speak of Iruva as 'He who has all power'. Iruva is
believed to be almighty not only in the potential, but also in the
actual sense of the word. He is regarded as 'the acting Almighty',
he is also Giver of Gifts, Protector, Judge,

> acting in various ways within human life here and now ... *Iruva's* role as
> Creator of everything is general in character, but the birth of a child or
> meditating on the wonders of the landscape at times gives this role particular
> significance. In various human needs, *Iruva* is remembered and approached as
> Giver of Gifts and Feeder ... The name Helper describes *Iruva's* activity
> in general ...[58] The idea of *Iruva* as God of (over) all men and things
> indicates that his creative activity is not limited to the past, but he is
> 'Creator' also in the present. *Iruva* did not only create everything in the
> beginning, but he also continues his creative activity.[59]

The place of the divinities in the structure of African traditional religion will be discussed in the next section. We should, however, observe here that <u>the divinities owe their being and divine authority to Deity and that they are not to be confused with him in any way.</u> In Yoruba mythology, there is a remarkable story which brings out clearly the relationship between Deity and the divinities.

The one thousand seven hundred divinities conspired against Olódùmarè, and decided that he must abdicate power and authority. They went before him and demanded that he should hand over power to them, at least, for an experimental period of sixteen years. Olódùmarè suggested to them that it might be wise for them to experiment for sixteen days in the first instance. This suggestion they joyfully accepted. Olódùmarè then told them that the world was theirs to run the way they chose for that period of sixteen days. They immediately set about their task. But after only eight days they discovered that things had gone wrong – that the machinery of the universe was, in fact, at a standstill.

They devised every means they could think of to keep things going – but made no headway; they adopted all the tactics they knew but failed; the heaven withheld its rains; rivers ceased to flow; rivulets became glutted with fallen leaves; yams sprouted but did not develop; the ears of corn filled but did not ripen; the juice of trees was being licked to quench thirst; Ọrúmìlà was consulted but his oracle was dumb and the appliances of divination refused to work; the daily feasting in the houses of the divinities stopped; the whole world was certainly going to perish! The divinities thus found themselves at their wits' end. There was nothing else they could do but to go back to Olódùmarè. And so, in shame, and with drooping heads, they went back to Him and confessed their folly, acknowledging His absolute sovereignty and supremacy over all, and pleading for mercy. The Benevolent Father laughed at their foolishness and forgave them. Then He switched on again the machinery of the universe and it immediately resumed normal running. The divinities went away singing:

Be there one thousand four hundred divinities of the home;
Be there one thousand two hundred divinities of the market-place,
Yet there is not one divinity to compare with Olódùmarè:
Olódùmarè is the King Unique.
In our recent dispute,
Èdùmàrè it is who won.
Yes, Èdùmàrè.[60]

<u>With regard to the essential person, it is illuminating that the African concept is generally that it is only Deity who can put this into man and thus make him a person.</u>[61] According to the Konkomba, *Ungwin* is that part of man which God gives.[62] While the

[margin handwritten note: Only God gives the self to man.]

archdivinity may be charged with the task of moulding the physical part of man, and while African thought on the subject suggests a cross between the creationist and the traducianist ideas, the responsibility for the being of the inner man is the prerogative of Deity.

Man is the dominant force among all created, visible forces. His force, his life, his fullness of being consist in his participation to a greater or less extent in the force of God. God, the Bantu would say, possesses (or, more exactly, He is) THE supreme, complete, perfect force. He is the Strong One, in and by Himself ... In relation to the beings whom he has created, God is regarded by the Bantu as the causative agent, the sustainer of these resultant forces, as being the creative cause. Man is one of these resultant living forces, created, maintained and developed by the vital, creative influence of God.[63]

The absolute dependence of the essential man upon Deity is further emphasized by the fact that in certain localities, the names by which the inner man is called derive directly from the names of Deity. We have instances of this among the Yoruba and Igbo where respectively Deity is called ORISE and CHUKWU, and the essential person is called *ori* and *chi*. Ori thus derives from the name Orise = Ori-se, meaning the 'Source from which beings spring up or happen, Source-Being'; and *chi* from Chukwu = Chi-ukwu, meaning 'The Great, Immense, Undimensional Source of beings'. We should add to this the concept of man's destiny which is usually connected with the essential person: this is usually conceived as something which man obtains from Deity Himself, and ultimately, the account of how man uses his talent must be rendered before Deity.[64]

We shall conclude this sub-section on the note that with regard to the creation, control, and maintenance of the universe, only Deity is the absolute origin of all things, only he has absolute power and authority. In African thought, Deity is absolutely essential and cannot be disregarded: the notion of a god as so transcendent that he is not immanent is alien to African belief, even though, as we have observed, when pressed to express this in straightforward, prosaic terms, Africans may be confused – especially when the question is couched in awkward terms by people who should know that there are questions which cannot be answered in the terms in which they are asked. Africans are explicit about the divine rulership and absolute control of the universe. The Akan say that God is 'of all the earth, the King and Elder'.[65] The Edo name for God,

Osanobwa, means 'The Source-Being who carries and sustains the universe'. About the Lugbara concept it is observed,

> God is not outside society, but rather above it completely ... He is said to be 'behind' all people and all things, as their creator, and so may be in indirect contact with all forms of social action. His presence unites them into a single schema, of which the divisions are complementary and cannot be understood in isolation.[66]

The Nupe sing,

> A being which Soko did not create, neither did the world create it ... Should you do anything that is beautiful, Soko has caused it to be beautiful; should you do anything evil, Soko has caused it to be evil.

The transcendence-immanence of God is emphasized by the Nupe in the saying: 'God is far away'; 'God is in front, he is in the back.'[67]

(d) *God is One, the only God of the whole universe.* This is a significant part of the African concept of God which must be well understood if one is to understand African attitude to life with regard to personal relations.

All over Africa, there are places each of which is considered to be the sacred city, the sacred grove, or the sacred spot, especially because it is believed, according to the people's cosmology, that the place is the centre of the world, the place where creation began, where the human race has its cradle, and from where the race dispersed all over the earth.

Let us take the Yoruba cosmogony as an example. The Yoruba believe traditionally that the creation of the earth began at Ilé-Ifè. When the earth was ready and fully equipped, sixteen human beings, the first set to be created, were despatched under the guardianship of Orìsà-ńlá, the archdivinity and the headship of Orelúéré, the first human Head to inhabit the earth. Although this myth is complex in consequence of the immigrants who came to Yorubaland under the powerful leader who is now known as Odùdúwà, its basic motif remains unshaken. The part of it which is relevant to our topic is that which implies the basic conception that the human race is one, even though their places of habitation may be far apart and the colours of their skins and their manners of life may differ from one another. The mythology continues by saying that Olódùmarè vested Orìsà-ńlá with the power to create man perfect, comely, or deformed, and with whatever peculiarities of shapes and looks, or of whatever colours, he chooses. Hence the different types of human beings.

There is a separate myth which explains the colouring of the white man (which includes almost every person with colour typically lighter than the African's).

Ilé-Ifè ... is the earthly origin and foundation of all; it is also the earthly end to which all must return in order to be told what to do next ... Ilé-Ifè is the origin and centre, not only of the Yoruba world but also of the whole world of nations and peoples. At one time, a stone 'shoe' could be seen there, and it was said to be the primeval shoe, the archetype of the shoes worn by Europeans. There are two bodies of water in the city: One is called Ọsàrà (Ọsà) – 'The Lagoon' and the other Ọkun – 'The Sea'. These are said to be respectively the original sources from which the world's lagoons and seas and oceans derived.[68]

During the central ritual of at least one major festival in Ilé-Ifè, the invocation begins with the divinity concerned and proceeds to invite the ancestors, and then all peoples from every corner of the earth to *come home* (in spirit, of course) and worship.

Godfrey Lienhardt observes with reference to the Dinka:

All Dinka assert that Divinity is one, ... The implications of this affirmation are that ... Nhialic is the same Divinity as that which different peoples know under different names, the Divinity the Nuer call 'Kwoth', the Muslims 'Allah', the Christians 'God', and so on.[69]

According to the Nuer, Kwoth

made one man black and another white (according to one account [the Europeans'] white skins are a punishment by God ...), one man fleet and another slow, one strong and another weak. Everything in nature, in culture, in society, and in men is as it is because God made or willed it so ... God is the father of men in two respects. He is their creator and he is their protector.[70]

With regard to Lugbara belief, John Middleton observes:

God is concerned with the wellbeing of an entire tribe, a unit that is too large to recognize any ritual relationship between itself and any single body of ancestors ... At the beginning of the world men and God were in a direct relation, and men could move up and down from the sky ... (The) bridge between heaven and earth was broken and men fell down, scattering into their present distinct groups each with its different language; before that all men spoke the same language ... Only God can overcome this separation. The myth distinguishes the small-scale cosmos of Lugbara thought from the chaos, social and moral, that surrounds it in space and time; and it also enables both spheres to be seen as a single whole, the universe ... God even made the Europeans ... Every lineage has its own ancestors, but God is everywhere, in a relationship of equal intensity with all lineages.[71]

The Igbo of Nigeria call Deity by the appellation of *Chi di n'uwa* –

God of the world or universe. Here again, we meet the conception of the unrestricted universality of God.

One important aspect of this topic is found in the African sense of the justice of God – justice with particular reference to the social and the moral order. Before God, there is no favourite. He is no respecter of persons: He made each one and all are of equal value before him.

> A client ... is a man without a lineage, a refugee from elsewhere. Before acceptance by a host or sponsor he has no kin, and is a 'thing'. When he is accepted he becomes a kinsman. Before this he may be killed as a 'thing', without fear of vengeance. Yet he is still regarded as a creature of God, and indeed as a Lugbara, even though his clan is unknown or unrecognized.[72]

A discovery about divine justice is also made by Godfrey Lienhardt in relation to the concept:

> If creativity and fatherhood are attributes of Divinity most commonly referred to, justice ... follows them closely. Divinity is held ultimately to reveal the truth and falsehood, and in doing so provides a sanction for justice between men. ... Lies, and the misunderstanding, suspicions, hostilities, and malice which accompany them, are mentioned to show that Divinity is especially needed to intervene in human affairs, to put them straight by making the truth appear. ... Divinity is made the final judge of right and wrong. ... Divinity is thus the guardian of truth. ... The Dinka have no problem of the prospering sinner, for they are sure that Divinity will ultimately bring justice ...[73]

The concept of *cuong* among the Nuer is illuminating here. The word may be translated 'righteousness' in reference to God's dealing with men, man's relation to God and to his fellow men. 'What, then, Nuer ideas on the matter amount to is ... that if a man wishes to be in the right with God he must be in the right with men ...'[74] The concept implies also that while goodness will never miss its reward in blessing, wickedness will not go unpunished. The Yoruba have an identical concept in Òtító – the plumb line by which man should take and measure his bearings in relation to God and to his fellow-men and the social order in general; and as the watch-dog of which God has set in perpetual operation a retributive principle known as 'the rewarder – avenger'.[75] According to the Meru, Iruva is 'God of (over) all things' and 'God of (over) all men'. 'Iruva knows' embraces for the Meru the only possible answer to the inexplicable issues of life as well as the unique omniscience which makes God the highest judge.[76]

David Tait appears to have discovered among the Konkomba of Northern Ghana a system of social justice which is restricted to the clan even when God is involved:

But there is no authority able to compose quarrels between men of different clans. There are special relations between neighbouring clans, which mitigate but do not obviate quarrels between neighbours ... To kill a fellow-clansman is an offence so awful that nothing can be done either to punish the killer or to save him from God's anger. To kill a man of a different clan 'does not matter' ... The sorcerer can, if he will, cease to be a sorcerer. Indeed to avoid the anger of God he must make that decision; and the problem of sorcery is therefore a moral one.[77]

It is but fair that we should mention this apparent exception, lest we should appear to be generalizing unduly. We should, at the same time, register our doubt as to whether the whole fact has been revealed here about the people's concept of God, especially as Tait's reference to God appears to be rather casual: his concern in his book is not the study of religion.

One element of God's justice that is emphasized very much, of which Africans are ever-conscious, is that of 'the Wrath' of God. We see the fact about this implied in the quotation made above from David Tait. The conceptualization of 'the Wrath' takes on concrete manifestation in the affliction connected with thunder. Usually, there are neolithic 'axes' to be found in shrines as cult-objects to represent the instruments of the affliction. The 'axes' belong to Deity himself, to be hurled at the children of disobedience. '*Nyame akuma*' – God's axe – 'is generally to be found' in the shrine of Onyame among the Akan. Imana is often associated with thunder and lighting by the Bantu, 'as the Zulu lord of Heaven and the Thonga Tilo are'; but often 'the Thunder is treated as a distinct personage'.[78] In Nigeria, there is always a divine minister of justice who is the solar and thunder divinity. God is called Soko by the Nupe, and the thunder divinity is called Sokogba (= *Soko egba*) – 'God's axe', which means that he is an expression of 'the Wrath' of God. Jàkǔta[79] (now commonly called Sǎngǒ) among the Yoruba is the same conception as Sokogba. The name Jàkǔta means literally 'one who hurls, or fights with, stones'.

The whole African concept of justice is based upon the fact that the world belongs to Deity; that the social and the moral orders are his ordinance, and that he is far above all divisions into races, ethnic groups, clan differences, or political partisanships. The political invention known as 'the God of Africa', in answer to what appears to be the Europeans' raciocentric God, is alien to the traditional, genuine, African concept of God.

The correct African belief about God is well expressed by implication in the following dialogue:

> 'What is the word for God?' he asked.
> 'Which one?' inquired Esther innocently.
> 'The only one,' he said severely.
> 'Theos,' she replied, after a little pause.[80]

2. Belief in the divinities[81]

As I have indicated, it is not easy to discuss this element freely for the whole of Africa because it is not everywhere prominent. West Africa may be said to be the home of divinities; but even here, we have variations from a very crowded pantheon to a very thinly populated one, and even to a situation where they appear to be scarcely in existence. There seems to be a clear situation with regard to divinities among the Dinka.[82] The Uganda situation is not as clear, simply because the origins of the Batembuzi and Bacweeci are shrouded in doubt — were they divinities who once inhabited the earth and ruled it theocratically, or were they originally heroes, conquerors, or powerful immigrants who first inhabited the land? There are investigators who are ready — perhaps too ready — to assert that in most of Africa, there is only a two-tier conception of the divine, that of Deity and that of the ancestors. We have to be very careful here, however. Conceptual language can be confusing, and one has to make sure that one really understands what it is saying. For example, in consequence of complications the term 'spirits' has been used to cover in certain areas both the categories of divinities and the general, uncharacterized spirits.

First of all, in discussing the divinities, we are confronted with two basic issues: the first is that a pantheon implies pluralism and this brings up the question as to whether or not polytheism applies as an appropriate, descriptive term for African traditional religion in consequence of the incidence of the divinities; and the other (which depends on the way the first one is resolved) is of the nature of the divinities and their relationship to Deity.

First, then, let us consider the meaning of polytheism. According

Polytheism

to Paul Tillich, whom we quote with approval,

Tillich's definition

> Polytheism is a qualitative and not a quantitative concept. It is not a belief in a plurality of gods but rather the lack of a unifying and transcending ultimate which determines its character.[83]

This definition, when carefully considered, will shed a guiding light through the darkness of confusion which has bedevilled the study of religion in certain areas of the world. The fact of 'The One and the Many' has frequently posed a problem to a certain type of mind; and such a mind has tended to follow the line of least resistance by adding 'The One' to 'The Many' and conveniently arriving at the answer 'Plurality'. This offhand mathematical answer to a purely spiritual question has always been a bane to the study of religion, especially in the non-Islamic, non-Christian contexts.

A careful study of religion these days should make one wary of such hasty conclusions. This is so indeed as we bring to mind the fact that religion, as we have it, has passed through stages which may be development or retrogression. If we follow Rudolf Otto's thesis in *The Idea of the Holy* we shall find that it is necessary again and again to re-examine the theory or fact of primitive monotheism. For it is becoming increasingly accepted that what man first encountered by experience as divine was that of a unitary control of the universe, and that it was as a result of the development of material culture and the organization of society that man came to develop the idea of an order of divine powers, whether these be in subjection to one absolute controller or in the form of what is generally described as 'proper polytheism'.[84]

The Olympian situation has always afforded a veritable example of what may be described as proper polytheism. Here we have a system where the gods appear not to have transcended the universe of social cliques and inter-tribal conflicts. Not only were the gods *all* of the same rank and file in kind and in passion, distinguished from one another only by a hierarchy of status or power among more or less equals; but also they shared in the passions of men and tended to use their divinity in competing with, and beating, men in 'superfluity of naughtiness'. There was the ancient but not clearly defined figure of Kronos – Kronos whose three offspring conspired against him under the leadership of the eldest, deprived him of the kingdom of the universe which they proceeded to share among themselves, and then fell to quarrelling among themselves, and victimizing the less powerful. It has become clear, however, that in the Olympian myth we have a reflection of the syncretism which resulted from conflicts between states among the Greeks.

What is not usually remembered, or even known, is the fact that there was the concept of 'Zeus Hypsistos'.

Of Smyrna, the noteworthy fact is reported that certain Jews in this city, not particularly firm in their orthodoxy, worshipped Jehovah under the name of 'Zeus Hypsistos'. This idea is not so outlandish as it may at first seem. There was in Greek mythology a Father of gods and men, standing high above Olympian Zeus who with his amorous affairs was the butt of the comic poets. This 'All-Highest' Zeus – Zeus Hypsistos – was worshipped without an image.[85]

This calls to mind, and probably interprets, 'the Unknown God' of Athens, in whom 'we live and move and have our being; "For we are indeed his offspring" '. According to Plutarch:

'The true Zeus' has a wider survey than 'the Homeric Zeus' ... To judge from the motions of the heavens, the divine really enjoys variety, and is glad to survey movement, the actions of gods and men, the periods of the stars. Thus under the Supreme is a hierarchy of heavenly powers of gods ...[87]

The argument is taken further by Alfred E. Garvie:

Polytheism cannot be accepted as a permanent form of religious belief and worship. In the measure in which human personality realizes its own unity and recognizes unity in the world around must multiplicity in the object yield to unity. The mind demands one principle for the explanation of the world, in which the discovery is ever being made that 'all things work together' (Rom. VIII:28). The heart craves one object of devotion, as *Kathenotheism*, however imperfectly, shows. Conscience demands one supreme moral authority and one constant moral order; else morality is involved in perilous confusion. The attempt to revive polytheism in a philosophical form in pluralism seems to me a bad joke, a mere freak of intelligence ... it must be frankly conceded that the exposition and demonstration of divine unity amid the multiplicity of the world is beset with difficulty; to relate the many to the One is by no means an easy task. For the conception of the divine itself combines contrasts ...[88]

Paul Radin raises a pertinent question on the same topic:

Monotheism itself presents a number of phases. A recent classification of its history divides it into three stages; into monolatry, i.e. a belief in a Supreme Being but the persistence of the worship of other deities at the same time; implicit monotheism, i.e. a belief in a Supreme Deity yet no definite denial of other gods; and lastly, explicit monotheism, a belief in a

Supreme Deity and a denial of the existence of other gods. If this were true, it might at first glance follow that we have to deny the existence among any primitive peoples of anything except monolatry. But it might be asked, is it really the mere fact of the worship of other gods or spirits or culture-heroes that constitutes the fundamental difference between explicit monotheism and monolatry? What of those cases where lesser gods have been created by a Supreme Deity; where all their powers have been derived from him; where they are merely his intercessors? Are we to interpret every act of worship not directly addressed to a Supreme Deity but to his divinely appointed intermediary as contrary to the spirit of monotheism? I am afraid that we should then find ourselves confronted with great difficulties.[89]

Professor H. H. Farmer, in maintaining a thesis that every religion is a result of revelation from the *one* living God, said something rather curious:

There is, however, a difficulty which at once presents itself in relation to this line of thought. If we have been justified in saying that living religions come into being at the point where the *one* God makes Himself known to man by the initiative of His self-disclosure, where (it may be asked) can we really find living religion in the primitive, and indeed in the later-than-primitive world? *For primitive and early religion is definitely and thoroughly polytheistic; it apprehends, not one God but many gods.*[90]

An important question here is of the date of Farmer's 'primitive'. And how does he come to know so definitely and so thoroughly that 'primitive and early religion is definitely and thoroughly polytheistic'? Surely, a philosopher-theologian as careful as he usually is should know that his, in this case, is a very sweeping statement which assumes a scope of knowledge which one does not really possess.[91]

We shall now proceed to look specifically at the African scene. As we have already observed, African traditional religion cannot be described as polytheistic. Its appropriate description is monotheistic, however modified this may be. The modification is, however, inevitable because of the presence of other divine beings within the structure of the religion. But 'beings' in their case can only be spelt with the initial small letter 'b'; 'powers', when they are so described, can only be spelt with the initial small letter 'p'; this is because, in fact, they have no absolute existence and the African world is under a unitary theocratic government.[92]

... *nhialic* is also a comprehensive term for a number of conceptions which differ considerably from each other. Powers, of which the most important religiously are those I have called free-divinities and clan divinities, are distinct from each other, though of most of them the Dinka say simply *e e nhialic*, 'it is Divinity'. This unity and multiplicity of Divinity causes no difficulty in the context of Dinka language and life ...[93]

The question of the relationship between Deity and the divinities defines the place of the latter within the whole system.

First, from the point of view of the theology of African traditional religion, it will not be correct to say that the divinities were created. It will be correct to say that they were brought into being, or that they came into being in the nature of things with regard to the divine ordering of the universe. Oriṣa-nlá (archdivinity among the Yoruba) is definitely a derivation partaking of the very nature and metaphysical attributes of Olódùmarè. Hence he is often known as Deity's son or deputy, vested with the power and authority of royal sonship. And this is why it has been possible in Bahia to syncretize his cult with Christianity and identify him as Jesus Christ. Olokun (Benin) is known as the *Son* of Osanobwa – the Son vested with power and majesty by his Father. All Akan divinities are called sons of Onyame. It is in consequence of this derivative relationship that these divine 'beings' are entitled to be called divinities or deities.

Secondly, the divinities are derivatives from Deity. This we have already illustrated.[94] It is necessary, however, to re-emphasize the fact in this context. It is not always that the fact of the derivation can be proved from the linguistic connections between the names of Deity and the generic names of the divinities. It is generally theologically provable that the divinities have no absolute existence – they are in being only in consequence of the being of Deity. All that we have said about the unitary control of the created order by Deity applies here. Because the divinities derive from Deity, their powers and authorities are meaningless apart from him.

Thirdly, each divinity has his own local name in the local language, which is descriptive either of his allotted function or the natural phenomenon which is believed to be a manifestation or emblem of his being. Among the Yoruba, the divinity who is believed to be the divine representative of 'the Wrath' is called Jàkŭta – 'one who hurls or fights with stones; and in Nupe he is called Sokogba (= *Soko egba*) – 'God's axe'. In each case the phenomenological reference is to the thunderbolt which is believed to be the instrument of execution. Among the Igbo, the archdivinity is called Ala (or Ana, Ani, according to the locality in Igboland); this is the same word

used for 'earth' or 'ground' – Ala is the Earth-goddess, and is the
archdivinity.

Fourthly, the divinities were brought into being as functionaries
in the theocratic government of the universe. According to Dahomey
belief, the whole set-up makes this clear.[95] Mawu-Lisa (the archdivinity) apportioned the kingdoms of the sky, the sea, and the earth
among six of his offspring, and to the seventh, Legba – who is the
same as the divine messenger and inspector-general in African
pantheons[96] – is assigned the office of being the liaison officer between
Mawu-Lisa and the other offspring and between the offspring themselves. Here we have an apt illustration that the divinity system
is a reflection, usually, of the sociological pattern in the conception
of the divine government of the Universe. Godfrey Lienhardt makes
a discerning observation in connection with the divinities:

> None of the free-divinities, with the possible exception of MACARDT,
> also called COLWIC, is thought to exist independently of the particular name
> by which the Dinka know it. That is, unlike Divinity, who is thought to
> be universal and known by various names to different peoples, the free-
> divinities are active only where their specific names are known and where
> effects in human life can be attributed to them.[97]

We shall be getting this accurately if we see the divinities in each
pantheon as intimately connected with the local situation, and each
of them believed to be specifically 'the god of' the particular people
with particular reference to a specific function in the ordering of
the total life of the community. The divinity, therefore, has a local
name which linguistically appears to limit his scope to the locality.
It will be discovered, however, upon careful study, that several of
the principal divinities are common to several parts of Africa although under different linguistic names. Jàkǔta (or Ṣàngǒ), representing 'the Wrath' among the Yoruba, appears as Sokogba among the
Nupe, as Xevioso in Dahomey and among the Ewe-speaking peoples.
Thus, even though the divinities are named in the various languages
and appear to be confined to localities, the actual conceptions which
they represent are not as confined, especially where such conceptions
are made universal by the universality of phenomena – earth, sky,
thunder, sun, water, agriculture, etc.

Fifthly, the divinities are ministers, each with his own definite
portfolio in the Deity's monarchical government. Each is in his own
sphere an administrative head of a department. They are also intermediaries between Deity and man, especially with reference to their

particular functions. Consequently, in course of time, they have become conventional channels through which man believes that he should normally approach Deity. It is this accepted role of the divinities according to African beliefs and practices which has lent weight to the notion which results in the sweeping and erroneous assertion that Deity is never approached directly by Africans; or that if he is called upon directly at all, it is only in moments of crisis and desperation when all other aids have failed.

The correct interpretation of the position of the divinities is that they constitute only a half-way house which is not meant to be the permanent resting place for man's soul. While man may find the divinities 'sufficient' for certain needs, something continues to warn him that 'sufficiency' is only in Deity. Technically, the divinities are only means to an end and not ends in themselves.

Sixthly, the divinities under their various generic names form the pantheon in each locality. The pantheons vary in sizes according to the sociological set-up or other factors which may influence the concept of the divine ordering of the government of the universe among each people. Over each pantheon is usually an archdivinity who is more closely related in attributes to Deity. For example, Òrìṣà-nlá (great – or archdivinity) is the deputy of Olódùmarè and derives his attributes from those of Deity. Ala, the archdivinity among the Igbo, is variously described as the wife or the daughter, and more firmly, the terrestial expression of Chukwu; the status is held by Mawu-Lisa in Dahomey: Mawu-Lisa is a result of the merger of two cults, an androgynous divinity who bears the combined nature of the father and mother of divinities and a derivation of the universal Mawu or Nana Buluku – the generic, divine name Mawu (feminine) in combination with Lisa (masculine) another generic, divine name, emphasizes not only the derivation from Deity but also the African sense of the male-female principle.

Seventhly, we still have to answer an important question. Are the divinities real or not? We may get round the question by saying that to those who believe in them and believe that they derive succour from their ministration or afflictions from their machinations, they are real; and to those who have outgrown them or to whom they have never had significance, they have no real, objective existence. But this is a question so subtle and of such a tremendous importance that it cannot be so slightly dismissed. First, it is wrong to hold that a certain experience is impossible simply on the ground that certain people have not had such or are incapable of it. Secondly, it will be sheer presumption to claim that we know already all that there is to know about the fact of spiritual powers and of the supersensible world.[98]

This much we can deduce from African belief with regard to the reality of the divinities:

(a) There are those who may be described as the 'divinities of heaven'. That is, they are the principal divinities who are a part of the original order of things. Whereas traditions may *know* times when they used to be on earth *in human form*, their very origins belong to the divine secret which is beyond man's probing.

(b) Some of them are conceptualizations of certain prominent attributes of Deity, especially as discerned through natural phenomena. This explains why the cult of the 'Solar and Thunder' divinity is so universal and why these phenomena are usually linguistically or notionally connected or (confused) with Deity.

(c) There are several of the divinities who are no more than ancestors and heroes who have become deified. More often than not, the deification occurred through their absorption of the attributes of certain earlier divinities.[99] (In a few cases there may be ancestors or heroes whose prowess during their life-time earned deification for them.) Here is another source of confusion in the study of African belief. Very often, we are treated to the offhand assertion that the divinities in African belief are *all* deified ancestors, whereas this is far from the truth.

Now, the census of the divinities.

In certain areas, the number of the divinities in the pantheons are not easy to assess. For example, Yoruba oral traditions put them variously at 201, 401, 600, or 1700.[100] On the other hand, in Dahomey and among the Ashanti, the numbers seem to be fairly certain. The reason for the uncertainty about original numbers may be attributed to certain factors, among which are migrations and fusion of cultures. When people moved from one territory to another, they naturally took their cults along with them. Although a *new* divinity thus introduced might be of the same nature and function as another existing divinity of the new home, the cult of the new divinity would be established as that of a completely new one; and in that way a duplication or even a triplication would occur.[101] Thus differences in names often appear as differences in divinities and we have additions, which are not really additions, to existing pantheons. To this must be added the deification of ancestors and heroes.

The main shortcoming of the divinity system is that <u>it very easily lends itself as a tool to priestcraft</u>. This is one other factor which makes for an increase in the number of divinities because, as is well known in the history of religion, priestcraft is quite capable of inventing spurious objects of worship.[102] <u>It is also in consequence of priestcraft that the divinities have largely tended to become ends in themselves instead of the means to an end which they are meant to be.</u> Thus, even though Deity is an ever-present, immanent reality in African belief, Africans are <u>**often**</u> led to accept the half-way houses as permanent resting places, the means as the end, to the impoverishment of religion and degradation of human life.

3. *Belief in spirits*

This element in the structure of African traditional religion has already been mentioned in our examination of the term *animism*.[103] We observed there that 'animism' was applicable to African traditional religion only because it formed an element in its structure; that is, provided we restricted the term to its basic definition as a <u>belief in, recognition and acceptance of the fact of the existence of, spirits who may use material objects as temporary residences and manifest their presence and actions through natural objects and phenomena.</u>

The previous sections in this chapter, as well as the sections that will follow, inevitably render this section rather brief.

<u>We refer to spirits here as those apparitional entities which form separate category of beings from those described as divinities.</u> We distinguish them also from the ancestors since we are dealing with those under a separate sub-heading. Divinities and ancestors come under the general nomenclature of spirits, no doubt. But divinities and ancestors form separate homogeneous categories of their own. Divinities and ancestors could be described as 'domesticated' spirits – the ancestors have always been a part of the human family, and the divinities are intimately a tutelary part of the personal or community establishments. But under our particular reference, spirits are not as clearly defined. <u>They may be anthropomorphically conceived, but they are more often than not thought of as powers which are almost</u>

abstract, as shades or vapours which take on human shape; they are immaterial and incorporeal beings. They are so constituted that they can assume various dimensions whenever they wish to be 'seen' – they may be either abnormally small or abnormally tall, fat or thin. It is believed that especially when they appear beside the natural object which is their residence, they may appear in the form or shape or dimensions of the object. For example, a man describing his experience of the spirit residing in a tall sacred tree said that he saw the shade as tall as the tree, but rather slender; when the spirit knew that it had been seen, it collapsed with a terrifying groan and dissolved into a mist.

Spirits, according to African belief, are ubiquitous; there is no area of the earth, no object or creature, which has not a spirit of its own or which cannot be inhabited by a spirit. Thus, there are spirits of trees, that is, spirits which inhabit trees. There are special trees which are considered sacred by Africans and these are believed to be special residences of spirits. The Yoruba *akòko*, also called by the Igbo *ogilisi* or *ogirisi* (*Newboldia Laevis*, according to R. C. Abraham) is a sacred tree which is an emblem to several divinities; it is also reputed to be a residence to certain nondescript spirits which congregate and chatter like birds among its leaves in the middle of the night.

Such a tree as spirits inhabit becomes their emblem; at the foot of it, offerings are made to them, and people make ejaculatory prayers as they pass by.

In the same way, there are spirits which inhabit rocks, mountains and hills, forests and bushes, rivers and watercourses, which natural objects are accepted as their emblems and the mediums by which they are approached.

Although the spirits we are considering are generally described as nameless (except that there is a common generic name by which they are called collectively in each locality), nevertheless, they have categories by which they can be described. For example, there are ghost-spirits. It is believed by Africans that a person whose dead body is not buried, that is, with due and correct rites, will not be admitted to the abode of the blessed departed ones, and therefore will become a wanderer, living an aimless, haunting existence. This is also the fate of those who die bad deaths – by hanging or drowning, of bad diseases, or during pregnancy; since they are accursed, they will not be acceptable in the abode of the blessed. This category of wandering spirits include also those who had been wicked while on earth and are therefore excluded from the fellowship of the good. The haunt of the ghost-spirits are trees, rocks, rivers and water-courses, or hills. In certain areas, the possibility is not ruled out that they may enter into animals or birds or snakes in order to destroy things or molest people.

There is a strong belief about another curious category of spirits. It is not certain whether these began as spirits of deceased persons or not. But they are the spirits known to the Yoruba as Àbíkú or to the Igbo as *Ogbanje*: that is, spirits 'born-to-die'. The belief here is that there are wandering spirits who specialize in the sadistic mischief of finding the way into wombs to be born in order to die. The traditional explanation is that there is a company of spirits whose members are under an agreement to undertake in turns this errand of mischief: before those who are thus assigned leave the company temporarily, they enter into a pact that they will return, that is, die, at certain named dates and times. Africans, where this belief prevails, are always seeking protection against this category of spirits, especially when women are pregnant. It is believed that a child who is an incarnation of one of such spirits may be detected through divination. When this is done, a step is taken by medicine or magic, often combined with maltreatment, to prevent it from ever again attempting the prank on the same woman – for one such spirit could plague the same woman several times and perhaps eventually leave her altogether childless if there is no means of controlling the situation. Sometimes, the spirit may be made to 'decide' to break the pact with its spirit-companions and remain a human being on earth.

One important human spirit with which Africa has had to reckon very painfully, very disastrously, is the spirit of the witches.[104] In Africa, it is idle to begin with the question whether witches exist or not. The observer from elsewhere outside African culture may hold whatever theory appeals most to him on the subject. To Africans of every category, witchcraft is an urgent reality. There are African investigators who have come to the realization that in speaking or writing about witchcraft, the *actual* belief of Africans must come first. African concepts about witchcraft consist in the belief that the spirits of living human beings can be sent out of the body on errands of doing havoc to other persons in body, mind, or estate; that witches have guilds or operate singly, and that the spirits sent out of the human body in this way can act either invisibly or through a lower creature – an animal or a bird.

The question how witches operate must be connected with the problem of evil in general. And so the secrets of witchcraft may never be altogether clear to non-members of the guild of witches. The Yoruba, in fact, designate the witches and sorcerers and those who belong together to the category of those who exist mainly for evil machinations as *aiyé* – 'the world' in the sense of the fallen, evil-ridden world of St John's Gospel and First Epistle. In the Yoruba concept, *aiyé* is the concentration of the power of evil in the world. Here we meet unmitigated evil in its essence, malignant, obstructing, spoiling, out-and-out diabolic.[105] Thus, until we can unravel the problem of evil, the question of the methods and techniques of witchcraft will remain a perplexity to a great extent. However, there is enough experience about witchcraft to enable us to have something of the facts of the situation.

It is generally believed that the guild of witches have their regular meetings and ceremonies in forests or in open places in the middle of the night. The meeting is the meeting of 'souls', 'spirits', of the witches. In several places in Africa, it is believed that the spirits leave the bodies of witches in form of a particular kind of birds. Their main purpose is to work havoc on other human beings; and the operation is the operation of spirits upon spirits, that is, it is the ethereal bodies of the victims that are attacked, extracted, and devoured; and this is what is meant when it is said that witches have sucked the entire blood of the victim. Thus, in the case of witches or their victims, spirits meet spirits, spirits operate upon spirits, while the actual human bodies lie 'asleep' in their homes.

The fact of spirits operating thus on spirits may be interpreted in various ways.

There is no doubt that there are persons of very strong character who can exude their personalities and make them affect other persons. The Yoruba concept of *àṣẹ* – the personality force by which one impresses one's authority or will effectively upon another, or upon a situation – hinges on this. Here lies also the power of the word – the word coming out by force of, and backed by, the personality of the one who utters the word.

In Africa, there are people who possess this ability to exude themselves and impose upon others psychologically or by words. These are people who will go to any length in self-denial and in seeking every means in order to develop their personalities – fasting, abstention from coition and from eating certain things which are believed to be psychically debilitating, and using appropriate medicine to strengthen the inner man ...[106]

The fact of telepathy is to be connected in Africa with that of the exudation of personality. Here, the psychological situation favours effective telepathy very much. The priest, the doctor, or any person of very strong will-power can impose upon the personalities of others psychologically to bless or to curse. The witch with this pervertedly strong will-power always operates psychologically to cause, first psychical, and then physical disasters. The 'compulsion neurosis' so much dwelt on by Sigmund Freud will apply aptly here.

The point here is that of the spirits to be reckoned with according to African belief, those of the witches are of urgent, painful, very often disastrous importance.

There is also the fact of the guardian-spirit or man's double. The belief here is either that the essence of man's personality becomes a sort of split entity which acts as man's spiritual counterpart or double, as among the Yoruba, or Igbo, or that the guardian-spirit is a separate entity as among the Edo. This double is bound up with the issues of man's destiny on earth; that is, destiny depends on how far this entity is in good state itself. The *ori* (Yoruba) or *chi* (Igbo) or *ehi* (Edo) guards one's steps and brings prosperity, or else puts obstacles in one's paths. A husband's double may make or mar the wife's fortune; so a father's or a mother's the children's. Thus, there is a cult of the double, by whatever local name it is called, in most places in Africa. For example, among the Yoruba, *ori-inú* is the essence of being – the essential person, and it also designates the double; the physical head is its symbol. But there may be other symbols, and sacrifices offered to the counterpart may be placed at the cross-roads or at the foot of a sacred tree. When a Yoruba makes an offering to his father's counterpart, the right big toe is the symbol, and when to the mother's double, the left big toe is the symbol. A wife who is dogged by misfortune may be told to make an offering to ọko-ọrun – the spirit-husband, that is, the husband's counterpart.

Persons, animals, or birds are believed to be instruments of possessions by spirits of all descriptions – good or bad, vengeful and helpful. Spirits may cause insanity or diseases, miscarriages in women, or deformity in human beings.

Most diviners are believed to be under possession by spirits when engaged in divination; and doctors claim that they are chosen by

<u>spirits, taught medicine by spirits, and guided in their profession</u> of <u>diagnosis and healing by spirits.</u>

We may appropriately summarize this section by saying that of spirits in Africa, there is no end. On the whole, they are regarded with dread, although it is believed that one can bargain with them or that they can be controlled by magic.

4. Belief in the ancestors

Using the phrase ancestor-worship in its broadest sense as comprehending all worship of the dead, be they of the same blood or not, we reach the conclusion that ancestor-worship is the root of every religion.[107]

This is how Herbert Spencer concludes a sweeping theory about the connection between what he calls ancestor-worship and religion in general. As has been shown earlier, Spencer has not enunciated a new theory: he has only restated the theory with which, generally, the name of the Greek Euhemeros, who lived between 320 and 260 BC, is connected.

Our concern here is not whether or not Spencer's theory is tenable (although it has now generally been exposed as untenable). We are concerned with the way in which the theory has been exploited by certain writers, especially when they are dealing with religion in Africa and other non-European areas of the world.

The first question of importance is, 'Is the term ancestor-worship correct?' That is, do people anywhere *worship* their ancestors? This is a question which may never be fully answered, inasmuch as we do not possess complete data with regard to the practice of man from the dawn of consciousness. <u>It is certain that the irrational fear of</u> <u>the dead is not uncommon and is still with us in every culture.</u> There are people who relate their dreams, their experiences of haunting, or even what they believe to be ocular evidence of the movements or doings of the deceased. Modern sophisticated man may wish to laugh off the reported doing of Marley's ghost in Charles Dickens' *A Christmas Carol*, or to dismiss as puerile stories of experiences of ghosts and of haunted places; but deep down in the minds of thousands of men and women of every level of spiritual or intellectual attainment is the belief or, at least, the persistent notion, that the deceased still have a part to play, for better or for worse, in the lives of the living. For the purpose of practical illustration, we may mention spiritualism – which is a respectable name for man's concern and endeavour to establish communication with the deceased. Spiritualism is growing strong in influence in Europe and America in spite of all that has been written to debunk it – treatises on, for instance, 'the faking of phenomena' in the form of inflated rubber gloves, or clever manipulation in such a way that there is rapping or rocking of the table, or the tricks that could be played with the knees or the elbows. There are those who keep open minds about it and will even allow that 'there is a certain amount of evidence to show that, in certain cases and under strictly guarded conditions, there is possibly some foundation of truth beneath the spiritualists' claims'; and there are those who are faithful devotees of it and will maintain stoutly that it is all true. 'Occultism' in its various forms involves some amount of purported trafficking with the dead.

Thus, there is the general belief that communion and communication are possible between those who are alive on earth and the deceased, and that the latter have the power to influence, help, or molest the former. We may call to mind here the popular story about the Englishman who went to place a wreath on the tomb of a deceased relative at the same time that a Chinese was putting rice on the tomb of his own deceased relative: the Englishman characteristically asked the Chinese, 'My friend, when is your relative going to eat the rice that you are offering?' To which the Chinese promptly replied, 'When yours is smelling your flowers!'

Still, the fact of the relationship between those who remain on earth and the deceased leaves our basic question unanswered, and we therefore have to search further. Should the means by which this relationship is realized be described as 'worship'? Professor H. H. Farmer examines this question and concludes:

The ancestor is a departed spirit who stands in peculiarly close relation to the tribe or the family: the life of the latter has been derived from him, and because he is still in existence he is still in a sense one with it; his favour or disfavour has therefore a sharply focussed relation to it and is more urgently to be sought or avoided. In addition to this, of course, is all that might be brought to the relationship by the sense of social solidarity and of kinship-ties, as well as – on occasion at least – by natural affection and filial piety. The commonly-used phrase 'ancestor-worship' must not mislead us here, nor be allowed to suggest a distinctly religious significance in the cult of ancestors which it does not necessarily possess.[108]

The English word 'worship' is an ambiguous term, as Farmer has pointed out.[109] 'His Worship the Mayor', 'The Worshipful Master' of Freemasonry, and 'Your Worship' used in addressing a judge, all show that the word 'worship' is not confined to the specifically religious.

Those who set up the cult of ancestors inside churches are careful not to use the term 'worship': they choose 'veneration' instead. It is however, needless to say that between worship and veneration in religious buildings or precincts, the dividing line is often only a hair's breadth, the human mind being what it is. Anybody who has watched with discernment this type of 'veneration' in the Roman Catholic Church, the Russian Orthodox Church, or at Westminster Abbey, or at household or wayside shrines in Europe, will appreciate this fact.

In Africa, the first obstacle to the understanding of what is involved in the cult of the ancestors is not so much that foreign investigators see what is called 'ancestor-worship' as connected with religion, but that they often see it as either the very basis of religion, or *the* religion in Africa. Thus, armed with Spencer's theory and being on the sharp look out for 'evidence' to substantiate preconceived theories, they are ever-ready to exaggerate and distort with regard to Africa what is, in fact, a universal phenomenon. It is amusing, and at the same time disappointing, that a person as careful and sympathetic in his approach to culture and religion in Africa as Edwin Smith could be fascinated by such a specious statement as

Akan knowledge of God (Nyame) teaches that He is the Great Ancestor. He is a true high God and manlike ancestor of the first man. As such ancestor He deserves to be worshipped, and is worshipped in the visible ancestral head, the good chief of the community ...[110]

This quotation is from J. B. Danquah's *Akan Doctrine of God*; it is in effect, saying that all that there is to Akan religion is 'ancestor-worship', however it may adorn the ancestor with the masquerade of 'a true high God' (in itself a very obnoxious term!), and that Onyame deserves to be worshipped only because he is a worthy ancestor.

In Genesis 2.7, we read, '... then *Yahweh Elohim* formed man of the dust from the ground, and breathed into his nostrils the breath of life; and man became a living being'. We are not saying that, in consequence of this, *Yahweh Elohim* is the great ancestor, father of Adam and grandfather of Cain and Abel, apparently by physical generation, are we? I know that in Luke 3.23-38, there is a genealogy drawn up backwards; it ends with '... the son of Adam, the son of God.' But no one has ever taken this to mean 'son' by physical generation; <u>it means 'son' in the sense in which in Yoruba we call a person an offspring of a particular divine being to mean the close intimacy of a covenant relationship; in the same sense as we say that Christians are sons of God</u>.

*[handwritten margin note: God not a Father by physical generation *]*

Evans-Pritchard's observation is apposite here:

> Either explicitly or implicitly, explanation of the religion of primitives was made out to hold for the origins of all that was called 'early' religion. ... Thus, as Andrew Lang put it, 'the theorist who believes in ancestor-worship as the key of all creeds will see in Jehovah a developed ancestral ghost, or a kind of fetish-god, attached to a stone – perhaps in the sepulchral stele of some desert sheikh.[111]

There is a mental confusion in this kind of thinking. Here is a case in which we must be careful not to read into any particular word more than it actually means, as we have warned all along in this book. We have many words available to us; it is only a matter of finding and using the suitable ones in proper contexts, rather than overloading any one word with forced meanings. Christians call God Father or even Mother; so are divinities designated father or mother; but there is always a distinction between the divine beings and the pure ancestors. <u>Because God is Father, he does not thereby in African thought become 'demoted' to the rank of ancestor</u>s.

E. Geoffrey Parrinder discusses usefully the topic of ancestral cults in his book, *African Traditional Religion*.[112] He brings together the views of certain writers who have given thought to the subject. These writers include those who think that the gods according to African traditional religion are only ancestors: 'The gods of the Lovedu are their ancestors.' 'The family divinities [of Ba-ila] are ghosts of one's grandfathers.' On the other hand, there are those like Cullen Young who believe that the term 'ancestor-worship' is highly misleading. J. H. Driberg is categorical:

> What we have mistaken for a religious attitude is nothing more than a projection of [the Africans'] social behaviour ... For no African prays to his dead grandfather any more than he 'prays' to his living father. In both cases the words employed are the same: he asks as of right, or he beseeches, or he expostulates with, or he reprimands, or (as the Eastern Ewe word *epode* puts it) he gives an address to, his ancestors, as he would do to the elders

sitting in conclave: but he never uses in this context the words for 'prayer' and 'worship' which are strictly reserved for his religious dealings with the Absolute Power and the divinities. The Latin word *pietas* probably best describes the attitude of Africans to their dead ancestors, as to their living elders.[113]

Parrinder also quotes Dr Kuper as saying of the Swazi:

> Ancestral spirits are not worshipped. Swazi address them in much the same way as they speak to the living, and the word *tsetisa* (to scold) is frequently used to describe the manner of approach. Swazi rarely express gratitude when they think the ancestors are blessing them, and they are more indignant than humble when they find they are being punished ...

On both sides of the argument, there appears to be much wishful thinking. On the one hand, those who are chronically addicted to 'ancestor-worship' as the religion in Africa or hold categorically that Africans worship their ancestors are victims of theory-fulfilment. Very often, they are taking appearance for reality or are arguing exclusively from one particular angle of a rather complex phenomenon.

On the other hand, those who say categorically that Africans do not worship their ancestors are forgetting the complex nature of the working of the human mind. Worship and veneration, as we have observed, are psychologically closer than next door to each other: the emotional indicator is always trembling between the two, swinging to the one or the other in accordance with the emotional pressure or the spiritual climate of the moment. This is something that happens anywhere, everywhere, in the world, and with peoples at every level of development.

A book entitled *The Deliverance of Sister Cecilia*[114] depicts an aspect of the persecution of the church. The heroine is a hospital nurse, a nun who has chosen for herself a patron saint to whom she is very devoted. Throughout the book which eulogizes Cecilia for the faith, courage, and perseverance which she maintains unflinchingly until her miraculous deliverance, her appeals and supplications and complaints are directed only to her patron saint, thus creating the strong impression that salvation for her begins and ends with that saint. At the end of all her troubles, it is the patron saint that she has to thank for her deliverance.

One has only to look at the set-up in certain churches to appreciate the fact that a hard and fast line cannot be drawn between what may be described as worship in the religious sense and what may be called veneration within the setting of religion. It often becomes the more difficult to distinguish between the two where, in churches, chapels or shrines are dedicated to saints or hero-ancestors and people meet there for what cannot be described by any other name except worship.

For example, in the *Church Times* of Friday, 1 June, 1962, the following item appeared:

Three thousand church people are expected to take part tomorrow in a pilgrimage to Westminster Abbey which has been planned by the Church Union and the Dean and Chapter of Westminster to encourage the use of the shrine of St Edward the Confessor as a place of prayer.

Led by the president of the Church Union (the Bishop of Crediton), the pilgrims will assemble at Lambeth Palace in the afternoon and then march to the Abbey for Evensong, at which Fr David, Father-Minister of the Society of St Francis, will preach. Some will have walked through the night from parts of Essex in order to be present ...

A rota of clergy will be on duty at the shrine of St Edward (which is behind the High Altar) from 9.30 a.m. until 6.30 p.m. in order to conduct prayers ...

Not unusually, in a situation like this, the human mind plays a trick with itself by choosing that by which for the moment it reaches easy spiritual or emotional satisfaction.

So, some do worship

The situation of alternation between pure veneration and what has, in fact, become an act of worship should be appreciated with regard to Africa. It is definitely wrong to say that 'ancestor-worship' constitutes religion in Africa: and the term itself is questionable; very much so. Nevertheless, there is no doubt that caution must be exercised in making a statement about the total situation involved. Among the Igbo in Nigeria, the morning ritual begins with the invocation: 'Chukwu (Deity), come and eat kola-nut; Ala (Earth Goddess), come and eat kola-nut; Ndiche (Ancestors), come and eat kola-nut.' This shows indisputably that the ancestors are assigned a significant place in rituals. The Yoruba use the same word, bọ, indiscriminately with reference to the worship of Deity or divinities, as well as with reference to the making of offerings to the ancestors. Here we see a justification for M. J. Herskovit's observation:

Speaking from a strictly theoretical point of view, the ancestors must also be included in the Dahomean religious system, where they comprise the third category of gods. For though the ancestral cult, when looked at in terms of its setting in the total configuration of Dahomean life, must be treated as an aspect of social organization, yet, in the final analysis, it is as fundamental a part of religious life as it is of social life . . .[115]

Africans make a distinction between Deity, the divinities, and the ancestors: Deity and the divinities are distinctly, out-and-out, of the super-sensible world, while the ancestors are of the living persons' kith and kin. The ancestors are related to the living community in a way that cannot be claimed for Deity or the divinities who are definitely of a different order. The ancestors are regarded still as heads and parts of the families or communities to which they belonged while they were living human beings: for what happened in consequence of the phenomenon called death was only that the family life of this earth has been extended into the after-life or super sensible world. The ancestors remain, therefore, spiritual superintendents of family affairs and continue to bear their titles of relationship like 'father' or 'mother'.

Nevertheless, it is of importance for the assessment of their status to know that they are no longer living human beings according to earthly assessment. They have become spirits – spirits whose sphere is the spirit world reserved for good ancestors and in consequence of which communion and communication with them is possible only at the spiritual level. A Yoruba dirge says:

> My father (or mother) is become a spirit of Olufẹ[116]
> who wears palm fronds;
> My father (or mother) is become a spirit of Olufẹ
> who wears palm fronds as clothes.

That is, the deceased are truly members of the families on earth; but they are no longer of the same fleshly order as those who are still actually living in the flesh on earth. They are closely related to this world; but are no longer ordinary mortals. Because they have crossed the borderland between this world and the supersensible world, entering and living in the latter, they have become freed from the restrictions imposed by the physical world. They can now come to abide with their folk on earth invisibly, to aid or hinder them, to promote prosperity or cause adversity. To some extent, they are intermediaries between Deity or the divinities and their own children: this is a continuation of their earthly function whereby they combined the headships of the families or communities with the office of family or community priests or priestesses. During their earthly days, it was their duty to help, to ensure domestic peace and the well-being of the community, to distribute favours, to exercise discipline or enforce penalties, to be guardians of community ethics and prevent anything that might cause disruption. In Africa, it is the general belief that a living father or a living mother, by virtue of his fatherhood or her motherhood, is endowed with the power to bless or curse an offspring effectively. That is why every passage of life and every undertaking by the offspring require parental blessing. It is believed that parental dissatisfaction or displeasure may upset an undertaking or cause it to fail. It is no wonder, then, that it is believed that such power in a father or a mother who has passed into the ancestral world has become infinitely enhanced and continues to be actively effective accordingly.

The ancestors are factors of cohesion in African society. This is a fact well illustrated in the sacred stools which are the ancestral symbols of the Ashanti, especially the Golden Stool. R. S. Rattray describes the Golden Stool as 'the shrine and symbol of the national soul'; the great umbrella covering the Stool when brought out in a procession, or during an open-air ceremonial is known as *katamanso* – 'the covering of the nation'.[117] It is the supreme symbol of the ancestral genius of the nation and is thus that which gives the nation a sense of cohesion.

Because the ancestors are no longer in the world of ordinariness, the way they are approached must be different from the ordinary approach to them during the time of their earthly life. They are spirits and are approached as spirits, even though they are spirits with a difference in consequence of their family ties with their earthly folk.

In Yorubaland and among the Edo of Nigeria, the festivals of the ancestors have in certain cases become definitely religious festivals. The cults of Orò and Egúngún and what in Benin is called Agwe are illustrations of this fact. Orò or Egúngún[118] represent either the fact of the spirit-ancestors in general or particular ancestors. Agwe prefixes either an ancestral festival or the festival of Osanobwa (Deity). The Odwira ceremony among the Ashanti is clearly a festival in honour of the ancestors; but there is no doubt that certain items connected with it can only be described in terms of a religious ritual.

The Friday following was a *Fofie*, i.e. a sacred Friday which comes round once every forty-three days; this was a day of purification for all. The king and his court, dressed in their best, and preceded by the Golden Stool and the ancestral blackened stools, the *odwira suman*, the *Bosommuru suman*, the shrines of the gods, together with all the paraphernalia of the household, stools, chairs, drums, horns, etc., were marched to the stream, near Akyeremade. Here the war-chair ... was set up, and upon this was placed the Golden Stool. The numerous blackened stools, the shrines of ancestral spirits, were held in front of the bearers, each by its respective stool-carrier.

The king held in his hand a branch of the plant called *Bosommuru adwira*; this he dipped into a large brass basin that had been filled with sacred water, and with it sprinkled the Golden Stool, repeating as he did so the following words:

> 'Friday, Stool of Kings, I sprinkle water upon you,
>   may your power return sharp and fierce
>
> .   .   .   .
>
> The edges of the years have met ...
> May the nation prosper.
> May the women bear children.
> May the hunters kill meat.
> We who dig for gold, let us get gold to dig, and grant that
>   I get some for the upkeep of my kingship.'[119]

As we conclude this section we must not forget the fact of the apotheosis of certain ancestors which is an indisputable fact all over Africa. It must be observed, however, that in almost every case, an ancestor became a divinity only by absorbing the attributes of an original divinity. There is usually a foundation cult with which the strong person had been closely associated as a priest or king-priest before his death. This, as we have observed elsewhere,[120] is the explanation of Sàngǒ, a human king who became deified with the attributes of Jàkǔta, the original Yoruba solar and thunder divinity.

Our conclusion is that while technically Africans do not put their ancestors, as ancestors, on the same footing with Deity or the divinities, there is no doubt that the ancestors receive veneration that may become so intense as to verge on worship or even become worship. Certainly, the cults of the ancestors do not constitute African traditional religion; and it is a gross error to equate them with the religion. The proper meaning of the ancestral cults derives from the belief of Africans that death does not write 'finish' to life, that the family or community life of this earth has only become extended into the life beyond in consequence of the 'death' of the ancestors. Thus the cults are a means of communion and communication between those who are living on earth and those who have gone to live in the spirit world of the ancestors.

[margin note: Note the variety of views]

In conclusion, two questions must be settled: Who are qualified to be ancestors? Have the ancestors a permanent 'abode' in the after-life?

In answer to the first question, African belief is generally that only good people become ancestors after they have received the 'Well done!' judgment of Deity or of 'the court of the ancestors'. Bad or wicked people will be cast into 'a place of rubbish heap', the 'hell' of midden, or into the 'hell' of potsherds. In some cases, they become random wanderers in a place of 'no abode'.

Generally, it is only those who have offspring and become old before their departure who become ancestors. But it appears that even those who depart in the prime of life or relatively young can become ancestors, provided they have offspring before their decease.

It appears also that there are those who although they are not strictly qualified in the way described above, may be admitted into the spirit world of the deceased because they are good and their days on earth are done, even though they may be young and childless. In certain areas of Yorubaland and Igboland, belief in the continued existence and influence of this category of deceased persons is symbolized in *Egúngún, Orò, Mmo, Ayaka*[121] which are various manifestations of the fact that those who have passed into the spirit world of departed members of the community are still a part of the social structure.

In answer to the second question we shall examine, first, the question of reincarnation. In African belief, there is no reincarnation in the classical sense. One can only speak of partial or, more precisely, apparent reincarnation, if the word must be used at all. There is the belief in certain areas that ancestors return in one or several children in the family. This, I have discussed elsewhere:

The specific belief of the Yoruba about those who depart from this world is that once they have entered After-Life, there they remain, and there the survivors and their children after them can keep unbroken intercourse with them, especially if they have been good persons while on earth and were ripe for death when they died.

Nevertheless, we find ourselves confronted with the paradox involved in the belief of the Yoruba that the deceased persons do 'reincarnate' in their grandchildren and great-grandchildren. In the first place, it is believed that in spite of this reincarnation, the deceased continue to live in After-Life; those who are still in the world can have communion with them, and they are there with all their ancestral qualities unimpaired. Secondly, it is believed that they do 'reincarnate', not only in one grandchild or great-grandchild, but also in several contemporary grandchildren and great-grandchildren who are brothers and sisters and cousins, aunts and nephews, uncles and nieces, *ad infinitum*. Yet, in spite of these repeated 'rebirths' (which should be rather exhausting), the deceased contrive to remain in full life and vigour in the After-Life.[122]

The Nupe meet the problem of the apparent reincarnation with their conception that each person has two souls. After death, one of the souls goes and resides permanently with the Maker, while the other one reincarnates. It seems that an interpretation of this delicate topic is that what Africans are trying to express is that the genius of the family never dies and that it keeps manifesting itself in unbroken sequence in offspring.

Secondly, the life of the ancestors in the after-life is a reality: it does not depend on the remembrance of them by those who are living on earth. They have their own independent existence; and their being is in no way a fulfilment of the theory that 'To live in hearts we leave behind is not to die'.[123] It is believed that they complain about, and even punish, dereliction of filial duties on the part of their offspring; but they do not for any reason fade into nothing or lapse into any kind of durational retirement. In the invocation of ancestors in certain African localities, the liturgy embraces those remembered and unremembered, those known and unknown. It is often said specifically, 'We cannot remember all of you by name, nevertheless, we invoke you all.' Further, ancestors connected with certain professions like medicine, crafts, or priesthood are mentioned as far back as the first one who initiated the practice. So also are those who were the aboriginal heads of clans. During annual festivals, or special rituals, ancestors are traced as far back as the beginning of things. This is a fact well substantiated in the practices of Yoruba and of the Anlo-Ewe people of Ghana. This may, of course, be difficult in cases where racial memory has been disturbed or disrupted in one of the ways described above; but what is happening to those who are on earth should not be projected to those who are resting permanently in the place of no-change of the after-life. In fact, the place where the ancestors live permanently is the 'paradise' for which Africans yearn as their final home – a 'heaven' in which they have a happy, unending reunion with their folk who are waiting for them on the other side. The belief of the Dahomeans will be an illuminating example in this connection: when a person leaves this earth, he makes a final journey to the after-life. He crosses over three rivers, and clambers up a mountain to reach the valley where his forbears live. There he takes his place as the lowest, sitting at their feet on a stool. He is able to fill a permanent place when the burial ceremony on earth is completed.[124]

5. The practice of magic and medicine[125]

From all that we have discussed or discovered so far, it is clear that since the dawn of consciousness, man has been confronted with a sense of need with which he knows that his own unaided power cannot cope. The complications and riddles of life have been such as urge upon him the need for succour, for deliverance, and for mastery over environmental circumstances.

He recognizes that behind phenomena is a power 'wholly other' than himself. His approach to this power depends on his conception of the power and the way which he believes would lead to the goal of his soul's sincere desire. There are two principal ways in which he has tried to avail himself of the resources of this power for the fulfilment of his needs. Where he recognizes the power as a divine being with whom man may have communion and communication, his approach has been one of submission and appeal; where he conceives of the power only as the reservoir of elemental forces, he has sought to tap and harness it and make it subserve his own end. The principle upon which he works in this case is one of technique, seeking to secure the proper means to the end that he may have control over these elemental forces. Magic is that second course by which man seeks to reach the goal of achievements of self-effort and his own independent devices. It will, however, be deluding ourselves that, anywhere in the world, man always makes a clear distinction in practice between these two courses.

With particular reference to Africa, we cannot discuss magic and medicine with understanding, however, except as seen in the light of religion. This is especially so as here we are discussing it as an element in the structure of a religion. It will therefore be proper at this stage to attempt definitions.

When we were trying to define religion, we saw how A. C. Bouquet reached the conclusion that *religio* came to mean 'a communion between the human and the superhuman' with the implication of 'a mixed relationship between the human self and some

non-human entity' which may be variously designated.[126] The definition by J. B. Pratt we considered to be an improvement on this –
'the serious and social attitude of individuals or communities towards
the powers which they conceive as having ultimate control over their
interests and destinies', 'the attitude of the self towards an object
in which the self genuinely believes': an attitude towards the
Determiner of Destiny, which must not be mechanical, nor coldly
intellectual, but must have such quality as we expect in a relationship of responsive love.[127] A definition which we consider more
appropriate and comprehensive than the above is: 'Religion in
essence ... is the means by which the Divine Spirit and man's
essential self communicate.'[128]

Thus, religion is essentially a matter of reciprocal relationship in
which man depends upon Deity for the fulfilment of personal, basic
needs which are more than material (although those are included)
with the belief that the transcendental Being on whom he depends
is capable of fulfilling those needs. Religion implies trust, dependence
and submission. At its basis is a sense of appeal and submission to
a divine intelligence.[129] And its motto is, therefore, 'Thy will be
done'.

Magic, by definition, is an attempt on the part of man to tap and
control the supernatural resources of the universe for his own benefit. It is a 'resort ... to supercausation by means of spell and rite'[130]
and rests 'on the manipulation and enforcement of supernatural
benefits ...'[131] Magic serves man's egocentricity and is for him a
short cut to spiritual bliss. We can take with reservation a definition
by J. B. Pratt that 'magic includes those supernatural devices em-
ployed to gain one's end without the help of spirits or gods ...[132]
We have taken this with reservation because, as we shall see, magic,
like religion, takes account of the transcendental. There is no
question, however, but that it operates on the belief that supernatural power can be controlled by mechanical techniques devised
or discovered by man.[133] Its motto, therefore, is 'My will be
done.'

Now to the question of the relation between religion and magic.
Are they the same in origin? Does one spring from the other? And
which of the two is older? These questions are all of a piece and
have been age-long. An all-embracing answer is that they both arise
out of man's sense of need, and it is very probably on this that some
scholars have based the theory that religion and magic have a

common origin. J. B. Pratt maintains that they sprang from the same matrix:

> The felt relation of the individual to the cosmic power and the responses to which it led developed ... into two interlocking though distinguishable phenomena, which may be called private magic and private worship.[134]

Franz Cumont says, 'Magic is religion in origin, and always remains a bastard sister of religion', as they both grow together.[135] John Oman thinks that magic is bad religion:

> As evolution and degeneration in the physical life are in the same environment, and the difference only concerns the uses to which it is put, so with the spiritual ... At its creative stage [magic] is religion because its effective setting is sacred tradition, its feeling is at least akin to the sense of the holy, and its power of the nature of the Supernatural ... Magic might even be described as mysticism in the fetters of fixed idea, because both alike work with the sense of the holy as awe-inspiring in itself ...[136]

There are those, however, who think that religion sprang from magic. According to Pliny,

> Magic ... embraces the three acts that most rule the human mind, medicine, religion, and mathematics – a triple chain which enslaves mankind.[137]

Then there is the school of thought which thinks that they are distinct both in origin, and in character. E. O. James believes:

> Magic is not ... the disreputable sister of religion. It is essentially a child of its own tradition, living its own life and effective in its own pedigree.[138]

It is this distinction that J. B. Pratt seeks to establish when he says:

> At some higher stages religious cult, though still intertwined at times with magical rites, is at least fairly distinguishable from magic ... the religious ceremony seeks to gain its end through the assistance of spirits or gods, while magic aims at its goal through no such indirect channel, but by immediate control of the mysterious powers of the universe ... the religious attitude is always in some degree social, whereas the attitude of magic may be purely mechanical.[139]

The question which of the two is older is also bound up with the question of their possible origins. And here also we have contradictory opinions. E. O. James quotes a few authorities in this connection. Frazer asserts that religion is 'the despair of magic and merely succeeds it in time'. This is in agreement with Hegel who declared that magic preceded religion. To this opinion Marrett subscribes by saying that prayer came as the magician became frustrated in the achievement of his end; as he came to personify the instruments and symbols of his magical performance, then 'the imperative passes into the optative', and spell became prayer. On the other hand, Jevon says that belief in the supernatural, which is the characteristic mark of religion, was prior to magic, and that magic was only a degradation or a relapse in the evolution of religion.[140] John Oman lent his support to this when he said that

> Magic, when it ceases to be religion and becomes a routine of superstition, ... when it no more stirs the feelings which originally produced it, but is a purely formal and ossifying ritual, ... is moral as well as intellectual stagnation ... [141]

We agree with those who say that religion is prior to magic: it would appear that those who think to the contrary are ignoring the element of the *mysterium tremendum et fascinans*. It cannot be doubted that this was the primordial or elemental basis of belief. And this is something before which man is given no time for immediate reflection with regard to a course of action. Spontaneity was the nature of man's reaction of abasement and submission. By its nature and definition, magic presupposes reflection and planning in order to secure an expected end. There can be no doubt that religion operated in this same way later on; but that is precisely why religion in fact often tends towards magic. Moreover, our judgment in this matter must be moderated by the fact that none of us were there at the beginning of things and we must therefore admit that we cannot have a categorical knowledge with regard to their origins.

This much is certain. Religion and magic have been very closely connected from the earliest times. In accounting for this close connection the Pythagoreans enunciated the principle that all souls were homegeneous, and that therefore worship virtually consisted only in the science and art of using certain means – sacrifice, formulae, and ceremonies – so that the gods being carried away in the current of events might change that current in man's favour. They held that man had two souls, one emanating from the Deity, and a natural one in affinity with the natural beings: on the strength of these, man was able to exercise influence on other souls and to exercise magical power on nature. Besides, the residence of the two souls in one and the same person enabled him to alternate easily between worship and magic, or even to commingle both.[142]

There is no doubt also that both religion and magic recognize the transcendental power, the supernatural, a power beyond man, and made this the basis of operation. 'I do think with Plato,' said Apuleius, 'that between gods and men, in nature and in places intermediary, there are certain divine powers, and these preside over all divination and the miracles of magicians.[143] In the early times 'man never doubted that power is the monopoly of the Deity'; '... appeal to the gods is based upon the fundamental principle of all magic. Magical rites and ceremonies have no inherent power of their own. They depend for their efficacy upon the supernatural power which is utilized by the magician.'[144] This is still the belief in most of the world today, and to this is to be added the increasingly recognized fact that science can never achieve *all* that man originally expected of the Deity.[145]

The difference between religion and magic may be found in their individual attitudes and techniques. As we have observed, the approach of man in religion is one of submission and appeal – there is always a prevailing sense of an infinitely higher power to whom man is subject and under whose domination and control are all the affairs of life. The religious man proceeds, therefore, from the premise that the affairs of this world are not in his own hands and that the ultimate issues of rituals do not depend on what he does or says so much as on the will of the Determiner of destiny. Thus, when the worshipper says 'Amen' [Àṣẹ] to prayers, he is saying by implication, 'I leave my life and its affairs in your hand' – the hand that controls all destiny.[146]

Magic, on the other hand, is self-contradictory in its attitude and approach. Although it admits the fact that man needs divine power to aid his inadequacy for certain issues of life, that, inevitably, he needs a supply from the supramundane resource of power, it only seeks to wrest the power for its own end. It seeks to serve no other will but its own. The purpose for which it sets out is to control the process of nature 'by sheer force of spell and enchantments'. For this reason, Freud thinks that magic disregards spirits: it can be used in dealing with spirits, its set aim being the subjection of natural phenomena to the will of man, for the protection of the individual from his enemies and from dangers, and to give the individual power to injure his enemy.[147] It would, however, be more accurate to say that magic seeks to bring spirits under control, or to persuade spirits by coercion.

Further, while essentially religion is for the individual and social well-being of man, magic could be for man's well-being or for man's undoing. It can serve for social benefit or be anti-social. Magic can be licit or illicit.

With regard to techniques, the difference may be summarized as follows. In religion, the technique is through a system of rituals which create an atmosphere of worship and constitute a means of approach, the end of which is that worship may be an offering, and a communion between Deity and man. Religion speaks to one who hears, one who listens, one who accepts, and one who blesses. In magic the technique consists in spells and enchantments made up of secret or archaic language or cryptic terminology, and expressions which may be utterly unintelligible even to the operator – but calculated to have the efficacy of fulfilling the will of man.

Thus, while religion addresses itself to Deity in a spirit of appeal and submission, magic goes by the operative factors based on the principles of similarity, contiguity, and unusualness.

It will be necessary for the purpose of elucidation to explain these principles. The principle of similarity is based on 'similarity between the act performed and the result expected'. Hence the term 'imitative' or 'homoepathic' magic. Although, according to John Oman, Marrett objects to an unreserved application of the term on the ground that 'to suppose that first there is a belief that "like produces like"', and that this guarantees symbolic ritual is ... putting the cart before the horse ... since no savage rite ... is purely mimetic', there can be no doubt but that actual practice justifies something of the term. There is, for example, the universal practice of making the effigy of an enemy and either sticking needles in the wax or clay image, or placing the effigy in a hot oven or fire, with the belief that the enemy would suffer the pain of needle-pricks as long as the needles remain in the effigy, or a burning agony as long as the effigy remains in the oven or fire. A love-magic practised among the Yoruba of Nigeria is a simple one. The ingredients are compounded with the woman in mind; when it is ready, the preparation is stuck on the face of a looking-glass, an incantation with the name of the woman being pronounced during the operation. The belief is that any time the woman looks at a mirror, she would invariably see the man's face; she would see the man's face also in her dreams and maybe in trances. Gradually, her resistance would be weakened through this constant mirror-presence of the man and she would eventually consent to the suit.

The principle of contiguity works on the notion that 'things once ② contiguity in contact with each other would continue to interact even when the contact is broken'. On this notion is based the belief behind the practice of lacerating an enemy's footprint with a poisoned knife, or pricking it with a needle that has been dipped in poison: the belief is that the foot which had made the print would thus be effectively poisoned. A person's chewing-stick or a woman's menstrual pad, according to the belief, may be used to the same end. On the same principle, the magic may be used to a good end.

It is also believed that the magic of unusualness would, for ③ unusualness example, have the desired effect of warding off or foiling an opponent's evil plan. For example, supposing a person fears being called to account about a misdeed, he could perform this kind of magic in order to ward off trial and judgment. A ritual believed to be effective towards this end is as follows: a shallow hole is dug in the earth, a quantity of palm oil is poured into it; immediately in front of the hole is spread a new white piece of cloth; the client is asked to squat over the hole and ease himself: while easing himself directly into the palm oil, he makes sure that his urine falls on the white cloth; the operative words in the incantation which accompanies the process are 'I, X, have eased myself into palm oil and urinated on white cloth; the case under reference will never come up unless the plaintiff or prosecutor eases himself into palm oil and urinates on white cloth'. The implication here is that none of those concerned on the opposite side would go out of their way and engage in a practice which normally would be considered mad.

The essential distinction between religion and magic may be summarized in the words of M. J. Field:

> Religion usually postulates a deity who is good and who demands goodness, whereas magic is of two kinds, good and bad. Magic, unlike deities, makes no moral demands and, above all, will operate automatically and inexorably for any operator, provided only that he operates correctly.[148]

She is writing on the beliefs of 'rural Ghana'.

Nevertheless, we must admit the fact that, more often than not, religion and magic are intermingled or even confused with each other in practice. For example, prayer often becomes so repetitive that efficacy comes to be attached to the correct repetition rather than to the spirit and content of prayer. It is also believed that certain elements of prayers must be repeated a stated number of times, the whole prayers a prescribed number of times a day at prescribed hours, special divine names called a number of times in a certain order. There are Christian denominations which believe that certain rituals must be said in a particular language or in archaic or cryptic formulae. In Islam, all the main rituals must still be universally said in Arabic. In each of these cases, it is believed that efficacy depends on the form rather than the spirit; and this is magic.

In African traditional religion, rituals have come to follow certain set patterns in consequence of their long traditions. And these patterns have in many cases been mistakenly accepted as the very essence of the rituals.

> In Yoruba worship ... a priest approaches his appointed task with awe, ever conscious of the dreadful fact that if the wrong step should be taken or the right order of service be not followed, everything might be lost and his own life and the life of the worshippers jeopardized ... Most of the dances ... are of fixed patterns and must be done correctly – which foot goes forward first, which movements of the hands and body accompany it, which turns are taken next, and how many times each component of the pattern is to be repeated ... This correctness is more than a matter of form ...; it is a sacred obligation the default in which, the Yoruba believe, may be ruinous to the efficaciousness of the ritual.[149]

Thus although African traditional beliefs recognize a clear distinction between what is man-made and what is of the spirit, the intermingling of religion and magic is always present in every ritual, in the fact that certain things *must* be done according to definite prescriptions or certain words said repetitively and in a particular order. There is also a definite practice of magic connected with the cults of certain divinities. The divinity Èṣù among the Yoruba, Agwu or Ekwensu of the Igbo, in Nigeria could be invoked as a tutelary divinity in connection with licit or illicit magic.[150] Ọsànyìn, tutelary divinity of doctors among the Yoruba, also serves the cause of magic. At the same time, most divinities do not regard magic in the sense of fetish favourably. One of the praise titles of Ṣọpọ̀ná, the divinity whose scourge is smallpox, is 'One who causes medicine or magic designed for wicked ends to be thrown away'.[151] This is true of the Dahomean counterpart, Sagbata. Tano, the archdivinity in Ashanti, hates magic. '*Suman* (fetishes) [it is said] spoil the gods'.[152] M. J. Field observes that in rural Ghana, strictly consistent priests do not look favourably on magic and the possession of suman. To use or even possess a bad suman is a major sin, punishable by deity with death. Good suman is not encouraged but tolerated.[153]

On the whole, it is the general admission of African traditional religion that while magical elements often intrude themselves into the practice of religion, magic in the sense of 'fetish' is not really necessary for those who are upright. In the strict sense, the aid of magic is sought by those who are not sure of their character or those who are positively wicked. This is why in African thought 'black magic' is always associated with witchcraft and sorcery, and considered anti-social. A Yoruba saying is apposite here:

> One who sleeps girdled with knives
> and pillows his head in a quiver.
> It is a person's character that drives him
> to dabble in the magic of immunity.[154]

Thus, we have grounds to believe that licit or illicit magic as practised in Africa is due to weakness in man's concept of God, or the weakness of man's faith, or impatience on the part of the man, which all come to practically the same thing. Religion does not need magic to keep it going; and man's self-reliance by way of magic will fail him and does fail him. Here, in fact, we find some truth in the saying that Africans turn to Deity when all other aids have failed them. 'In the final analysis, man can only appeal and supplicate', it is in submission that he finds *shalom*. 'For thus said the Lord God, the Holy One of Israel, "In returning and rest you shall be saved; in quietness and in trust shall be your strength".'[155] Essentially, this is also the belief of Africans.

Now, we shall see how medicine fits into the pattern.

MEDICINE

The *Concise Oxford Dictionary* defines medicine as 'Art of restoring and preserving health'. It is logical that in the definition, the preservation of health is mentioned after the mention of its restoration, because man must have learnt that health could be lost or impaired only through practical experience. The purpose of medicine is essentially to help the body to help itself. It is curative, in that it helps the body to return to its normal state; it is preventive, in that it builds up resistance against infection by toning up its organs.

In the ancient world, medicine was closely associated with religion, because it was the possession of a divine healer who dispensed it through the agency of a priest. According to Babylonian beliefs, Ea, the father of Marduk, 'is the great physician of humanity who has under his control all the remedies needed to cure diseases inflicted by demons'.[156] In Rome (as in Egypt) 'men and women slept in the temples of Isis and Serapis ... to recover their health'.[157] Of the many illustrations available from the ancient world we shall quote this telling one.

In the priesthood of Poplius Aelius Antiochus.
I, Marcus Julius Apellas of Idrias and Mylasa, was sent for by the God (Asklepios) for I was a chronic invalid and suffered from dyspepsia ... When I reached the Temple, he directed me to keep my head covered for two days; ... I was to eat bread and cheese, parsley with lettuce, to wash myself without help, to practise running, to drink citron-lemonade ... to pour wine into hot water before I got in ... to offer in public sacrifices to Asklepios, Epione and the Eleusinian goddesses, and to take milk with honey. When for one day I had drunk milk alone, the god said to put honey in the milk to make it digestible.
When I called upon the god to cure me more quickly, I thought it was as if I had anointed my whole body with mustard and salt, and had come out of the sacred hall and gone in the direction of the bath-house, while a small child was going before me holding a smoking censer. The priest said to me: 'Now you are cured, but you must pay up the fees for your treatment.' I acted according to the vision, and when I rubbed myself with salt and moistened mustard, I felt the pain still, but when I had bathed, I suffered no longer ... The god also touched my right hand and my breast ...
As I prolonged my stay in the Temple, the god told me to use dill along with olive-oil for my headaches ... After I used the olive-oil, I was cured of headaches. For swollen glands the god told me to use a cold gargle, when I consulted him about it, and he ordered the same treatment for inflamed tonsils. He bade me inscribe this treatment, and I left the Temple in good health and full of gratitude to the god.[158]

The point of this quotation is that whatever happened through the agency of the priest, or priest-doctor, in the Temple, the patient believed that healing came directly from the god. And here we have the origin of what we know as hospitals or infirmaries. When in the fourth century AD, Fabiola, a Roman lady, founded in Rome what is described as the first Christian hospital and St Basil founded another one of great celebrity in Caesarea, they were in fact carrying on the healing work which had been a concomitant of religion from time immemorial.

In the passage quoted above, one may discern the spirit which gave birth to magic. Apellas said '... I called upon the god to cure me more quickly ...' This might be an urgent importunity, man still casting himself upon divine mercies; but it might also be a coercion to get the divinity to do what otherwise he would not have done or would have been tardy in doing.

Magic certainly finds a place in the practice of medicine. In fact the two can become so interlinked as to make it difficult to know where one ends and the other begins. This is because both are connected with the transcendental power. Ea, whom the Babylonians believed to be the great physician of humanity, is also said to play the most prominent role in the incantation texts.[159]

It would be this apparently inevitable intermingling of magic and medicine in Africa that has led certain investigators to conclude that the term 'medicine' should be used to embrace both. For example, Nadel uses 'medicine' in this way and justifies himself by saying,

The Nupe word [translated] 'medicine' ... is ambiguous in that it refers both to skills of an esoteric and miraculous kind, and to healing practices which are public, profane, and acquired by ordinary learning ...

Further:

Let me say first of all that 'medicine' is the literal translation of the vernacular term, which is applied not only to 'magic' substances but also to medicinal herbs or drugs of any kind, native as well as European, whose properties are assessed essentially empirically.[160]

To this, in general, M. J. Field would agree:

Magic or, as it is more often called in West Africa, 'medicine', always involves concrete apparatus ... and a ritual in which this apparatus is handled. There is no activity in life which cannot be assisted by medicine. A hunter can medicine his gun and his bullets to make them unerring, his dog to make it fleet, himself to make him invisible.[161]

In Africa, by and large, the oral traditions have it that the basis of medicine is religion, inasmuch as it came directly from the Supreme Deity, and operated through a tutelary divinity or spirits. Nadel argues that Nupe belief contradicts this general conception. He thinks that the Nupe do not think of medicine as being part of the primordial gift of God. It exists through man's endeavour. Nadel has probably misunderstood the situation. It is significant that he found out that among the Nupe, 'In preparing or administering "medicine" the name of Soko (God) is mentioned ...' and that medicine is applied with reference to God. Further, he admits, 'On one plane, there is an empirical "normality", valid for all ordinary intents and purposes. On another, this normality is part of divine creation which includes, with the natural order of things, also that mystic order of which ritual is an item.'[162] Under this reference, he includes medicine.

According to R. S. Rattray, the Akan have the saying that 'If God gave you sickness, he also gave you medicine.'[163] Among the Yoruba, the tutelary divinity of medicine is Ọsányìn, believed to be the younger brother of Ọrunmila, the oracle divinity, the divine consultant with regard to everything related to human destiny. Agwu among the Igbo holds the divine portfolio of medicine. From the tutelary divinity the doctor receives his call to be a doctor, and he therefore practises his science always with reference to the divine healer. Besides, every divinity has in his possession a particular set of remedies for the care of his 'children'. A Yoruba supplicatory hymn goes as follows:

> Father of children (our father)!
> Prepare medicine for children (us);
> Children (we) have no medicine.

It is also significant that more often than not, the collection of ingredients and the dispensing and application of medicine are accompanied by some form of ritual.

Invocations proper also have their place in *cigbe* (medicine) practice. The *cigbeni* (doctor) ... may add some new medicine to those already known ... And whenever he discovers or invents a new remedy, he must perform a sacrifice ... speaking thus – 'God, the medicine that has been prepared, here it is. May the medicine be successful. I am sacrificing to Kpara, I am sacrificing to Twana Malu, I am sacrificing to Twako Dzana.'[164]

The mention of invocation of ancestors in connection with the practice of medicine is a common feature in the practice of medicine in many parts of Africa. It is an accepted practice that apart from God and/or the divinity, the ancestors who first practised medicine or who were past masters and teachers of medicine must be given due honour. It is believed that this makes still more for the efficacy of medicine. Thus in Ilé-Ifẹ̀, the Sacred City of the Yoruba, Elèṣìjẹ̀, the first doctor and ancestral genius of medicine, is always invoked.

Traditional doctors in Africa often claim that they are taught medicine by divinities or, more generally, in dreams or in trances, or during meetings with spirits in forests. There was a Yoruba doctor named Àjànàkŭ, a man very well versed in Yoruba pharmacopoeia. This man claimed to have been carried away by the whirlwind into the world of spirits where he remained for seven years, feeding on alligator pepper and being taught medicine. His deformity he attributed to the twisting of his body during his painful ride in the whirlwind. Àjànàkǔ certainly had a phenomenal power of memory. Whatever may be the truth of his story, there is no doubt that it emphasizes <u>the generally accepted belief that spirits do teach medicine to men of their own choice whom they have called to be doctors</u>. It is, of course, to be taken along with this that 'observations of nature and the discovery of causal links are certainly at the root of many magical (and medicinal) procedures'. One fact which Àjànàkǔ's story underlines is that a really good African doctor is usually a person who lives close to nature and has the opportunity of close observation even of the medical habits of animals and birds.

Nadel, I believe, misunderstands the connection between ritual and actual medicine.

At the same time the procedure belies its own efficacy ... For there one employs a 'medicine' which is in itself automatically powerful ... yet one also prays – 'May God cause ...'; the prayer simply duplicates the other features in the ritual performance.[165]

<u>The point of the ritual is simply that unconsecrated medicine has no meaning for Africans</u>. That is why divine and ancestral sanctions are considered necessary before and during the preparation and application of medicine. This is also the reason why, in cases of serious ailments. European medicine without augmentation with the traditional remedy appears to Africans by and large as inadequate. It is common knowledge that relatives of patients who are admitted to hospitals 'smuggle' in for them medicine obtained from traditional doctors. And it not infrequently happens that African doctors trained in the European methods advise relatives of patients in hospitals, 'This is not a case for this place', or, 'This case, as I see it, cannot be treated successfully in this hospital; why don't you take the patient home and try "the native way".' This they say either because they genuinely believe in the efficacy of 'the native way' for certain forms of sickness, or because they believe that the patient would respond psychologically more easily to 'the native way' and so assist his own recovery. Everywhere and anywhere in the world, one cannot ignore the factor of 'faith' in the practice and application of medicine. This is being increasingly appreciated today.

<u>By the nature of things</u>, it is inevitable that medicine and magic should intermingle in Africa. The reasons may be stated as follows:

(a) In most places, the same divinity has both within his portfolio. We have already mentioned Ọsányìn among the Yoruba and Agwu among the Igbo.

(b) The same designation in the vernacular is often used to cover medicine and magic. For both, the Nupe use the word *cigbe*, and the Yoruba use the word *oògùn*, the Igbo the word ọgwu, for example.

(c) Medicine is more often than not prescribed with the instruction that it must be used at stated times, compulsorily under certain conditions, accompanied with certain prescribed gestures (which may be repetitive), and with incantations. And from the point of view of the patient, it is often difficult to know whether it is the actual medicine or the accompanying ceremonies, or both together, that effect a cure.

(d) There is no doubt that, at times, what is described as medicine is little more than sympathetic magic. For example, it is believed that a person who is timid or cowardly may be cured in this way: a stone is placed in the fire until it becomes very hot; then it is placed in a basin of palm oil and left to cool; the patient then drinks the oil. It is believed that in this way 'his heart will be as strong as stone'. Based on the same principle is such a practice as the 'washing away' of sickness with medical soap in a stream; or the killing of a snake that bites a person, reducing it to powder by burning and grinding, and giving the powder to the patient to drink in water or eat with porridge.

Here, as in the case of magic and religion, magic appears to be the odd one out. African elders will declare that certain 'magical' ceremonies which accompany medicine are not essentially necessary, except in so far as they aid the mind of the patient and thus enable the mind to influence the body to respond favourably to treatment. Religion, on the other hand, is considered necessary to medicine, since the belief is that only the Maker can remake, repairing the damage to mind and body and effecting wholeness in man's being.

VI

The Prospect of
African Traditional Religion

This chapter is, naturally, a speculative exercise; but it keeps an observant eye on the actual scene in Africa and is, therefore, entitled to be called an assessment and a prophecy.

Religion has an organic life of its own which results from divine activity and man's response. It is a life which comes into being and grows in the atmosphere, not only of man's response, but also of his constancy in loyalty to an accepted faith. Without this loyalty on man's part, the manifestations of divine creative and saving activity will be short-circuited and religion will thus become ineffectual or a thing of the past. It has always been the predicament of religion that whereas the activity of the living God is constant, man's loyalty can become uncertain in consequence of several factors – the vagaries of man's mind; the phenomena of change which may mean upheaval and disruption with the consequence of partial or total destruction; and, of course, death.

One of two things has happened to man's religion in any given situation: modification with adaptation, or extinction. The first may be said to have been the fate of religion throughout the world, of any religion. There is no living religion that has not taken into itself elements from other religio-cultures. Influences from other cultures and contacts with immigrant religions have brought, not only changes in the complexion of religion, but also modification of its tenets. The most particular of religions have not been able to escape this factor: they have been forced by the nature of things to give and take elements to and from even those religions which they regard as their enemies or rivals. As for the fact of extinction, it is well known that the religions of ancient Egypt, Greece, and Rome, to quote certain obvious examples, are no longer in existence today. All that remains of them is what can be read from ruins and monuments or observed as having been absorbed into the total character of the living successors of the ancient races or taken over into a successor-religion. Christianity is an adept in such takeovers.

With particular reference to Africa, we have outlined in chapter III of this book certain factors which had affected the traditional religion in certain areas adversely, to the point either of extinction or of the confusion of its tenets. We may look at the current situation through one or two snapshots.

First, for about fourteen years now, I have lectured on African Traditional Religion in the University of Ibadan. During that period, it has been my experience that the majority of my students have come to learn for the first time about the tenets of the religion even as practised in their several native localities. And, by and large, they have been learning their lessons from books written by foreigners. It is only recently that books on the subject written by African scholars are becoming available. African students have, therefore, hitherto entered upon their studies with an academic temper dictated by the attitudes and terminologies of foreign writers. This happens, not only with students but also with lecturer and professors who have been captured by Westernism and have not yet been able to find their way out of its spiritual and intellectual bondage. Such can only discuss African Traditional Religion by quoting from books. A case in point was that of an African Professor who made a questionable statement about the religion. After his attention had been called to his error, he remarked at an open lecture: 'I consulted Parrinder's book and discovered that Africans considered it offensive to use such a term ...'! Thus, we see that as far as the youth of Africa who are being brought up in the Western system of education, as well as Africans who have attained higher learning, are concerned, it appears at first sight that the religion as *religion* is no longer a matter of ultimate concern.

Secondly, the details of the census of Nigeria will show that those who hold the traditional faith and practise the religion are in the minority as compared with those who are Muslims and Christians. The indication is that this would be the pattern throughout Africa. And this has emboldened certain academic soothsayers to assert categorically that African Traditional Religion is on the decline and that it is only a matter of time before it will be stamped out altogether.

This apparent situation has occurred because it has become unfashionable, by and large, for any one except an old person to declare himself an adherent of the traditional religion. In public records, like those of the hospitals, where religion is still indicated, people will claim to belong to either Christianity or Islam; and the same thing happens in any other situations where people have to answer the question 'What is your religion?' Here again, it is easy to conclude that African Traditional Religion has had its day.

We must not, however, take mere appearance for reality. If we return to the subject of university students, we shall find that what we have said is not the end of the matter. Their studies have led several of the students to what they consider to be a joyful discovery of a valuable heritage which had been lost; some even feel that, somehow, the foreigners who brought their own religions and cultures to displace African indigenous ones have only come to cheat them of their own God-given heritage. They have often, therefore, expressed cheerful surprise in their discovery that Africa is blessed with so many indigenous spiritual and cultural treasures. And an oft-repeated question is, 'Since we have such a wealth of indigenous spiritual and moral values, why have we abandoned them for imported ones?' Often, they want to stop their teacher and ask him to say precisely in what way the imported values are better than the indigenous ones, and why 'we' cannot bring back the religion of our forbears to its own, refining it, if need be. Words like those of R. S. Rattray fascinate them:

I sometimes like to think, had these people been left to work out their own salvation, perhaps some day an African Messiah would have arisen and swept their pantheon clean of fetish ... West Africa might then have become the cradle of a new creed which acknowledged One Great Spirit, Who, being One, nevertheless manifested Himself in everything around Him and taught men to hear His voice in the flow of his waters and in the sound of His winds in the trees.[1]

While, as we have said, every African may wish to be regarded as connected with one or the other of the two 'fashionable' religions, most are at heart still attached to their own indigenous beliefs. It is now becoming clear to the most optimistic of Christian evangelists that the main problem of the church in Africa today is the divided loyalties of most of her members between Christianity with its

Western categories and practices on one hand, and the traditional religion on the other. It is well known that in strictly personal matters relating to the passages of life and the crisis of life, African Traditional Religion is regarded as the final succour by most Africans. In hospitals, for example, people who, on admission, have declared themselves Christians, and indeed are 'practising' Christians, have medicine prepared in the traditional way smuggled in to them simply because, psychologically at least, that is more effective in that it is consecrated medicine with the touch of the divine healer, in contrast to the Europeans' *mere* 'coloured water' or *mere* pills. In matters concerning providence, healing, and general wellbeing, therefore, most Africans still look up to 'their own religion' as 'the way'.

A new interest has, of course, been born with regard to everything African in consequence of nationalism, the independence of African nations, and the general search for identity throughout the continent. Kwame Nkrumah, the advocate of the philosophy of 'African personality', took as one of his first official steps in his effort to restore the soul of Africa the introduction of the traditional foundation ritual into government affairs. Such a ritual precedes anything to be done by Africans in their own traditional setting – its purpose is always to acknowledge the divine lordship over the whole earth: man is a tenant on God's earth and, therefore, must not undertake anything without divine sanction. To replace the formal opening of Parliament with Christian prayers as instituted by the Colonial rulers, Nkrumah ruled that libation should be poured and the prescribed details of a foundation ritual carried out. In various other ways, what I shall describe with the broad title of 'Ethiopianism'[2] has come into expression throughout Africa to emphasize that the Continent is moving actively and purposively to recover her 'enslaved soul'. 'Ethiopianism' has taken various forms, ranging from attempts at the indigenization of the Christian church, the founding of churches by charismatic, Christian African leaders, and the establishment of splinters from the European-dominated churches as separatist churches which are completely free from any form of foreign interference. The significant aspect of 'Ethiopianism' for our purpose is the coming into being of 'churches' which are positive repudiations of Christianity, even though they use the scaffolding of the Christian church to erect new structures for the self-expression of the traditional religion. From Nigeria we quote three examples. There is *Orunmilaism* which adopts the oracle divinity according to

the Yoruba as *the* prophet of God to 'the black race', has founded a church in his name and worships Olodumare *through* him. The emphasis here is the replacement of the 'God/prophet' element of Islamic faith with a 'God/prophet' element of the traditional faith, even though the behaviour of the church is patterned after Christianity. We have the <u>Aruosa Church of Benin-City</u> which was founded ②
by the Ọba of Benin with the avowed purpose of helping the Edo people to worship God in the language which God understood! To that end, Osanobwa is worshipped *through* his son Olokun. The emphasis here is a replacement of the 'Father/Son' element of Christianity with a 'Father/Son' element of African Traditional Religion. Again, there is the political church which began as the ③
National Church of Nigeria and the Cameroon, changed its name to the <u>National Church of Nigeria with the separation of Cameroon from Nigeria</u>, and has since moved between a politico-philosophical kind of Africanism and a kind of theosophy called <u>Goddianism.</u> The main emphasis here is a total condemnation of the adoption of any 'foreign' or 'imported' religion by Africans: Africa must recover her soul; she must give the first and supreme position to her own God-given heritage, and be obedient to the teachings of her own God-appointed prophets. With 'Goddianism' in mind, it is now permissible, however, to appropriate the best element in any culture or religion for the enrichment of the African culture and beliefs; but always, African Traditional Religion *must* be the religion of every African.

We notice that the new interest in African Traditional Religion is not a phenomenon restricted to Africa. It has become global. <u>'African Traditional Religion' is finding its way into the curriculum of every higher institution of learning throughout the world;</u> there are European and American professors and lecturers in the field, even though they may never have visited Africa or may have had rather slight contact with the actual scene in any locality in Africa; doctoral these are being written and accepted on the subject almost throughout the world.

This interest is not only academic. While the academic interest has moved on from the attitude of the anthropological or sociological curio-collection and is now entering a new phase of seriousness and respect, there is also the deeper interest of those who have come to believe more and more that the religion has satisfying spiritual values to offer. A study of the situation in the Caribbean, the United

States, Latin America, or anywhere else where there are people of African descent will convince one of this fact. The religion is being practised at home and abroad.

'It does not yet appear what we shall be.' This sums up what can be said with certainty about the future of African Traditional Religion. Nevertheless, we maintain that this is the religion of the majority of Africans today. We can add that there is every indication that the processes of modernization, and of syncretism with the religion as the senior and predominant element in the mixture, will continue. Not long ago, two Europeans (both Austrians, and one of them definitely an Austrian Jew), Ulli Beier and Susan Wenger adopted a cult of the religion in Yorubaland and gave it a European artistic reorganization and renovation in the locality where they lived. Ulli Beier is now a Professor and the Director of African Studies in the University of Ifẹ̀, Ile-Ifẹ̀, and Susan has become a wife of the chief drummer of Ṣàngó, living with her husband at Oṣogbo where one can see today the sophisticated marks of her artistic devotion on temples and shrines. Also, it appears that those who outwardly profess faith in other religions but are constantly resorting to the traditional religion for succour may not decrease substantially in numbers for a long time to come. It appears also that there will always be the 'faithful remnant' whose loyalty to the religion of their forbears will continue steadfast.

Notes

NOTES

CHAPTER I
The Study of Religion

1. A. C. Bouquet, *Man and Deity*, Heffer, Cambridge, 1933, p.23.
2. Julian Huxley, *Science, Religion, and Human Nature*, Watts, London, 1930, pp.12, 8.
3. Bouquet, op. cit., p.4.
4. Quoted from *First and Last Things* by Bouquet, op. cit., p.20.
5. E. Bolaji Idowu, *Olódùmarè: God in Yoruba Belief*, Longmans 1962, p.67.
6. A. C. Bouquet, *Comparative Religion*, Pelican 1945, p.15.
7. Matthew 7.21.
8. Bouquet, *Comparative Religion*, p.14.
9. W. Cantwell Smith, *The Meaning and End of Religion*, Mentor Books 1964, p.12.
10. J. Estlin Carpenter, *Comparative Religion*, Williams and Norgate, London, 1913, p.24.
11. In *Proceedings of the XIth International Congress of the International Association for the History of Religions* (1965), Brill, Leiden, 1968, Vol.I, pp.95f.
12. See pp.116ff. below.
13. H. A. Williams, 'Theology and Self-awareness', in *Soundings*, ed. A. R. Vidler, Cambridge University Press 1966, p.73.
14. E. E. Evans-Pritchard, *Theories of Primitive Religion*, Oxford University Press 1965, p.6.
15. Ibid., p.106.
16. *The Meaning and End of Religion*, pp.9f.
17. E. Bolaji Idowu, 'The Study of Religion', *Orita: Ibadan Journal of Religious Studies* I.1, 1967, p.3.
18. Evans-Pritchard, op. cit., p.17.
19. Huxley, *Science, Religion, and Human Nature*, p.27.
20. Bouquet, *Man and Deity*, p.27.
21. Julian Huxley, *Religion without Revelation*, Watts, London, 1941, p.vi.
22. Huxley, *Science, Religion, and Human Nature*, p.9.
23. Bouquet, *Man and Deity*, pp.25f.
24. Bouquet, *Comparative Religion*, p.21.
25. Idowu, 'The Study of Religion', p.5.

26. Russell Brain, *Science, Philosophy and Religion*, Cambridge University Press 1959, p.31.
27. Huxley, *Science, Religion, and Human Nature*, p.11.
28. Huston Smith, *The Religions of Man*, Harper and Row 1965, p.13.
29. W. Cantwell Smith, *Proceedings of the XIth International Congress ...*, Vol.I, p.66.
30. William Temple in *Relations among Religions Today*, ed. M. Jung and others, Brill, Leiden, 1963, p.54.
31. Cantwell Smith, op. cit., p.68.
32. Ibid., p.62.
33. See Cantwell Smith's observations on this point, op. cit., pp.62f.
34. Acts 15.10.
35. Cantwell Smith, op. cit., pp.58f.
36. Cantwell Smith, *The Meaning and End of Religion*, p.10.
37. W. Schmidt, quoted by Evans-Pritchard, *Theories of Primitive Religion*, p.121.
38. Cantwell Smith, *The Meaning and End of Religion*, p.10.
39. Huston Smith, op. cit., p.10.
40. Bernard Shaw, *Major Barbara: a Screen Version*, Penguin 1945, p.137.
41. Steven Runciman, *The Great Church in Captivity*, Cambridge University Press 1968, pp.3f.
42. R. S. Rattray, *Ashanti*, Oxford University Press 1923 (reissued 1969), p.11.

CHAPTER II
Religion

1. H. Fielding Hall, *The Hearts of Men*, Hutchinson 1934, p.xxiii.
2. J. Estlin Carpenter, *Comparative Religion*, 1913, pp.42f.
3. A. C. Bouquet, *Comparative Religion*, 1945, pp.12f.
4. Carpenter, op. cit., pp.43f.
5. W. Cantwell Smith, *The Meaning and End of Religion*, 1964, pp.183f.
6. Ibid., pp.184f.
7. One should read the whole of this book in order to appreciate his genuine concern for a clear understanding of this all-important but very elusive and delicate subject.
8. Op. cit., p.175.
9. Ibid., p.176.
10. Ibid., pp.175ff.
11. From J. G. Whittier's hymn 'O Lord and Master of us all' (*Methodist Hymnbook* no. 103; *Church Hymnary* no. 513).
12. *Shaw on Religion: Irreverent Observations by a Man of Great Faith*, ed. Warren Sylvester Smith, Dodd, Mead and Co., New York, p.154.
13. Eugene Carson Blake, *The Church in the Next Decade*, Macmillan, New York, 1966, pp.15f.
14. Albert Camus, *The Myth of Sisyphus*, Vintage Books 1961, pp.49ff.
15. Quoted by T. R. Glover, *The Conflict of Religions in the Early Roman Empire*, Methuen 1932, p.25.

16. Cf. Helmut Gollwitzer, *Karl Barth's Church Dogmatics*, T. and T. Clark 1961, pp.49ff.

17. Dietrich Bonhoeffer, *Letters and Papers from Prison*, SCM Press 1953, revised 1967, revised and enlarged, 1971.

18. Bonhoeffer in letters of 16 and 18 July 1944 (op. cit., 1967 ed., pp.196 and 200; 1971 ed., pp.360 and 362).

19. Cantwell Smith, *The Meaning and End of Religion*, p.175.

20. Luke 18.8.

21. Cf. Aldous Huxley, *Brave New World*, Chatto and Windus 1952.

22. All that is implied in the very expressive German *Gottesdienst*.

23. Mark 2.21f.

24. A. E. Garvie, *The Christian Belief in God*, Hodder and Stoughton 1933, pp.88f.

25. E, E, Evans-Pritchard, *Theories of Primitive Religion*, 1965, p.15.

26. Carpenter, *Comparative Religion*, pp.45f.

27. See E. Bọlaji Idowu, *Olódùmarè: in Yoruba Belief*, 1962, p.69.

28. *Encyclopaedia of Religion and Ethics* 5, pp.572f.

29. Job 11.7.

30. Isaiah 45.15.

31. Matthew 7.16.

32. Idowu, *Olódùmaré*, p.19.

33. E. Bọlaji Idowu, 'Religion in Ibadan' in *The City of Ibadan*, ed. P. C. Lloyd, A. L. Mabogunjẹ and B. Awe, Cambridge University Press 1967, p.23.

34. The crucial test posed by the sceptic Sextus Empiricus. See A. E. Garvie, *The Christian Belief in God*, p.92.

35. *Totem and Taboo*, Eng. trans. by James Strachey in *The Complete Psychological Works of Sigmund Freud*, Vol. XIII, Hogarth Press 1955.

36. Op. cit., p.102 n. 1.

37. Ibid., p.141.

38. Ibid., p.142 n. 1.

39. Ibid., p.146.

40. Ibid., p.50.

41. Ibid., p.63.

42. Ibid., p.92.

43. Ibid., p.147.

44. Ibid., pp.147f.

45. Ibid., pp.156f.

46. Ibid., p.157.

47. *The Future of an Illusion*, Eng. trans. by James Strachey in *The Complete Psychological Works of Sigmund Freud*, Vol. XXI, Hogarth Press 1961, pp.15ff.

48. Ibid., pp.17f.

49. Ibid., p.30.

50. Ibid., pp.41f.

51. Ibid., pp.43f., 53ff.

52. Job 13.15 (AV).

53. Romans 8.35-37.

54. Quoted from the expression of the faith of a Muslim mystic named Rabi'a in C. R. North, *An Outline of Islam*, Epworth 1952, p.108.

55. Emile Durkheim, *The Elementary Forms of Religious Life*, Allen and Unwin 1915, (reprinted 1954), p.206.

56. Durkheim, quoted by J. B. Pratt, *The Religious Consciousness*, reprinted Macmillan, New York, 1947, p.11.

57. Durkheim, *The Elementary Forms of Religious Life*, pp.207-11.

58. H. H. Farmer, *Towards Belief in God*, SCM Press 1942, pp.145ff.

59. Isaiah 11.6ff.

60. Quoted by Pratt, op. cit., p.76.

61. C. Marnay, *Structures of Prejudice*, Abingdon Press 1961, p.48.

62. Idowu, *Olódùmarè*, p.145.

63. Garvie, *The Christian Belief in God*, pp.104ff.

64. Evans-Pritchard, *Theories of Primitive Religion*, p.111.

65. Garvie, op. cit., p.88.

66. Quoted by Maldwyn Hughes, *Christian Foundations*, Epworth 1948, p.4.

67. A. C. Bouquet, *Man and Deity*, 1933, p.29.

68. Rudolf Otto, *The Idea of the Holy*, 2nd ed., Oxford University Press 1950.

69. Idowu, *Olódùmarè*, pp.129f.

70. The title of A. C. Bouquet's contribution in *Proceedings of the XIth International Congress of the International Association for the History of Religions* (1965), Brill, Leiden, 1968, Vol. II, pp.1ff.

71. Mircea Eliade, *The Sacred and the Profane*, Harper Torchbooks 1961 pp.137, 10, 11.

72. See Charles Kegley, ed., *The Theology of Emil Brunner*, Macmillan 1962, Vol. III, p.83.

73. L. Harold DeWolf, *A Theology of the Living Church*, Hamish Hamilton 1960, p.36.

74. John Baillie, *Our Knowledge of God*, Oxford University Press 1941, p.26.

75. DeWolf, op. cit., p.33.

76. H. H. Farmer, *Revelation and Religion*, Nisbet 1954, p.28.

77. Paul Tillich, *Systematic Theology*, Vol. I, Nisbet 1953, p.133.

78. Baillie, op. cit., pp.42f.

79. Idowu, *Olódùmarè*, pp.39f.

80. Romans 1.20.

81. Acts 17.26-28.

82. Farmer, op. cit., pp.105, 109.

83. Bouquet, *Man and Deity*, p.85.

84. Genesis 28.16-19.

85. S. F. Nadel, *Nupe Religion*, Routledge and Kegan Paul 1954, p.11.

86. Isaiah 40.18,22.

87. Isaiah 59.1.

88. Bouquet, *Man and Deity*, p.21.

89. Bouquet, *Comparative Religion*, p.15.

90. F. B. Jevons, 'Anthropomorphism', *Encyclopaedia of Religion and Ethics*, Vol. I, p.576.

91. See pp.91ff. below.

92. E. Bọlaji Idowu, *God in Nigerian Belief* (October Lectures, 1962), Federal Ministry of Information 1963, p.9.
93. J. K. Parratt, 'Religious Change in Yoruba Society – A Test Case', *Journal of Religion in Africa* II.2, 1969, p.18.
94. A. B. Ellis, *The Yoruba-speaking Peoples*, Chapman and Hall 1894, p.34.
95. Leo Frobenius, *The Voice of Africa*, Hutchinson 1913 (reissued by Blom, New York, 1968), Vol. I, p.198.
96. James O'Connell, 'The Withdrawal of the High God in West African Religion: an Interpretation', *Man* LXII, May 1962, pp.67-69.
97. Here we go again! West Africa is the special habitation of a special breed of Supreme Gods.
98. Again, a multitude of them.
99. Bernard Shaw, *Back to Methuselah*, Penguin 1954, p.225.
100. M. J. Herskovits, *Dahomey*, Augustin, New York 1938 (reprinted Northwestern University Press 1967), Vol. II, p.289.
101. See pp.155ff. below.
102. See pp.161ff. below.
103. Tillich, *Systematic Theology*, Vol. I, p.142.
104. See pp.85ff. below.
105. Garvie, *The Christian Belief in God*, p.84.
106. Pratt, *The Religious Consciousness*, p.1.
107. Hall, *The Hearts of Men*, pp.vif.
108. The first three illustrative definitions examined here are based on quotations from the authors by Garvie, op cit., pp.49ff.
109. Tillich, *Systematic Theology*, Vol. I, p.47.
110. Pratt, op. cit., pp.2f.
111. Bouquet, *Comparative Religion*, p.13.
112. Farmer, *The World and God*, Nisbet 1935, p.42.
113. I am aware that I am excluding pseudo-religions or modern substitutes for religion, those phenomena based upon the 'all-sufficiency of man'.
114. Paul Tillich, *A History of Christian Thought*, SCM Press 1968, p.165.
115. Idowu, *God in Nigerian Belief*, pp.3f. (slightly modified). It may be worth while to read the whole chapter on 'Religion'.

CHAPTER III
The Study of African Traditional Religion

1. Laurens van der Post, *The Lost World of the Kalahari*, Penguin 1962, p.251.
2. David Tait, *The Konkomba of Northern Ghana*, Oxford University Press 1961, p.226.
3. See Ch. IV below.
4. E. B. Idowu, *Olódùmarè: God in Yoruba Belief*, 1962, pp.7ff.
5. Liddell and Scott, *Greek-English Lexicon*, abridged ed., Clarendon Press 1909.
6. *Olódùmarè*, pp.7ff.
7. Leo Frobenius, *The Voice of Africa*, 1913, Vol. I, pp.1f.

8. Ibid., p.xiii.
9. Edwin Smith, ed., *African Ideas of God*, Edinburgh House Press 1950, p.1.
10. See John Oman, *The Natural and the Supernatural*, Cambridge University Press 1931, pp.485ff.; A. C. Bouquet, *Man and Deity*, 1933, pp.101f.; E. E. Evans-Pritchard, *Theories of Primitive Religion*, 1965, pp.35, 50.
11. See Oman, loc. cit.
12. See Evans-Pritchard, op. cit., pp.103f.
13. Andrew Lang, *The Making of Religion*, Longmans, Green, 1898, p.181.
14. Oman, op. cit., p.486, quoting Lang, op. cit., p.179.
15. Bouquet, *Man and Deity*, p.101.
16. Evans-Pritchard, op. cit., p.104.
17. Oman, op cit., p.487.
18. Bouquet, op. cit., pp.101ff.
19. H. H. Farmer, *Revelation and Religion*, 1954, p.107.
20. Bouquet, op. cit., p.102.
21. See Nevil Shute, *A Town Like Alice*, Pan Giant 1961, p.60.
22. See pp.61ff. above.
23. Bouquet, op. cit., p.106.
24. Frobenius, *The Voice of Africa*, Vol. I, pp.xiii and 1f.
25. Ibid., p.xiv.
26. Ibid., p.187.
27. Ibid., pp.xivf.
28. In Yorubaland (Western Nigeria), Olokun is a goddess; in Edoland (mid-west) the divinity is a god. The cult of this divinity as a goddess (largely) or as a god is prevalent in Southern Nigeria. Olokun means 'Owner or Lord of the sea'.
29. P. A. Talbot, *The Peoples of Southern Nigeria*, Oxford University Press 1926, Vol. II, pp.14ff.
30. R. S. Rattray, *Religion and Art in Ashanti*, Oxford University Press 1927 (reissued 1969), p.vi, quoting a report of 1816.
31. Rattray, *Ashanti*, 1923, p.12.
32. *Religion and Art in Ashanti*, pp.vf.
33. See p.21 above.
34. Op. cit., pp.viif.
35. Edwin Smith, *African Ideas of God*, p.3.
36. A. C. Bouquet, *Comparative Religion*, 1945, p.24.
37. Edward B. Tylor, *Primitive Culture*, 5th ed., John Murray 1913, Vol. II, p.334.
38. Charles Williams, *Descent into Hell*, Faber and Faber 1949, p.39.
39. E. S. Waterhouse, *The Dawn of Religion*, Epworth 1936, p.41. He was a 'stay-at-home'.
40. Placide Tempels, *Bantu Philosophy*, Presence Africaine 1959, p.16.
41. *Biblical Revelation and African Beliefs*, ed. K. Dickson and P. Ellingworth, Lutterworth 1969, reviewed by F. B. Welbourn, in *Africa* XL.1, January 1970. I will not, in fact, use such a heretical term as 'a Supreme Being'.
42. See ch. V below.

43. S. F. Nadel, *Nupe Religion*, 1954, pp.1ff.
44. Ibid., p.10.
45. Tempels, *Bantu Philosophy*, p.78.
46. See pp.155ff. below.
47. W. Cantwell Smith in *Proceedings of the XIth International Congress of the International Association for the History of Religions* (1965), Brill, Leiden, 1968, Vol. I, pp.63f.
48. Ibid., Vol. II, pp.1f.
49. Ibid., Vol. I, p.67.
50. Edwin Smith, *African Ideas of God*, p.3.

CHAPTER IV

The Nature of African Traditional Religion

1. See E. S. Waterhouse, 1936, *The Dawn of Religion*, p.13.
2. Sigmund Freud, *Totem and Taboo, The Complete Psychological Works*, Vol. XIII, 1955, pp.102f.
3. Waterhouse, op. cit., p.17.
4. E. B. Idowu, *Olódùmarè: God in Yoruba Belief*, 1962, pp.120f.
5. Charles Williams, *Shadows of Ecstasy*, Faber and Faber 1965, pp.120f.
6. F. A. M. Webster, *Son of Abdan*, The Readers' Library 1947, pp.124f.
7. Denise Robins, *Gold for the Gay Masters*, Mayflower Paperback 1966, p.154.
8. Webster, *Son of Abdan*, pp.85f.
9. P. C. Wren, *Sinbad the Soldier*, John Murray 1958, p.148.
10. E. E. Evans-Pritchard, *Theories of Primitive Religion*, 1965, pp.18f.
11. On 'Abyssinia', *Encyclopaedia of Religion and Ethics* 1, pp.55ff.
12. Franz Cumont, *Oriental Religions in Roman Paganism*, Dover Publications, New York, 1956, pp.196f.
13. Ibid., pp.viiif.
14. M. I. Boas, *God, Christ and Pagan*, Allen and Unwin 1961, pp.7f.
15. Op. cit., p.7.
16. Hastings' *Dictionary of the Bible*, Vol. II, 1899, pp.319f.
17. Liddell and Scott, *Greek-English Lexicon*, abridged ed., Clarendon Press 1909.
18. Tylor, *Primitive Culture*, 5th ed., 1913, Vol. I, p.497.
19. *Encyclopaedia of Religion and Ethics* 7, pp.110f.
20. Ibid., pp.112ff.
21. J. B. Pratt, *The Religious Consciousness*, 1947, pp.273ff.
22. A. C. Bouquet, *Comparative Religion*, 1945, p.15.
23. *Olódùmarè*, pp.64ff. The whole of ch. 7 will be illuminating.
24. Quoted appropriately from R. R. Marett, *Sacraments of Simple Folk*, Clarendon Press 1940, p.146, by Edwin Smith, *African Ideas of God*, 1950, p.14.
25. *Olódùmarè*, pp.65f.
26. Tylor, *Primitive Culture*, Vol. II, pp.176f.
27. P. A. Talbot, *The Peoples of Southern Nigeria*, 1926, Vol. II, p.22.

28. *Encyclopaedia of Religion and Ethics* 7, pp.112, 114f.
29. Tylor, op. cit., Vol. II, pp.143ff.
30. E. G. Parrinder, *African Traditional Religion*, Hutchinson's University Library 1954, pp.15f.
31. R. S. Rattray, *Ashanti*, 1923, pp.9f.
32. Ibid., pp.24f.
33. H. W. Fowler, *Modern English Usage*, Clarendon Press 1957, p.178.
34. P. A. Talbot, op. cit., Vol. II, pp.20f.
35. Tylor, *Primitive Culture*, Vol. I, pp.424ff.
36. Ibid., pp.426f.
37. Ibid., pp.438, 442, 450.
38. Ibid., pp.448f., 457.
39. Ibid., pp.469, 474.
40. Ibid., Vol. II, pp.184f.
41. Ibid., pp.247f., 316ff.
42. Ibid., pp.331ff.
43. Ibid., Vol. I, p.426.
44. Talbot, *The Peoples of Southern Nigeria*, Vol. II, pp.15f.
45. Ibid., p.15.
46. E. G. Parrinder, *Religion in an African City*, Oxford University Press 1953, p.11.
47. S. F. Nadel, *Nupe Religion*, 1954, pp.2, 10.
48. Idowu, *Olódùmarè*, pp.202ff.
49. See pp.165ff. below.
50. See W. Cantwell Smith, *The Meaning and End of Religion*, 1964, pp.58f.

CHAPTER V

The Structure of African Traditional Religion

1. P. A. Talbot, *The Peoples of Southern Nigeria*, 1926, Vol. II, p.14.
2. See p.165 below.
3. See p.58f. above.
4. See pp.128ff. above.
5. See pp.178ff. below.
6. E. G. Parrinder, *West African Religion*, Epworth 1961, p.12.
7. See pp.61ff. above.
8. See M. J. Herskovits, *Dahomey*, 1938, Vol. II, pp.101f., 291.
9. R. S. Rattray, *Religion and Art in Ashanti*, 1927, p.11.
10. E. E. Evans-Pritchard, *Theories of Primitive Religion*, 1965, p.112.
11. See pp.79ff. above.
12. This is the name of the archdivinity in Yoruba belief.
13. P. Baudin, *Fetishism and Fetish Worshippers*, 1885, pp.9ff.
14. Diedrich Westermann, *Africa and Christianity*, Oxford University Press 1937, pp.65ff.
15. R. S. Rattray, *Ashanti*, 1923, pp.139ff.
16. Job 11.7.
17. I Timothy 6.15f.
18. Cf. Isaiah 6.1.

19. 'Systematic' as dealing with concrete experiences and situations, and as distinct from 'abstract'.
20. See pp.63ff. above.
21. See pp. 149ff. below.
22. See pp.51ff. above.
23. S. F. Nadel, *Nupe Religion*, 1954, p.11.
24. See pp.51ff. above.
25. See pp.189ff. below.
26. E. B. Idowu, *Olódùmarè: God in Yoruba Belief*, 1962, pp.116f.
27. David Tait, *The Konkomba of Northern Ghana*, 1961, p.226.
28. See below under (b), (c) and (d).
29. E. E. Evans-Pritchard, *Nuer Religion*, Oxford University Press 1956, pp.7ff.
30. Godfrey Lienhardt, *Divinity and Experience*, Clarendon Press 1961, p.29. But why does he use the pronoun 'it' for God?
31. John Middleton, *Lugbara Religion*, Oxford University Press 1960, p.258.
32. Raimo Harjula, *God and the Sun in Meru Thought*, The Finnish Society for Missiology and Ecumenics, Helsinki, 1969, p.28.
33. Alice Werner, *Myths and Legends of the Bantu*, Harrap 1933, pp.41f.
34. Harjula, op. cit., pp.40f.
35. Isaiah 40.18.
36. See p.63 above.
37. Idowu, *Olódùmarè*, pp.35f.
38. Middleton, op. cit., pp.253, 256.
39. Alice Werner, op. cit., p.51.
40. Ibid., p.44.
41. Evans-Pritchard, *Nuer Religion*, p.12.
42. Harjula, op. cit., pp.18, 46.
43. Alice Werner, op. cit., p.44n., pp.50f.
44. Harjula, op. cit., pp.29, 33.
45. Evans-Pritchard, op. cit., pp.1f.
46. K. Little, *The Mende of Sierra Leone*, Routledge and Kegan Paul, 1951, pp.217f.
47. Placide Tempels, *Bantu Philosophy*, 1959, pp.33-47 and *passim*.
48. Middleton, op. cit., p.27.
49. Evans-Pritchard, op. cit., p.4.
50. Harjula, op. cit., pp.34f.
51. Middleton, op. cit., pp.251f.
52. Lienhardt, *Divinity and Experience*, pp.29f., 41f., 54.
53. Alice Werner, op. cit., p.41 and note.
54. Ibid., p.44.
55. Evans-Pritchard, op. cit., pp.1-27.
56. Rattray, *Ashanti*, p.148.
57. Margaret Read, *The Ngoni of Nyasaland*, Oxford University Press 1956, pp.158ff.
58. Harjula, *God and the Sun*, pp.46f.
59. Ibid., pp.35, 38, 46f.
60. Idowu, *Olódùmarè*, pp.54f.

61. Ibid., pp.170f.
62. Tait, *The Konkomba of Northern Ghana*, p.226.
63. Tempels, *Bantu Philosophy*, p.65.
64. For this concept see Idowu, *Olódùmarè*, pp.169ff.
65. Ibid., p.44.
66. Middleton, *Lugbara Religion*, p.257.
67. Nadel, *Nupe Religion*, pp.11f.; cf. Isaiah 45.7.
68. Idowu, op. cit., p.14.
69. Lienhardt, *Divinity and Experience*, p.56.
70. Evans-Pritchard, *Nuer Religion*, pp.6f.
71. Middleton, op. cit., pp.258, 270, 27f.
72. Ibid., pp.27f.
73. Lienhardt, op. cit., pp.46f.
74. Evans-Pritchard, op. cit., p.18.
75. Idowu, op. cit., pp.146, 161, 198.
76. Harjula, *God and the Sun*, pp.35, 40ff.
77. Tait, op. cit., pp.63, 224.
78. Alice Werner, *Myths and Legends of the Bantu*, p.57.
79. Idowu, op. cit., pp.93f.
80. Lloyd C. Douglas, *The Big Fisherman*, Davies 1959, p.317.
81. I recommend the reading of *Olódùmarè*, chs. 7 and 8, in conjunction with this section.
82. Lienhardt, op. cit., pp.56-146. It would seem that some of those brought under divinities should be classed under spirits in general.
83. Paul Tillich, *Systematic Theology*, Vol. I, 1953, p.246.
84. John Oman, *The Natural and the Supernatural*, 1931, pp.191ff.
85. Peter Bamm, *The Kingdoms of Christ*, Thames and Hudson 1959, p.66.
86. Acts 17.23-28.
87. T. R. Glover, *The Conflict of Religions in the Early Roman Empire*, 1932, p.96.
88. A. E. Garvie, *The Christian Belief in God*, 1933, p.172.
89. Paul Radin, *Monotheism among Primitive Peoples*, Allen and Unwin 1924, pp.50f.
90. H. H. Farmer, *Revelation and Religion*, 1954, p.99 (italics mine).
91. See section 1 above on 'Belief in God'.
92. See pp.155ff. above.
93. Lienhardt, *Divinity and Experience*, p.56.
94. See pp.150, 155ff. above.
95. See Herskovits, *Dahomey*, Vol. II, pp.103ff.
96. Idowu, *Olódùmarè*, pp.80ff.
97. Lienhardt, op. cit., p.57.
98. See Idowu, op. cit., pp.62ff.
99. See section 4 below on 'Ancestors'.
100. Idowu, op. cit., pp.67ff.
101. Ibid., pp.68f.
102. Ibid., p.69.
103. See pp.128ff. above.

104. See E. B. Idowu, 'The Challenge of Witchcraft', *Orita: Ibadan Journal of Religious Studies* IV.1, June 1970, pp.3ff.

105. Idowu, *Olódùmarè*, p.178.

106. Idowu, 'The Challenge of Witchcraft', pp.12f.

107. Herbert Spencer, *Principles of Sociology*, London 1885, Vol. I, p.411.

108. Farmer, *Revelation and Religion*, pp.91f.

109. Loc. cit.

110. Edwin Smith, ed., *African Ideas of God*, 1961, p.28.

111. E. E. Evans-Pritchard, *Theories of Primitive Religion*, p.16.

112. E. G. Parrinder, *African Traditional Religion*, 1954, pp.63ff.

113. Quoted by Smith, op. cit., pp.25f., as well as by Parrinder, op. cit., p.64.

114. I have misplaced my copy of the book so cannot give the requisite reference here.

115. Herskovits, *Dahomey*, Vol. II, p.297.

116. Ile-Ifẹ is the sacred city of the Yoruba. It is one of their traditional beliefs that anyone who 'dies' anywhere in Yorubaland must report there immediately for further orders, and that the dead make an earthly rendezvous at the city. The title Olufẹ in this dirge refers to the genius of the city.

117. R. S. Rattray, *Religion and Art in Ashanti*, 1923, p.130.

118. Idowu, *Olódùmarè*, pp.193f.

119. Rattray, op. cit., p.138.

120. *Olódùmarè*, pp.92ff.

121. *Mmọ* and *Ayaka* are the Igbo counterparts of the Yoruba Egúngún and Orò.

122. *Olódùmarè*, pp.194f.

123. Thomas Campbell, in 'Hallowed Ground'.

124. Herskovits, *Dahomey*, Vol. I, p.195.

125. The substance of this section has appeared as an article in *Orita: Ibadan Journal of Religious Studies* I.2, 1967, pp.62,77. Acknowledgment is due to the Board of Editors of the journal for permission to use the material.

126. A. C. Bouquet, *Comparative Religion*, 1945, pp.12f.

127. J. B. Pratt, *The Religious Consciousness*, 1946, pp.2f.

128. E. B. Idowu, *God in Nigerian Belief*, 1963, p.4.

129. Nadel, *Nupe Religion*, p.261.

130. E. O. James, *Comparative Religion*, Methuen 1938, p.72.

131. Nadel, loc. cit.

132. Pratt. op. cit., p.310.

133. E. A. Nida, *Customs, Culture and Christianity*, Tyndale Press, London, 1963, p.147.

134. Pratt, loc. cit.

135. Franz Cumont, *Oriental Religions in Roman Paganism*, 1956, p.185.

136. Oman, *The Natural and the Supernatural*, pp.483, 384.

137. Glover, *The Conflict of Religions in the Early Roman Empire*, p.18.

138. James, op. cit., pp.71f.

139. Pratt, loc. cit.

140. James, op. cit., pp.54f.

141. Oman, op. cit., pp.484f.

142. J. J. I. Dollinger, *The Gentile and the Jew*, Gibbing, London, 1906, p.223.
143. Glover, op. cit., p.229.
144. Edward Langton, *Essentials of Demonology*, Epworth 1949, p.27.
145. M. I. Boas, *God, Christ and Pagan*, 1961, pp.18f.
146. *Olódùmarè*, pp.116f. See also H. H. Farmer, *The World and God*, 1935, ch. 8.
147. Sigmund Freud, *Totem and Taboo*, 1955, pp.78f.
148. M. J. Field, *Search for Security*, Faber and Faber 1960, p.40.
149. *Olódùmarè*, pp.9, 115.
150. Ibid., pp.83f.
151. Ibid., p.99.
152. Quoted by Rattray, *Religion and Art in Ashanti*, p.24.
153. Field, op. cit., pp.129f.
154. The word I have translated by the phrase 'magic of immunity' is *okìgbẹ́*. It is believed that anyone protected with this magic cannot be harmed by gunshot or by any sharp weapon.
155. Isaiah 30.15.
156. Langton, op. cit., p.27.
157. Glover, op. cit., p.22.
158. Ibid., pp.221f.
159. Nida, *Customs, Culture and Christianity*, p.148.
160. Nadel, *Nupe Religion*, pp.6, 17.
161. Field, op. cit., p.40.
162. Nadel, op. cit., pp.17, 19, 104.
163. Rattray, *Ashanti*, p.142.
164. Boas, *God, Christ and Pagan*, p.18.
165. Nadel, op. cit., pp.104f.

CHAPTER VI

The Prospect of African Traditional Religion

1. R. S. Rattray, *Religion and Art in Ashanti*, 1927, pp.vf.
2. See Psalm 68.31. I shall be discussing 'Ethiopianism' in a future book.

Index

Abasi Ibom, 150
Abdera, 121
Abednego, 48
Abel, 181
Àbíkú, 175
Abraham, 31
Abraham, R. C., 174
Africa, 5-8, 28, 38, 67-9, 76-80,
    82f., 85-8, 90-2, 94-104, 106,
    108f., 111, 113f., 116, 119, 127,
    131-5, 139, 144-6, 148, 150-2,
    155, 161, 165, 170, 175-8,
    180, 183, 185f., 197, 201, 203-7
  religion in, 6, 15, 60, 93, 105,
    108, 123, 127, 134, 140, 180,
    182
  universities of, 10
  personality of, 79
  practices of, 86, 103
  beliefs of, 101
  religion of, 103f.
  human sacrifice in, 112
Africanism, 207
Africanists, 77
Africanness, 28, 103
Africans, 63, 68, 80, 82, 92,
    98-9, 101, 103, 106f., 113, 139,
    144-7, 149-50, 154f., 160, 171,
    173-5, 181f., 184, 186, 188, 197,
    201, 204-8
  belief of, 175, 197
  generation of, 82
Agwe, 185
Agwu, 196, 200, 202
Àjànàkù, 200f.
Akamba, 151
Akan, 20, 104, 136, 151, 160, 164,
    169, 180, 200
Akyeremade, 186
Ala, 169-71, 183
Alcibiades, 35
Allah, 26, 62, 117f., 142, 163
Alpha, 141, 147
America, 76, 110, 112, 114, 179
Americans, 7, 60, 110
Ana, 169

ancestor, 165, 172f., 178, 180-7,
    200
ancestor-worship, 38, 138, 178-83
Anglo-Saxon, 88
Ani, 169
animatism, 133
animism, 40, 128, 130, 134, 137, 173
Anlo-Ewe, 188
Anselm, 74
anthropologists, 7-9, 49f., 85, 92, 114
anthropomorphism, 59-61, 132f.,
    137
Antiochus, Poplius Aelius, 198
Apellas, Julius Marcus, 198
Apuleius, 193
Arabian Mullahs, 117
Arabic, 196; Arabs, 87
Aruosa Church, 206
Ashanti, 21, 97, 127, 137-9, 141,
    147f., 158, 172, 185, 196f.
Ashtoreth, 117
Asia, 5, 100, 111, 114
Asklepios, 198
atheists, 28f., 34
Athens, 167
Atkinson, J. J., 39
Atlantis, 94f.
Australia, 112
Automaton, 47
Ayaka, 187

Babylonia, Babylonians, 100, 197,
    199
Bacweeci, 165
Badagry, 19
Baganda, 127
Bahia, 169
Baila, 151, 154, 157, 181
Baillie, John, 56
Balbus, 23
Bantu, 102, 104, 155, 157, 160,
    164
Bapedi, 151
Barbarians, 120
Barth, Karl, 30
Basil, St, 198